MEDITATION
FOR THE MODERN MAN

MEDITATION
FOR THE MODERN MAN

An Introduction to
COGNITIVE MEDITATION

Pestonji K Sholapurwala

Non-religious, non-cultic,
Spiritual, humanistic,
Extra-traditional, perennial,
Empowering,
Science-oriented, evolutinary

PARTRIDGE
A Penguin Random House Company

Print information available on the last page.

To order additional copies of this book, contact
Partridge India
000 800 10062 62
orders.india@partridgepublishing.com

www.partridgepublishing.com/india

Published in Loving Memory of

"Our Dear Pesi Kaka"

by
Firdosh H Sholapurwala

With the participation of

Roshan F Sholapurwala
Hilla H Sholapurwala
Aspy B Talati
Farida A Talati
Rukhshana F Sholapurwala
Zarir H Sholapurwala
Kainaz X Mistry

TABLE OF CONTENTS

"Mrs. Tehmina Sholapurwala" "Mr. P.K.Sholapurwala"
(1902 – 2009) (1919 – 2009)

Dedicated to my mother Tehmina, a great observer of the world, particularly plants and animals. She never tires of watching monkeys and can regale others with her endless simian stories. She passed on this trait to me, but with a slight twist. I grew up watching the flowers and beasts within. However, like my mother, monkeys played a important part for me too. By and by, learnt to deal with them, starting a long journey called meditation.

Dr. Cyrus S. Poonawalla
Ph.D.

9/11, Poonawalla Park,
Pune 411 037, India.

Tel. - Res. : (020) 24271348
Off. : (020) 26993900
Fax - Res. : (020) 24261368
Off. : (020) 26993921
email : csp@seruminstitute.com

FOREWORD

I take great pleasure to write this Foreword for the book on "Meditation for the Modern Man" written by my dear friend, philosopher and advisor Pesi.

I had the good fortune of meeting Pesi when I first visited Haffkine Institute in Bombay in 1964 along with another dear friend, Dr. Jal Mehta. This memorable first meeting finally culminated into the long journey in making Serum Institute as the world's largest vaccine manufacturer.

Now when I hold this book in my hand, nostalgic memories come back to me on this selfless human being; Pesi. I recall a memorable incident at the time when he joined Serum Institute on his retirement from Haffkine Institute. He came to me during the course of his engagement as an Advisor to the Company with an unusual personal request. He said – I would like to meet you when you can give your full attention. *I was worried*....... Pesi said, that the terms of remuneration that I had fixed were bothering him! I looked up and said to myself... *"the man sitting in front of me was not money minded. What's he talking about?"* Pesi said ..."*I do not deserve the remuneration that you have offered. I will feel happy and go home peacefully if you half my remuneration"*. I was astonished! This is the first and last time anybody has said this to me in all my years upto now. I accepted his proposal and then my conscience made me to make up to him in later years.

Whenever I lost my temper – rightfully or wrongly – Pesi found solutions without losing his cool. This obviously was the result of his belief in Meditation and Yoga, which gave him the ability to lead a self-less life.

The book is a celebration of free thinking, uncluttered by the fetters of religion or standard practice or cults or Godmen.

It truly depicts the way Pesi was and I am sure it will continue to guide others on to the true path of discovering themselves towards inner peace.

Dr. Cyrus S. Poonawalla

ACKNOWLEDGEMENTS

I have to thank Dr. Cyrus S Poonawalla for his support all along which enabled me to complete this book.

Amy Fernandes of Times of India for guidance and help with the manuscript. Fali Hirji for helping me in a number of ways. Narayan Shanbhag of Strand Book Stall for helping me with the production of the book and my niece Dr. Farida. A. Talati for her assistance whenever required.

I would also like to thank Prof. Mrs. Vispi R. Balaporia, Former Chancellor's Nominee, Senate, University of Mumbai, for her immense contribution in editing the manuscript.

PREFACE

On the morning of the 8th October 2001, my friend Jal stepped into his bathroom and never returned. He had suffered a massive cerebral haemorrhage, with a systolic blood pressure of 240.

Jal was a dedicated leprosy worker of the country. As a medical doctor, he gave new life to thousands of leprosy patients in his work spanning decades. Not only did he cure them, he also rehabilitated them economically. He gave them cottages to live in – a luxury in India for those otherwise on the streets. Families who had ostracized these patients on the streets returned to stay with them. A cottage and a steady income were irresistible. To run the show, Jal indefatigably raised funds from all over the world. He probably also contributed from his own pocket.

Apart from the occasional blood pressure episodes, common for high placed executives, Jal had no chronic hypertension trouble.

Jal`s passing away raises so many questions. He was a good man. Is this the way God treats angelic humans? (Earlier, his only son, a young doctor, died on an Himalayan expedition). Does God exist? If He does exist, what is His composition? (In my book which is not religion oriented, God does not figure).

On a less emotional level, a more pertinent question is; why did Jal get a massive brain haemorrhage? He had talked to me the previous day in the most normal fashion.

Because of his age (75), and growing administrative problems, his friends persuaded Jal to hand over the charge of his leprosy mission to others. I developed serious reservations about this. Knowing Jal`s deep involvement in his work, the very idea of handing over his life-work to somebody else would have been anathema. But Jal apparently was all co-operation. 10th October 2001 was fixed as the day of handing over charge. On the morning of 8th October Jal was struck by cerebral haemorrhage. We all concluded that the emotional stress of handing over his life`s work to someone else was too much for him to bear, whatever his conscious and apparent cooperative attitude. In order to appear cooperative, Jal would not accept, even to himself, the gravity of parting with his deep passion. That suppressed passion hit back that fatal morning as a blood pressure episode, which killed him. I submit that had Jal cultivated meditation, particularly the variety elaborated in this book, he could have defused his passion, instead of being killed by it. Passion is passion. A good passion can be as devastating as a bad one.

Apart from the moral of the story, it also illustrates that the living flowers of meditation springs from the soil of our day-to-day joys and sorrows.

The origin of meditation lies in man`s endeavour for conscious and voluntary spiritual evolution. But modern times have found new and pressing uses for meditation, particularly to cope with the deadly stress of today`s life.

Meditation is the skill behind all other skills and another of its modern uses is the excellence it brings to our professional activities.

I believe meditation has been a trial and error procedure for mankind. Religious meditations are now seen as mistaken approaches. True spiritual exercise is as non-religious as physiological exercise.

It will not be surprising that a dynamic activity like meditation can be multi-dimensional with different practitioners contributing different concepts and procedures. Naturally, I consider my version nearest to the truth. I am well practiced, well informed and in touch with the current relevant thinking about the human psyche. The model of meditation that has arisen from my heart and brain will be found comfortable by the modern man. Ancient, modern and my original concepts are integrated and repackaged experientially, in the emerging model.

It is not possible to practice meditation and yet not be confronted with problems like the mind-body relationship, the physio-psycho-spiritual anatomy, the problems of change from the lower to the higher, the meaning of lower and higher, the contrast between the religious and the spiritual, conscious evolution, and above all, the birth and development of self-awareness. I have tried to address such problems and provide answers based on my experience or on informed hypothesis.

There is a preponderance of quotations from Buddhism or Vedanta or Sufism. This does not mean that I am either a Buddhist or a Vedantin or a Sufi. These disciplines are deeply involved in meditation and hence the preponderance of their concepts. Some of these concepts click with my own thinking and hence their inclusion here.

WALK WITH THOUGHTS

I know that the multitude walk in darkness. I would put into each man's hand a lantern to guide him, and not have him set out upon his journey depending for illumination on abortive flashes of lightning, or the coruscations of transitory meteors.

William Wordsworth

We've conquered outer space, but not inner space; we've split the atom, but not our prejudice. We have higher incomes, but lower morals; we've become long on quantity, but short on quality.

R.W. Emerson

I must create a system, or be enslaved by another man's; I will not reason and compare, my business is to create.

William Blake

The intricate maze of different schools of philosophy claim to clarify matters and reveal the Truth. But they, in fact, create confusions where there need be no confusion. To understand anything, there must first be the person who understands, that is the Self. Why worry about other things? Why not remain yourself and be in peace? Fortunate is he who does not entangle himself in the labyrinths of philosophy but goes straight to the source, the Atma from which all have sprung.

Sri Ramana Maharishi

My heart leaps up when I behold a rainbow in the sky.

William Wordsworth

The whole of science is nothing more than a refinement of everyday thinking.

Albert Einstein

As a man abandons his worn-out clothes and acquires new ones, so when the body is worn out, new one is acquired by the Self, who lives within.

Bhagavad Gita 2.12-25
S. Radhakrishnan

With the mind thus composed, quite purified, quite clarified, without blemish, without defilement, grown soft and workable, fixed immovable, I directed my mind to the knowledge and recollection of former habitations .....
Thus I remember diver's former habitations in all their modes and details.

Buddha

Would you learn the secret of the sea? Only those who brave its dangers, comprehend its mystery.

H. W. Longfellow

If you would be a real seeker after Truth, it is necessary that at least once in your life you doubt, as far as possible, all things.

Rene Descartes

Thou takest on thyself the shame of hemp and wine
In order that thou may`st for one moment escape from thyself.

Jalal-ud-din Rumi
Quoted by Prof. E. G. Brown
In A Year Amongst the Persians

One must be his own awakener, that is, no one can awaken another by the mere instruction of Sufism.

Rumi, the Persian, the Sufi
A Reza Arasteh

The legend of Rabi'ah al-Adawiyyah. One day in spring-time she entered her house and bowed her head, " Come out", said the woman-servant, "and behold what God hath made." Rabi' ah answered, "Come in and behold the Maker."

Quoted by R. A. Nicholson in
Rumi, Poet and Mystic

INTRODUCTION

One day while roaming on the rainbow, I jumped, or slipped, I cannot remember, and fell on earth. Since then, I have been trying to get back. This book is the story of what I think needs to be done to return.

If you have read books on meditation, you will find this one different.

To know the difference, we need to get acquainted.

I have undergone extraordinary exposure to any number of contrary influences; ancient and modern; eastern and western; religious, scientific and above all, spiritual.

Thanks to the meditative process constantly going on, these influences have neither neutralised each other, nor made eclectic. The meditative fire has been continuously melting these influences, blending them, fusing them, homogenising them. I receive rays of innumerable colours which, while passing through the prism of my self-awareness, emit a colourless light. By the end of the day I remain neither ancient nor modern, neither eastern nor western.

I am deeply imbued with the concept of six archangels (symbols of spiritual states) of Zarathrustra, in whose faith I was born. The Upanishads and Sufism, particularly Rumi (a great Sufi Sage) excite my utmost respect and enthusiasm. Because of my unbounded admiration for Freud, I am likely to be mistaken for a Freudian. There is a core of Freud`s thinking, the depth of which only a true meditator will appreciate. In spite of his 19th century baggage, he will remain the greatest modern pioneer of insight and of the eventual triumph of the conscious over the unconscious. He has tried to civilize man, not by theological morality, not by political indoctrination, but by self-knowledge, by making the unconscious conscious. In his own way, Freud was a lifelong meditator.

I have always held that a person who has not read Freud`s "A General Introduction to Psychoanalysis" suffers from gross intellectual lacuna. On the scientific side Freud was the first to show how one can travel from the pathological to the normal, by self-knowledge. Had ten more years of productive life been granted to him, he would have further shown how the normal can travel to the super-normal, again by self-knowledge. His theories of de-sexualised libido, transmutation of the id into the ego, and his ego psychology, are pointers in this direction.

Most detractors of Freud are a source of amusement. But one can't say the same about Karl Popper, perhaps the greatest philosopher of science. Is there any truth beyond scientific truth? Popper accepted the possibility of scientific truth only. And it was to be established by his test of falsifiability. Any other entity, even if it be the truth, if it cannot be subjected to the test of falsifiability, is not science. For example, Popper did not consider Darwin's work as science. (I wonder whether creationists have harnessed Popper's stand). This is because it does not satisfy the test of falsifiability. However, it seems this did not prevent Popper from factually accepting Darwin's contribution. One is tempted to think that there are truths beyond scientific (Popperean) truths.

I have raised this discussion here because I like to believe that activities like meditation or the pursuit of the spiritual should be subject to some kind of validity testing if not of falsifiability. Some day when the definition of science is broadened, it would be worthwhile considering whether meditation is a science or not. Meanwhile, I treat meditation as science-like, if not science. For example, if you carry out meditation steps A, B and C, spiritual results X, Y and Z, should predictably follow.

I consider Raman Maharishi to be the greatest spiritual genius of the 20th century; a fantastic combination of intellect and spirituality. I have always remained dazzled by his utterances. I took quite a long time to understand the relationship between the ego and the 'I', which turned out to be simplicity itself. Perhaps Raman Maharishi has helped me in this particular endeavour. As you will see later, I eventually arrived at the concept of three 'I's – the ego, the current I and the future higher I.

I find myself addressing an audience which does not belong to any religion, at least not vehemently, much less a sect, or a cult or a godman. I am addressing an audience, liberal in its outlook. An audience with vague stirrings of the spiritual. An audience inclined and ready to experiment with various states of consciousness. An audience eager to explore the inner world. And above all, an audience in search of self-improvement.

Even though I consider myself pro-science, I believe in ESP, survival after death and even reincarnation. In my case these beliefs have nothing to do with religion. Till they are proved factually they should be entertained only provisionally. As far as ESP in the area of telepathy is concerned, I have direct, repeated, unimpeachable experience. And as you will see later, if telepathy is established, survival would be a logical corollary. Those who practice meditation would be naturally attracted to the concept of reincarnation. They eventually realise that one lifetime is not enough to reach the distant heights of meditation.

I recently came across a work 'The End of Science' (Horgan, 1996). The main thesis was this: whatever worthwhile scientific discoveries could have been made have already been made. Now there is no scope in any discipline of science to make any further seminal discoveries. At the most only advanced technological progress would be possible. I believe the great adventure of science has not yet been initiated. It is the study of the nature of consciousness. Until now, this study has remained the preserve of philosophers. Now it is the turn of scientists, As usual they start such studies with the help of scientific gadgetry upon the consciousness of others. But one day, they will realize that consciousness is best investigated upon oneself. And that will be the beginning of a new chapter in the history of meditation. In my theory and practice of meditation, only three entities are involved. The I, the mind and the body. (The higher self turns up later). There is no reference to, or dependence on, entities like God, gods, godmen, gurus, secret doctrines, religious rituals and ceremonies or any other similar non-scientific elements. Whatever statements I have made relating to the technique and practice of meditation are verifiable. And whatever hypothesis I have drawn can be legitimately derived from this practice and experience.

At no stage will I ask you to believe in me. I will not invoke obedience, faith, grace and such other enslaving devices. I maintain that, given reasonable physiological and psychological health, if the technique presented here is practiced, results must follow.

That ancient wisdom anticipated the discoveries of modern science is a favourite theme of some gurus. I believe, the need of the hour is to reformulate the ancient wisdom, to bring it in line with modern science. Even ancient truths shine brighter if the patina of tradition is scraped off. Most gurus (they like to be called so) expound meditation, as if human knowledge came to a standstill 2500 years ago.

I am a creature of the 20th century, now into the 21st. I believe that even in the field of meditation there is scope for new concepts and techniques, perhaps even for new objectives. Today, a business executive may practice meditation to advance his professional career!

By now you must have guessed I am not a godman. I am a shirt-and-pant man. Japanese and other robes, lockets, beads, exotic hair styles, painted foreheads, chantings, prancing about, are a perennial source of entertainment. Pseudo-spirituality, thy name is exhibitionism.

I am a complete breaker with tradition. My ashram is my office. I was associated with a unit involved in production, marketing and other related activities. Although my prime goal in life is one of the most ancient – spiritual evolution, to support it, I seek my livelihood in a very modern way.

You will find my approach to meditation, both for theory and practice, altogether different from that of others. In fact, you may not find any theory at all in other systems!

You will find me attacking many holy cows. I will be contending with Patanjali`s Yoga Darshan, modern concepts of relaxation and inspirational talks on positive thinking, to mention a few.

More dangerous would be my non-acceptance of religion. Its fate is already sealed today in Northern Ireland, Bosnia, Middle East, Pakistan, India, Srilanka and so on. I am fully aware of the occasional good, religion contributes. But this is because of a certain admixture of the spiritual with religions. In his march, man is already leaving behind religion, but it would be a great catastrophe if the space vacated is not filled with the spiritual. In the world of meditation conventional morality has no place. It is gradually replaced by a higher morality. But those who do not meditate should continue with conventional morality, lest they fall between two stools. In any case conventional morality is not to be discarded. As meditation progresses, it will fall off by itself and its place occupied by higher morality. Higher morality cannot be formalised. It is the unpredictable, spontaneous, creative, individualised response of the higher self which will be established by meditation. Conventional morality is a crude amalgam of the superego, expedience and even hypocrisy. It is the way of the stagnant. Higher morality is the way of the free, soaring towards the final destination.

I must have devoted about 20,000 hours to meditation which gave me an opportunity to try out various approaches. It is but natural that some theory will have emerged from such practice. Hence, the book is divided between theory and practice, which you may not find in any other meditation treatise. I have not been on a sabbatical while writing this book. It has taken shape in the thick of professional involvements. One of the consequences has been repetition for which I apologize to the reader.

Meditation involves several psychological and spiritual states which are not part of our usual consciousness. And hence, there are no terms for them in our current language. Since I am not in a position to coin new terms, I have made use of existing lexicon for the new experiences by attaching to them special meanings. I have, therefore provided a glossary of such terms and the special meanings attached to them. The reader is requested to make repeated use of this section to understand me better.

I find that my treatment of various themes has been concise, which is but appropriate for an introduction. If I get an opportunity, I would like to elaborate on these themes in the future. More importantly I have not `researched` any of my concepts from other books, except for quotations. The various concepts are expressions of my own experience, some of them reinvented and some of them original. Their integration into one unitary whole, which constitutes my theory of meditation, has deeply satisfied me.

There are many kinds of meditations. I have christened my brand "Cognitive Meditation". It means meditation in which the I takes cognizance of the non-I, i.e. the inner world of thoughts, desires, cravings. It is found that the exercise dissolves the non-I, and the `solute` homogenizes with the I. With such regular inputs of new energy, the I becomes more and more self-aware, powerful, blissful, free and eventually transcendent. Such an empowered I without mumbling auto-suggestions and positive affirmations is ready to take on this world and the next.

Before concluding this introduction, I would like to touch upon a subject about which considerable misunderstanding prevails. It is believed that the meditative experience can be easily replicated with the help of drugs and without undergoing the labours of training oneself in meditation. Instant nirvana!

I find this an irresponsible stand and a downright lie. A state produced by the activity of drugs bears no comparison whatsoever with that produced by meditation. The former is drug- dependent and the latter self-generated. The former is a case of bondage, the latter that of freedom. The former leads to pathological states of body and mind and to their eventual destruction. The latter leads to psychological and spiritual health.

I hold people like Aldous Huxley responsible for romanticizing the use of drugs (Huxley, 1959). He recommended the use of mescaline as a substitute for alcoholism! A classical recipe for jumping from the frying pan into the fire. Timothy Leary (Leary, 1968) institutionalized the drug culture, promising chemical samathis. Another classical instance, this time, of the blind leading the blind.

There are many ways a change can be brought about in human beings. I understand that there are over 3000 self-improvement centres in America. With so many centres, there is bound to be a variety of techniques. Some are quite prominent. Auto-hypnosis, auto-suggestion, gestalt therapy, behavior therapy, yoga, Sufism, positive thinking, relaxation systems, stress removal techniques, self-analysis, shamanism, tantra, Tibetan meditations, kundalini, music, dance, prayer....

The technique I advocate is rigorously based on self-awareness and self-awareness alone. The term 'gnana' used by Shankaracharya is usually translated as 'knowledge'. A more sensitive translation would be 'self-awareness'. For Shankaracharya, 'gnana' is only remedy for spiritual development. Thus, at least on the issue of potency of self-awareness, I am in exalted company. This introduction is not the place to undertake a comparative study of the various methods. I may attempt it some other time. Meanwhile, I will content myself with the statement that further evolution of man is possible only through self-awareness.

Not everyone is fond of theory. In such a case one may proceed directly to the practice chapter. In any case, in all undertakings, practice precedes theory.

I will close this introduction with a humanistic prayer.

May you be curious as to what you are,
May you be curious as to who you are,
May you be curious as to what I say,
May you be curious as to find out for yourself.

AN EXTENDED GLOSSARY

Since the process of meditation unfolds new states of consciousness not otherwise experienced by humans, no terminology identifying these states has yet been developed. Whatever new terms exist are not standard. 'Atma' is common to both Jainism and Vedanta, but has altogether different meanings in both the disciplines.

Since I have no background to create new terms from classical sources, I have resorted to using existing terms, attributing to these specific, exclusive meanings, to describe specific meditation states.

There are also common terms like 'mind', 'soul', 'consciousness' which over centuries have lost all semblance of exactitude and hence I am constrained to shun them altogether. I have standardized loose concepts and substituted them with terms having extra meanings. 'Mind' has become 'Psychological Self', 'Spirit' has become 'Higher Self', 'Consciousness' has become 'Self-awareness' and so on. The main purpose of glossary is to clarify how common terms have now been made technical and pegged to their exact meanings.

If I have occasionally used terms discarded by me, it is only to improve communication, at the non-technical, colloquial level.

This is an extended glossary of terms. Some of the terms continue to have standard meaning and some of them have been refined from their current loose connotations and given standardized meanings, with a view to improving the quality of the communication and the dialogue which may follow.

Glossaries normally come at the end of the work. This one appears at the beginning, so that my concepts, which frequently are quite unconventional, can be better understood.

In case a reader finds this glossary over-technical and difficult to grasp the terms, it would be advisable to start directly with the first chapter, and more profitably return to it later.

Action

An act performed by the I. same or similar to voluntary or proactive action. Opposite of Reaction.

Allotrope

Modified manifestation of the two basic energies of Non-Self-awareness and Self-awareness. For example, some of the allotropes of self-awareness are insight, mindfulness, awakening, understanding, meaning, wisdom.

Ananda

Bliss. A state in which psychological drives are transmuted by Self-awareness into a homogenised pool of energy, which is equipoised at all points. It is effortless, stillness or movement. In this state, there is nothing to want or to reject.

Opposite of pain (tension) and pleasure (discharge).

Atma

A term not used by me. It is the highest spiritual entity, having varying meanings. For example, the 'atma' of Vedanta, is an illusively detached entity, from the Brahman, the Vedantic Ultimate Reality, in which it is perennially merged. For the Jains, there is no merger for the 'atma', which on realisation, continues to shine in splendid isolation. The Jain 'atma', seems nearer to the 'Purusha' of Samkhya.

The highest spiritual entity envisaged by me is modestly described as the Higher Self. It also merges in the Ultimate Reality, THAT, but its origin and earlier history is altogether different.

The starting point of the Higher Self is the Physical Self, which is a Reality by itself, from where, by dialectical leaps into the opposite and the higher, it reaches the Higher Self status. Vedantic atma has nothing to do with the physical and the psychological.

Also see Selves and Spiritual Self.

Awareness – See Self–awareness.

Becoming

The Physical, Psychological, Instinctual and Psychological selves are coiled and constantly try to uncoil and unfold. The Physical tends to unfold into the Physiological and the Physiological into the Instinctual and so on.

They are all in a state of unstable equilibrium in search of equilibrium, which is attained when the Spiritual is reached.

This movement from the Physical to the Spiritual is Becoming. It is constant flux and movement. It is what makes a certain phase of manifestation, subject to transience.

It is the opposite of Being.

Being

Same as Higher Self, Higher "I" or Spiritual Self, Spirit, Highest spiritual state.

Pool of homogenised energy transmuted from various psychological drives, which are de-individualised.

State of dynamic (not passive) self-generated stillness or movement.

Opposite of Becoming.

Cognitive meditation

A term I have coined.

A meditation based on the cognition (observation) by the "I" of the "Non – I", i.e. of impulses, thoughts, desires, passions.........

Such cognition transmutes the Non-I into the Higher I or Higher self.

Building of the Higher Self and its dynamics is the objective of Cognitive Meditation.

Cognitive meditation is different from other meditations which are based on suppression or expression.

Conscious

A term not used by me except colloquially where context demands it. The term I use is self-aware.

Consciousness

A term not used by me but generally used by all including those who do not believe in its existence.

Everybody has a rough idea as to what it means but cognitive psychologists and neuro-scientists raise a lot of controversial dust about it. They cannot make out what it is or even whether it exists.

And when they accept its existence, they mistake 'conscious' thoughts, feelings, desires for consciousness. Thoughts, feelings are never conscious. They appear to be conscious because they are lighted up by

Self-awareness. (Those thoughts, feelings, etc. which are not lighted up by self-awareness are called unconscious. Actually they are not even unconscious. It is only because they are not accessible to the I and its Self-awareness that they are called unconscious).

I use the term Self-awareness for Consciousness (reasons explained elsewhere). For me, it means the sense of I-hood, awareness of one's own existence. In its pure state it contains nothing except pure Self-awareness, not even a semblance of a thought. When Self-awareness (Consciousness) is 'contaminated' by impulses, thoughts, feelings, desires, it becomes impure. Modern day 'Scientific' psychologists know only the impure variety. Pure Self-awareness (Consciousness) can be experienced only by meditators, which is the ultimate experiment of science.

Pure Consciousness is the equivalent of the Higher I or the Higher Self. Also see Self-awareness.

Conventional Morality

Morality of the conventional, religious, wordly person. Ostensibly derived from God, it is mainly a product of the superego. The superego is an unconscious entity, which is a moral code, injected into the child, by the parents. It is not a divine but an acquired morality, varying with time and place. The superego morality may be mixed with social expediency and even hypocrisy.

The superego, being an unconscious, non-self-aware entity, is oppressive and enslaving. It has none of the freedom and choice of the Higher Morality, which flows from Self-awareness. Conventional morality is bondage, whereas higher morality is liberation.

Cosmic Evolution

Evolution is usually understood to be Darwinian. Its span spreads from the primeval vegetative structures to man. It is also called organic evolution.

The span of Cosmic Evolution is much, much wider. It begins with the big bang from THAT and ends with the merger of the Spiritual Self into THAT. In between, it encompasses the physical, physiological, instinctual, psychological and psycho-spiritual stages. It is a journey from THAT to THAT.

Currently, man is in the psycho-spiritual phase, progressing towards the spiritual.

Cosmic Evolution, which starts with extraordinary concentrated and 'coiled' matter (the physical phase), starts unfolding through the various phases. This movement or flux is called Becoming.

Man's destiny is to unfold from the Psycho-spiritual to the Spiritual and eventual merger into THAT. However the unfolding from the Psycho-spiritual to the spiritual is different from the unfolding from the physical to the Psycho-spiritual. The former is self-aware and by choice and the latter non-self-aware and compulsive. Also, the former is undertaken by the I, while the latter belongs to the non-I. Cosmic Evolution starts with inertia and bondage of the physical and ends in self-generation and freedom of the Spiritual.

The movement from the physical to the physiological to the instinctual, to the psychological, to the psycho-spiritual, to the spiritual is by dialectical leaps into the opposite and the higher.

Current I

Today's man is designated as the Current Man and his I, as the Current I.

Wherever there is Self-awareness there is I-hood. Both can be considered synonymous.

The I is an evolving structure. It starts as the ego of the primitive or psychological man, evolves into the Current I of the Current Man and finally, evolves into the pure or Higher I of the Spiritual Self.

The Ego which is just sprouting from the Psychological Self, is highly contaminated with impulses, thoughts, desires, cravings, passions....... The Current I of the Psycho-Spiritual Self is partly contaminated, and the higher I of the Spiritual Self is free from all contamination.

It is the Current I which undertakes the worldly and the higher enterprises. It is also the Current I which undertakes the great adventure of Meditation and in the process, becomes the Higher I.

Current Man.

Very roughly, man passes through three evolutionary levels: Primitive Man, Current Man and the Higher Man.

Primitive Man is just evolved from the animal kingdom. In addition to instincts, which manifest at the animal level, Primitive Man also has drives. Drives are psychologised instincts, giving the Primitive Man the psychological level. The psychological level consists of impulses, thoughts, desires, carvings, passions......

The animal level has no I-hood. It is a creature of instincts. The Primitive Man has a faint glimmer of I-hood in the form of the Ego. The Ego is a partially transmuted structure of the psychological and the accompanying non-I makes its first debut as the I in the form of the Ego.

The Primitive Man evolves into the Current Man, which is a Psycho-spiritual level. The 'Psycho' component is from the psychological of the Primitive Man and the 'Spiritual' component is from the Ego of the primitive Man, which has matured into the Current I.

The Current Man, in the course of time, will evolve by choice and voluntary decision into the Spiritual Man.

The Current Man is an intermediate stage between the Primitive and the Higher Man.

Current Self – See Current I.

Dialectical Leap

Cosmic Evolution has six levels – physical (physical entities), physiological (plant), instinctual (animal), psychological (primitive man), psycho-spiritual (current man) and the spiritual (Higher man).

The transition from the lower level to the higher level, for example, from the physical to the physiological, is neither gradual nor a purification. It is sudden and therefore a leap. Also, it is leap into the opposite and the higher. Therefore, a dialectical leap. It is because of dialectical leaps that higher and higher levels of evolution are achieved.

The dialectical leaps from the physical to the Psycho-spiritual are Non-Self-Aware or caused by nature. The dialectical leap from the psycho-spiritual to the spiritual is Self-Aware, voluntary and by choice. Once the spiritual component is involved, Self-awareness automatically steps in.

However, the dialectical leap is only a structural rearrangement, the underlying Reality remaining constant. For example, the stinking manure is restructured into a fragrant flower, the underlying stuff remaining the same.

Drive

Animals have instincts. Men have both Instincts and Drives. Instincts are energy of a physiological nature. Drive is energy of a psychological nature. Some of the Drives are psychologised Instincts, for example, sex into love. Sex is physiological, love is psychological. There is a one to one relationship, both are distinct and structurally different. However one can pass into the other. Where sex becomes love, the former decreases and the latter increases. (Love can also become sex).

Drives can be in the conventional sense 'good' or 'bad'. Sympathy, compassion, altruism, pity, unselfishness are some of the 'good' Drives. Acquisitiveness, selfishness, aggrandisement, cruelty, violence are some of the 'bad' Drives.

However, both the varieties are psychological. The so called 'good' Drives have nothing spiritual about them. This is because all Drives are Non-Self-Aware and therefore non-spiritual. The Spiritual is equipoised and completely free from not only any kind of Drive, but even an involuntary thought, which is only a mini-drive. The Spiritual is by choice. The non-spiritual (Non-Self-Aware) is compulsively silent or noisy.

Ego

Ego carries different meanings for different people. Its popular meaning is the vehicle of egotism. For psychoanalysts, it is the equivalent of what I have called the current "I". The psychoanalytic Ego manages the Id, the Superego and the external world. For me, the ego is the I, but of a very primitive type.

There are three 'I's. The Ego, the Current I and the Higher I.

Perhaps I am using the term Ego in its original sense. It is the small bud of I-hood, which sprouts on the surface of the Psychological the vehicle of Drives. It has a sense of I-hood, but only as a faint-glimmer. Having sprung from the Drives, it is entirely surrounded and contaminated by them. It is more of drives than I-hood.

The Ego has a mean beginning but ends up as the highest structure in the universe — the Higher or Spiritual self.

Equipoise

Equipoise is an allotrope or state of the Higher I. In it, energy is equally distributed all over without any pockets of tension or relaxation.

It is effortlessly and dynamically still or active, being free from all pulls, i.e. good or bad, from every direction. It is self-generated stillness or action.

It is free from all wanting and non-wanting. It is bliss itself. It is the source not only of psychosomatic health but of unalloyed wisdom itself.

Once experienced, it leaves behind a permanent impression.

Evolution

Movement from lower to higher forms of life and existence — see Cosmic Evolution.

Fractionating Column

The human unit is like a Fractionating Column. The starting material is the Physical. The first fraction from the physical is the Physiological. The next fraction from the Physiological is the Instinctual. The next fraction from Instinctual is Psychological. The fraction from the Psychological is the Psycho-spiritual. The Psycho-spiritual yields the last fraction, the Spiritual. Including the physical, there are 6 fractions. Each of these fractions has been designated as a self. Also see 'Selves'.

Fragmentation

Unlike the Higher Self which is homogenized and whole, the lower self is fragmented.

The Lower Self comprises the Physical, the Physiological, the Instinctual and Psychological selves.

Each of these selves is fragmented into dualistic and conflicting forces. The negative and positive charges in the atom, growth and decay in the plant, life and death instincts in the animal, love and hatred in man. In man, at the psychological level, many more conflicting dualities are operating. All this leads to the fragmentation of man.

Man can be both fragmented and whole, depending upon the level. Also see Wholeness.

Freedom

One of the allotropes of self-awareness. Most of the man, in all his selves, except the Higher Self, is conditioned, determined, bound.

There are two schools of thought – that man is free or that man is bound.

The truth is man is part bound and part free. In the Lower Selves from the Physical to the Psychological, man is bound. In the Higher Self, man is free

Higher I – See Ego and the Current I.

Higher Man – See Current Man.

Higher Morality

The source of Higher Morality is the Higher Self. Opposite of Conventional Morality – see Conventional Morality.

Higher Self – See Spiritual Self, Selves.

I– see Current I.

ID

A term very occasionally used by me. It has the same meaning and significance as in psychoanalysis. The id is the reservoir of the drives, which are genetic and innate. It is unconscious, i.e. Non-Self-Aware.

Immortality

Generally confused with survival after death.

That which survives is a psychological complex, subject to rebirth.

Immortality refers to the Spiritual or Higher Self, which is no more subject to birth, death or rebirth. It would eventually merge into THAT, The Ultimate Reality

Impotence

This term, as used here, is not in any way related to sexual impotence.

It is one of the principal allotropes of Non-Self-Awareness. It is the absence of the power of will, i.e. it is the dualistic counterpart of Power.

However, this Impotence has got its own explosive, violent, mad strength of Instinct/Drive.

Impurity

This term, as used by me here, is not referring to physical, physiological or moral impurity.

I am talking of impure or pure Consciousness. When Consciousness is cluttered with impulses, thoughts, desires.....good or bad, moral or immoral, it becomes impure. When Consciousness is free of all involuntary impulses, thoughts, moral or immoral, it becomes pure. Pure Consciousness (Self- awareness) is not known to anyone including modern psychologists. It can be experienced by meditators alone. It is a clear pool of energy with only a sense of I-hood.

Impurity is a principal Allotrope of Non-Self Awareness and Purity that of Self-awareness.

Involuntariness

These are physiological and psychological movements, which take place by themselves and cannot be controlled by the I. They are expressions, allotropes of the Non-I or Non-self-awareness.

Examples on the physiological level include the nature of movements of organs like the heart, stomach, kidneys and other organs. Similarly, the nature of myriad physiological reactions going on in the brain and the rest of the body.

On the psychological plane, the nature of movements of thoughts and complexes, which cannot be controlled by the "I". the entire working of the unconscious and preconscious components of the psychological self is involuntary. Even the nature of the movement of the thought spray is involuntary.

From the spiritual perspective, it is bondage.

It is the opposite of voluntariness in which muscular and thought movements are under the control of the I.

Examples are movements of arms and legs. Or controlled movements of thoughts. The working of the higher self is voluntary, it being under the control of the I. It is an expression, aspect or allotrope of Self-awareness.

From the spiritual perspective, it is freedom.

The objective of meditation is to transmute involuntariness, both physiological and psychological, particularly the latter, into voluntariness. This is done by subjecting physiological and psychological involuntary movements to observation by the I.

Lower Self – See Selves.

Middle Self – See Selves.

Mind

A term not used by me in my presentation because, in the course of time, it has lost any definite meaning. Nowadays, it can mean the lowest desire, highest intellectual properties or the highest human component like spirit or the Buddha-nature.

My term nearest to 'mind' is the 'Psychological Self'. It is a conglomerate of all kinds of impulses, desires, carvings, passions. In short, all the drives. It does not include any intellectual or spiritual functions, which are spread over the Psycho-spiritual self and the Spiritual self (higher self).

Preconscious

The region between the Unconscious and the Thought Spray (the apparently conscious). Unlike in the case of the Unconscious, the "I" can recall the contents of the Preconscious. The Drives, which originally reside in the Unconscious before they become the Thought Spray, pass through the Preconscious. Similarly, the down-flow of the Thought Spray also returns to the Preconscious. The Preconscious arises from the Unconscious and the Thought Spray from the Preconscious. My Preconscious is similar to that of psychoanalysis. See Psychological Self, Selves.

Psyche

A term not used by me. It can be roughly equated to the Psychological Self. See Psychological Self or Selves.

Psychological Self

This self is composed of impulses, desires, cravings, passions. These are of various kinds. All these are energies. A common term for all these is Drive. Thus, there is drive for hunger, drive for sex, drive for fear..... Drives are energies in a coiled or compressed state, seeking discharge. In a compressed state, a drive causes tension and when discharged, causes relaxation.

Intellectual faculties like reason, comprehension, vision do not reside in the psychological self. They belong to the spiritual component of the Psycho-spiritual self. The I is also not a part of the psychological self. It belongs to the Psycho-spiritual self.

Drives have three levels of cognitivity: (1) The Thought Spray, (2) The Preconscious and (3) The Unconscious.

The Thought Spray is more popularly known as the stream of consciousness. It is also treated as a component of the conscious mind along with the I.

It is the third component of the psychological self and its topmost story. Anatomically, it is just below the Psycho-spiritual self and its I. The I takes cognisance of the contents of the thought spray because of the close proximity. This leads to a great misunderstanding. Because the I, which is conscious (self-aware) structure, is aware of the thought spray; even the contents of the thought spray are clubbed with the I and treated as conscious. Western cognitive scientists are consistently dubbing the thought spray and its contents as part of the conscious mind. The fact is thoughts, desires, impulses, i.e. the contents of the thought spray, are non-self aware and non-conscious. The illusion of their conscious nature arises from the close proximity of the I and the lightening up of the thought spray by its Self-awareness. It is a case of reflected glory. All thoughts, desires, etc. are mini drives and are as non-self-aware as the unconscious drives.

The impulses, thoughts, desires, cravings, passions, of the psychological self make their presence and needs known to the I, at the level of the thought spray.

The Preconscious is the second component and middle story of the psychological self. It is below the thought spray and above the unconscious. It contains drives which have back-tracked from the thought spray, as well as those drives from the unconscious, on their way to the thought spray. The I has partial cognition of its contents and can even recall some of them.

The Unconscious is the first component of the psychological self and its bottom story. It is just above the physiological self. Its contents are totally beyond the cognition of the I. It is the I, so to say, which is unconscious of the contents of the so called unconscious. The self-awareness of the I does not reach the caverns of the unconscious. This is the Achilles heel of man and his most important component-the I.

The Unconscious is the breeding ground of drives. It is here that the physiological instincts are transmuted into corresponding psychological drives.

These drives take cognisance of other drives, but are non-self-aware of their own selves. They are blind about their own activity, inertial, untamed, only interested in expressing themselves and having their own way.

The unconscious is dualistic. It has two kinds of drives i.e. the genetic and the acquired. To the former belong hunger, sex, aggression, greed, fear, gregariousness, etc.. These are hedonistic. The acquired drives are ascetic and anti-hedonistic. They monitor, inhibit, tame, control, culture the genetic drives.

The genetic drives approximate to Freud's Id and the acquired drives to the Superego. The Id and the Superego can be aware of each other but are non-self-aware of their own selves. It is an extraordinary blindness in which they can see others, but not their own selves.

As the cosmic evolution moves forward, a new set of genetic drives will emerge in the unconscious. In isolated cases, they have already emerged. These genetic drives are antagonistic to earlier genetic drives of hunger, sex, aggression, greed, fear, hatred..... They are the drives of compassion, love, sympathy, co-operation, sacrifice.... As meditation accelerates the cosmic evolution, such drives emerge earlier in the case of the meditator. These drives are far from common these days. No wonder they go unnoticed or are misclassified as acquired drives by psychological scientists like Freud.

These later genetic drives, like compassion, also suffer from another kind of misclassification. They are wrongly treated as spiritual entities. Spiritual entities are self-aware and have no compulsiveness, inertia, blindness, pressure. Entities like compassion, love, sympathy, etc. are, merely drives and, like any other psychological drive are compulsive, inertial, etc. the spiritual is not a drive at all.

See also Selves and Drives.

Reaction

Action by the Non-I, i.e. by the Physiological or Instinctual or Psychological selves. Same or similar to involuntary or reflex action.

It is an Allotrope of Non-Self-awareness and opposite of action.

Reincarnation

For me, reincarnation is not a religious issue. It can only be factual. Whether there is reincarnation or not is purely a matter of fact. Religious opinion either way has no validity.

Therefore, Stevenson's 'Twenty Cases Suggestive of Reincarnation' (1974) is a more valid approach.

Of the six fractions of the human unit, only two can survive and subsequently reincarnate. The Physical, the Physiological and the Instinctual are left behind. The Spiritual, which has already exhausted all the coiled up forces, no more dies or is born, much less reincarnate.

However, the two fractions, the Psychological and the Psycho-spiritual, survive and reincarnate.

All those who have made progress in meditation realise two things; (1) that it would not be possible, to fully realise the Spiritual in one lifetime and that (2) several lifetimes would be required to do so. Hence, they look upon Reincarnation favourably. But this could also be a wish-fulfillment mechanism. Hence, the significance of the work of people like Ian Stevenson.

Relaxation

Another buzz word. One of the consequences of tension and stress is the tensing of the muscles. So it is believed, if the muscles were relaxed, tension and stress would be removed. I believe differently. Relaxation only pushes back and suppresses the tension and stress and drives them underground. Hence, if practiced for long, it only serves to make the condition worse.

Take the case of anger, which is at the Psychological level. If expression is given to anger, energy is fritted away (apart from other serious consequences). If expression is not given, it gets suppressed and resurfaces in devious and toxic ways.

On the Physiological (muscular) level, a similar thing happens. Because of the anger muscles of the arm are tensed. If a slap is administered, the muscle will relax. However, if 'control' is exercised, muscular tension energy will continue to keep the arm muscles tensed. If this tension is 'removed' by relaxation of the muscles, it is pushed back into the Physiological system, apparently Relaxing the arm. But the suppressed muscular tension energy would continue with its toxic ways. Mere suppression cannot destroy it.

As will be seen later, the ideal way is neither expression nor suppression but transmutation into a Self-awareness allotrope, Equipoise. It takes care of both Psychological and muscular anger.

Thus, Relaxation can be obtained in three ways. (1) By expression, i.e. giving vent. This method can have serious social consequences, apart from the fact that it results in frittering away the individual's energies. (2) By suppression, i.e. muscular Relaxation. As seen above, a far from ideal solution. (3) By Transmutation, a process facilitated by meditation.

Safeguarding health, not only is the stress relieved, but the energy is conserved and transmuted to perform higher functions.

Religion – see spiritual.

Selves

There is a long tradition in the Upanishads that man is constituted of several selves. Taittiriya Upanishad talks of five selves. The number varies from thinker to thinker. My number amounts to six (1) The Physical Self, (2) The Physiological Self, (3) The Instinctual Self, (4) The Psychological Self, (5) The Psycho-spiritual Self and (6) The Spiritual Self.

Each Self has a different structure and dynamics.

The Physical Self – This is the first self and is composed of substances like air, water, food, etc. which are ingested inside the human body. Its structure is material and the various components are drived from the environment. The prototype is inanimate matter, symbolically called the 'mineral'. Its dynamic is Non-Self-awareness (see chapter X).

The Physiological Self – This is the second self and is the living body, loosely called the physical body. It is composed of various living tissues. It is drived from the physical self. It is subject to birth, growth, decay and death. The prototype is the plant.

The physiological self is composed of living matter and is derived from the physical self. Its dynamic is that of Non-self-awareness.

The Instinctual self -this is the third self and is a continuation of the physiological self. In the physiological self (plant), the two main forces are birth and death. Though there is no such tradition, these two forces could be called instincts. The main difference between the physiological and instinctual selves is the proliferation of instincts beyond life and death instincts. Instincts of hunger, sex, fear, aggression and several others appear for the first time. Instincts are specialized physiological substances producing related behaviour. The instinctual self is derived from the physiological self. The prototype is the animal. The dynamic is of Non-self-awareness.

The Psychological Self – this is the fourth self. It is a big evolutionary leap. Animal evolving into primitive man. The chief characteristic of this self is the emergence of the psychological substances.

These are drives of hunger, sex, fear, aggression, greed, love, hatred, compassion, sympathy and so on. The drives are psychologised instincts. Instincts are made of physiological substances and drives of psychological substances. The drives are derived from the instincts. On the physiological level, they are called instincts; on the psychological level, they are called drives.

The drives, though psychological, are still material, though matter of a much more refined nature. The psychological self is made up of specific drives in the form of impulses, desires, carvings, wanting, not-wanting, passions, emotional storms, etc.

The prototype is the primitive man. The dynamic is that of Non-self-awareness.

The Psycho-spiritual Self- This is the fifth self. It is derived from the psychological self. The psychological component remains the same and the spiritual component is derived from the psychological self.

It is obviously a hybrid entity. It is the predominant self of the current man; the bridge between the psychological self and the yet-to-evolve spiritual self.

The psychological component continues to be a bundle of energies (drives). The energy of the spiritual self is something altogether unique. It is a single energy. Psychological energies are coiled and always under pressure, trying to unfold and release themselves. This is how tension is created in the system. The single energy of the spiritual self is totally uncoiled and always in a state of equipoise. If one desires to remain in a state of equipoise, it cannot be done by forcing the turbulent psychological component to become quiet. It will only be suppressed and from deep down will bounce back with more turbulence when the opportunity arises. The psychological can only be transmuted into the spiritual through a technique involving Self-awareness.

The psychological component with its bundle of conflicting drives has no I-hood. Such a structure is called the non-I. All the preceding Selves – the physical, the physiological, the instinctual, have also no I-hood and belong to the category of the non-I. I-hood appears for the first time, at the level of the psycho-spiritual self (because of the spiritual component).

Thus, the psycho-spiritual self is part tense, part equipoised, part non-I, part I, part non-self-aware, part self-aware.

The spiritual self- This is the sixth and final self of the human unit, which has shed the psychological component of the fifth self. We have noted its characteristics above. It is a self of pure consciousness or Self-awareness. It is refulgent and the very opposite of the darkness of the physical self. One day it will take a leap and be merged into THAT.

The spiritual self as an independent entity is not known to the majority of mankind. It has to be consciously built from raw materials – like the desires and carvings of the psychological self and their transmutation, through the process of cognitive meditation. But we can always experience some of the spiritual through the spiritual component of the Psycho-spiritual self.

The Genealogy of Man

For some, the genealogy of man could be even more humble than that suggested by Darwin. Man might have immediately descended from the apes. But the apes themselves have descended from a long series of animal species. And in turn the animal kingdom has descended from the plant kingdom and plants from bacteria-like structures. These bacteria-like entities are derived from the 'primal soup' which in turn is derived from material physical substances.

This means the ultimate ancestor of all the selves, including the spiritual self of the human being, is inanimate, inert, non-conscious matter.

Recapitulation

Of the six selves of the current man, four selves have 'recapitulated'. Physical self from the material ancestry, physiological self from the plant ancestry, instinctual self from the animal ancestry, and psychological self from the primitive man ancestry. These are the sources of recapitulation.

When the 'plant' emerges from the 'physical', a fraction of the physical is retained in the plant and becomes a permanent feature of the plant by recapitulating the physical. When the 'animal' emerges from the plant fractions of the physical and the physiological are retained. When primitive man emerges from the animal, fractions of the physical, physiological and instinctual are retained. And in case of the current man, one additional fraction, the psychological is retained in addition to the physical, physiological and instinctual. Only two selves are original for man – the Psycho-spiritual and the Spiritual.

Thus, even though the cosmic evolution is a constant advance from the lower to the higher, due to inertia, a fraction of each lower level is just carried forward. Hence, the current man becomes a conglomerate of six selves. The last self – the spiritual – is ultimately derived from the first self- the physical, i.e. the material self. Of course, one can always argue that the physical, in the pre-big bang state was THAT- the final REALITY.

As far as history of this universe is concerned, spirit is derived from matter. However, this does not mean that it has the same characteristics and dynamics as that matter. Quite the contrary (steam may be derived from ice but its properties are opposite to that of ice). This is because the spirit is arrived at from matter through a series of dialectical leaps, a leap leading to a higher and opposite state.

Grouping of the Selves – The Six selves can be grouped into three formations; the LOWER SELF, the MIDDLE SELF and the HIGHER SELF. The

LOWER SELF is a bundle of the physical, physiological, instinctual and psychological selves. MIDDLE SELF is the psycho-spiritual self, and HIGHER SELF is the spiritual self.

This cosmic evolution of the selves explains how the current man comes to have the physical, plant, animal, primitive man components in his make-up, in addition to the last two selves.

Self — Awareness

One of the latest buzz words. If it were really understood, the world would have been a different place. As you will see, my entire presentation is based on Self-awareness.

There are three related terms — Awareness, Self-Awareness and Non-Self-Awareness.

In general usage Awareness and Self-Awareness mean the same. However I place great distinction between the two.

Non-Self-awareness is a term coined by me.

My definitions are as under.

Self-awareness means awareness by the self, i.e. the I. Please note, it is not the awareness of the self or the I. Non-self-awareness means Awareness by the non-self or the non-I, i.e. by the physiological or psychological selves without the knowledge of the I. It does not mean absence of Awareness.

In Self-awareness, the "I" knows that it knows. In Non-self-awareness the non-I knows, but it does not know that it knows. This is because there is no I which knows that it knows.

In my scheme, Awareness as a term does not exist. It is found either as Self-awareness or Non-Self-Awareness.

It is generally assumed that Self-awareness performs only a cognitive function. Most unexpectedly, it performs a cognative function also. It not only cognizes but also modifies. I have called it the Observation Effect. Since only energy can modify, Self-awareness turns out to be an energy.

This brings us to the term consciousness — a term I do not use, except where widespread usage and context compel me to do so. For me, it is the same as Self-awareness.

Soul

I have not used this term at all. Not even in a popular sense. It is used so loosely as to be useless for any technical discussion.

Spirit

This is a term I am occasionally compelled to use instead of the more congenial 'Higher Self'. I find that I cannot do without the adjective 'Spiritual' and if I have to use it, I have to accept the term 'spirit' also.

Needless to say, my use of 'spirit' is not identical to that used by theologians and the religious. For them, the spirit is something of independent origin from the body and mind somehow joined to them. For me, the 'Spirit' or the Higher I, or Higher Self, is the last and highest fraction of an evolutionary process, which begins with the Physical. Also see "Selves."

Spiritual

I make a sharp distinction between the religious and the spiritual. For theologians and priests, both are indiscriminately synonymous.

For me, religion means a fantasy activity. Propitiation of the unknown out of fear and greed. Expectation of something for nothing by a labour-saving device called prayer. Formation of groups in high sounding terms to counteract other groups for purely worldly advantages. Frequently, a method for exploiting others. At times, a device for releasing pent up hatreds against others. Hand maiden of politics to rule over others. Religion is perhaps the most hypocritical activity known to man- loftiest on rhetoric, lowest on motives.

In the name of religion, arson, murder and rape are sanctified. This is demonstrated even in the enlightened 20th century in North Ireland, Bosnia, Middle East, Sri Lanka, Pakistan, India, and Malaysia...

The God of the religious is an over-magnified image of the biological father or mother, projected into the sky. Even after the biological father is no more, physically or effectively, man perceives himself to be in dire need of protection, punishment and reward. The fantasy Father is moulded to take over these functions.

While religion is a product of psychological drives, the Spiritual is a dynamic non-drive activity, flowing from the Higher Self or the Higher I or the Spirit.

Whatever good occasionally flows out of religion is due to its admixture with the Spiritual.

Accustomed as man is to confuse religion with the Spiritual, a great lacuna persists in his being, It is not possible for man to experience or even to understand the spiritual unless he develops the Higher Self. And there is no way the Higher Self can be developed except by meditation. The Spiritual has to be worked out to be understood and experienced.

It is difficult to convey even its concept by definitions or commentary. For those who thirst for some explanation, however inadequate, the Spiritual is the Self-aware and its allotropes – Purity, Wholeness, Power, Higher Morality, Being and Transcendence.

Spiritual Self

The last of the evolving selves. (The previous ones being the Physical, the Physiological, the Instinctual, the Psychological and the Psycho-spiritual selves). It is positioned between the Psycho-spiritual Self and THAT. It is the culmination of the Cosmic Evolution, my term for this entity is the Higher Self.

As conceptualised by me, the spiritual self is the fully Self- aware Self with all its dynamics. It is fractionated from the previous selves. In it all the evolutionary uncoiling forces, instincts and drives are resolved, transmuted and homogenised.

The higher self is generated at three levels.

1. Transmutation of the Thought Spray. Possible in early stages of meditation.
2. Transmutation of the Preconscious, which harbours the upward flow from the Unconscious and backward flow from the Thought Spray. A long time meditative accomplishment, but possible in one lifetime.
3. Transmutation of the drives in the Unconscious, particularly the genetic ones. For most of us, this can only be an academic objective. To transmute the Unconscious, it would take several lifetimes with many ups and downs.

Practical meditators should be satisfied with the first two transmutations. It may not result in the ultimate development of the Spiritual or Higher Self, but sufficient to experience a new dynamic and a new existence.

It is not the spiritual self of the theologian. It is equidistant from vice and virtue, being neither. (both vice and virtue belong to the Psychological Self).

It is the spiritual self, which undertakes the final spiritual leap into THAT.

Apart from the spiritual journey, a milder version of the Spiritual Self is necessary for a healthy worldly journey also. It would be a great asset in professional life, because it confers capacities like voluntary energy, equipoise (protection from tension and stress), objectivity, impartiality, compassion, concentration, patience, clarity, problem solving, comprehension, creativity, vision...... also see Selves.

Stagnance

Stagnance is inertial movement or quiescence. Going round and round in circles, not breaking out of the groove.

The daily stagnancy is waking up, attending to the daily routine, going to sleep, waking up…. The final stagnance is birth, growth, decay, death, rebirth, growth, decay, death, rebirth…..

Stagnance is the ultimate expression of Non-self-awareness. The only way to break out of it is Self-awareness, which is generated by meditation.

Stream of consciousness

This phrase is not used by me. See Thought Spray.

Stress - see Tension.

Sublimation – See Transmutation.

Superego

Used in the same sense as in psychoanalysis. A structure in the unconscious, acquired during childhood. It represents the parents, particularly the father. It is a behaviour code, with a system of punishments and rewards. It is acquired morality.

Freud believed that the 'lower' the 'immoral' could be genetic in the form of the Id. But for him, there are no genetic, 'higher' or 'moral' forces. All morality for him is acquired morality. I believe otherwise. When the Cosmic Evolution unfolds, 'lower' or 'immoral' drives, in the form of the Id, are first to manifest. When this Evolution, unfolds further, 'higher' or 'moral' drives manifest. Examples – altruism, sympathy, compassion, tolerance, courage, cooperation…….

Thus, man has two sets of morality – acquired i.e. through the superego, and natural, through higher genetic drives. See Psychological Self.

Survival – See Reincarnation.

Tension

When the flow of a drive, say anger, is blocked, the energy concerned gets accumulated, tries to burst but cannot. This causes Tension and its accompanying pain. When anger gives way, the accumulated and blocked energy is discharged. Tension subsides and relaxation takes place, accompanied with pleasure.

Blocking of higher drives, like compassion, also causes tension.

Currently, the term Tension is substituted by the term stress. Most of the modern stress is related to the drives of fear and failure.

More elaborate concepts of stress are in vogue, but they do not affect our basic understanding of the phenomenon.

THAT

I may not believe in God, as popularly conceived. But I do believe in a higher and Ultimate Reality.

This reality is beyond all words and therefore beyond all description. As it cannot be named, I have just called it THAT.

THAT is the sources of all existence, past, present and future. Our universe is born from THAT, with a big bang.

THAT is the source of all contraries – evil and good, material and spiritual, non-I and the "I", Non-Self-awareness and Self-awareness and so on. THAT not only contains all the dualities but is also beyond them.

This universe is not only born from THAT but will eventually merge in it. All existence is in a state of disequilibrium and it will not rest till it finds equilibrium, which is a spiritual state. In the spiritual state, all drives are resolved. When this happens, the last vestige of separate identity ceases and the spiritual self merges into THAT.

All existence is from THAT to THAT.

Even for the highest evolved man, the nature of THAT can only be a speculation. He can experience it only when he merges in it. But once he is merged, he is dissolved and can no more communicate it.

Thought Spray

Comparable to the celebrated Stream of consciousness of William James. What James must have meant is the stream of thoughts. Because of Freud, we now know that thoughts can be unconscious or conscious. The difference between the two is that unconscious thoughts cannot be taken cognisance of by the "I", while the conscious ones can be. According to me, both varieties of thoughts, are non-self-aware, having no I-hood, i.e. consciousness (Self-awareness).

The cognising agent is the "I", i.e. its consciousness or Self-awareness. When the "I" takes cognisance of the succession of thoughts, it is mistakenly called the Stream of Consciousness. It is just a stream of thoughts, recognised by a stationary "I" and its consciousness or Self-awareness. The thoughts arise from the self, just below the "I", i.e. preconscious, a component of Psychological self. From the Preconscious, they arise to the "I". This constitutes a spray rather than a stream. Hence, the Thought Spray.

The Thought Spray is the third and last component of the psychological self the first two being, the Unconscious and the Preconscious.

The Thought Spray is equivalent to Freud's Conscious. However, the Thought Spray is really not conscious. It appears to be conscious, because of the light of self-awareness of the I which falls on the Thought Spray, it being adjacent to the I.

Transcendence

Transcendence is the last dynamic of Self-awareness. It is the opposite of Stagnancy. It is going beyond the Physical, the Physiological, the Instinctual and the Psychological.

The Spiritual is the transcendent. The leap beyond the transcendent is the final leap into THAT.

The Cosmic Evolution is from THAT (the big bang) to THAT (the merger).

Transmutation

Sublimation and Transmutation are two different processes.

When anger is converted to a sophisticated form like satire, it is sublimation. When aggression is converted into sports, it is sublimation.

In sublimation, the change is one of degree.

But when anger or aggression is converted into Equipoise, it is Transmutation. When stinking manure is converted into fragrance of a rose, it is transmutation.

Transmutation is a qualitative change into the opposite and the higher, by a dialectical leap.

The objective of religion and conventional morality is sublimation. The objective of the spiritual and its higher morality is Transmutation. The highest sublimation continues to be bondage. Transmutation leads to freedom and liberation.

Uncoiling

Uncoiling refers to a 'spring' which is built in the evolutionary process. The physical level is born with the big bang from THAT. The physical level is the most concentrated, 'coiled' state. It constantly tries to uncoil.

It is because of this uncoiling movement that the physiological is produced from the Physical – the living from the 'inanimate'. Because of the further uncoiling action, the Physiological gives birth to the Instinctual, which in turn gives birth to the Psychological which is followed by the Psycho-spiritual.

By the time, the Psycho-spiritual level is reached; the uncoiling pressure is exhausted and becomes minimal. The movement from the Psycho-spiritual to Spiritual is no more fueled by the non-I, non-self-aware forces. This grand enterprise is undertaken by the I itself, the process of which is called meditation.

When the Spiritual is reached, the uncoiling force is entirely spent. In the spiritual, no non-self-aware movement is possible anymore. The Spiritual is a state of self-generating Power, which is the Freedom to move voluntarily in any direction or to remain still.

Unconscious

It means the same as the psychoanalytical term. For me, the Unconscious is the deepest component of the Psychological self. The other two components are the Preconscious and the Thought Spray.

Voluntariness – See Involuntariness.

Wholeness

Another buzz word and opposite of Fragmentation.

In the fragmented state, man is moved by contrary drives like love and hate, cruelty and compassion, selfishness and selflessness, pride and humility, violence and non-violence, acquisitiveness and charity, exploitation and altruism and so on.

In the progressive establishment of Self-awareness, the fragmenting drives are attenuated and one day dissolved or at least partially dissolved. This happens because of the 'Observation Effect' taking place in Meditation. (This is dealt with later).

When Fragmentation is dissolved, a homogenous state sets in called Wholeness. In Wholeness, all inner conflicts are dissolved and an inner state of peace is established.

Wholeness is one of the dynamics of Self-awareness.

THEORY

CHAPTER I

WELCOME TO THE LAND OF MEDITATION

For several reasons, the last century turned out to be the age of anxiety, tension, stress and psychological turmoil.

One of the reasons was the receding of religion and its tranquilizing effect. Apart from its ostensible objectives, the main concern of religion is to provide protection against worldly misfortunes. It was fuelled by anxiety and fear. Also, it promised something for nothing by the convenient device of prayer. The advancement of science and education and their great benefits pushed religion into the background. However, even today, science with all its greatness is not in a position to satisfy man's spiritual hunger. Religion, with all its shortcomings, has a component of the spiritual, which meets a crucial need.

Today's science has no discipline to fill the vacuum by the shrinking of religion and its consolations. It has still to undertake the study of the higher states of consciousness and their processing. Man has still to wait for the science of the spiritual.

Meanwhile, the need for coping with a world without religion has spawned new techniques like progressive relaxation, positive thinking, auto-suggestion, visualization, etc. A large number of serious psychotherapies are also on offer. Unfortunate and dangerous were the aberrations relating to drugs, the hippie culture and suicidal cults.

Though the above highly abbreviated scenario roughly belongs to the second half of the twentieth century, the story really begins in the last decade of the nineteenth century. In the year 1893, Vivekananda, a spiritual activist from India addressed the Parliament of Religions held in Chicago. He literally overwhelmed and captured the American consciousness. He placed India on the spiritual map of the world. By no stretch of imagination was Vivekananda a godman, having nothing to do with dollars. But half a century later, his mission, inadvertently, opened up a broad highway for droves of godmen to descend upon the Western sensitivity, particularly the American. They brought with them exotic and esoteric (so called) secrets, the stock-in-trade of conmen. Their wares were packed under high-sounding labels – raj yoga, mantra yoga, tantra yoga, siddha yoga, kundalini yoga, bhakti yoga, not to mention of Tibetan lore. All these systems found cozy niches. The modern age of the guru and his disciples set in. The landscape was enriched by exotic garments, hair styles, beads, malas, swaying, dancing, and chanting ... the West had already lost its religion and now its balance too. There were a few sincere and serious entrants also, like Zen, Sufism, Vipassana.

In this boom, blasts and bangs, one sound emerged from all directions – Meditation.

Meditation mostly meant sitting on the floor, closing one's eyes, fixing attention on some internal or external spot, concentrating on some "divine" themes, repeating a mantra, all culminating in 'peace and tranquility'. For the harried American, peace and tranquility were obviously the highest good, occasionally accompanied with lowered blood pressure.

With increasing popularity, meditation became a group activity. The participants closed their eyes, leaned back in their chairs and relaxed. Lights were dimmed, soft and soothing music took over and everyone sank into his or her depths. The whole procedure had an uncanny resemblance to that of putting babies to sleep. Indeed, such meditations are only a variant of normal sleep – agreeable, pleasant, soothing, voluptuous, dulcet, seductive, enticing, and addictive. In other words, a pampered, cultivated non-self-awareness – the sleep behind all sleeps.

Most meditators are intent on peace and tranquility. One day, they shall learn that peace and tranquility are of two types – that generated by sleep and that generated by awakening. They shall also learn that in the manifested universe, there are ultimately only two states – sleep and awakening. They shall also learn that peace and tranquility from sleep-like states are stunting, whereas those from awakening, fecund.

There are meditations and meditations. For me, true meditation is based on cognition, self-observation, insight, transmutation, realisation and birth of the New Self, the Higher Self, with all its wondrous capacities. This cognitive meditation is Darkness restructured into Light – the ultimate spiritual alchemy.

What Meditation is not

Meditation is not sitting cross-legged. It does not make one a Buddha. It is not even a component of meditation. One can meditate sitting on a chair, standing or even lying down. All these positions are in use.

Meditation is not closing the eyes. People going to sleep also close their eyes. Besides, some meditate with their eyes open. If closing of any particular sense organ is meditation, then how can one 'close' the ears or the nose? If we need not close the ears, we may as well not close the eyes either. Even those who meditate with their eyes 'open' cease seeing and hearing after a certain stage. This is the real 'closing' of the eyes and the ears.

Meditation is not controlling the breath. In the sophisticated Vipassana meditation, there is no control of breath, only its observation. In any case, ultimately, it is meditation which modifies the breathing pattern.

Meditation is not concentrating, whatever it might mean. This is so notwithstanding what the celebrated second aphorism of Book First of Patanjali Yoga states 'Yoga (concentration) is the restriction of the fluctuations of mind-stuff: (Woods 1927). All such 'restriction' is suppression. And eventually suppression 'achieves' the very opposite. Not the destruction of the mind-stuff but its perpetuation in the deeper recesses of the unconscious. Even if Freud had discovered nothing else excepting this, he would have become immortal. As a matter of fact, even Patanjali himself suggested another method of dealing with subtle mental fluctuations — by the method of 'prati-prasava'. (Aphorism 10 Book II, Woods, 1927). The technical term "Prati-prasava" has been translated by different commentators in different ways. 'Prati' means towards and 'prasava' means birth, the term meaning '(moving) towards birth'. In other words, one must, in the case of subtle fluctuations, neutralise them by reaching their birth place. (Inverse propagation' as Woods calls it). In modern terminology, one can say by reaching and identifying the unconscious complex. In other words, mental disturbance is to be made quiet not by suppression but by insight — sight in the internal regions — of the unconscious.

Meditation is not relaxation of the popular type. Relaxation is of two types — from sleep and from awakening. So-called meditation in a dim room, reclining in a chair, with soothing music, leading to relaxation is variety of sleep. As already pointed out, this is how babies are put to sleep! As we shall see later, equipoise is one of the aspects or allotropes' of self-awareness or awakening. Operationally, it also relaxes, but this relaxation is altogether different from that produced by 'dim surroundings and soothing music' or by 'progressive relaxation' so popular nowadays. Both produce different results as we shall see when we come to 'The Dynamics of Non-Self-awareness and Self-awareness'.

Meditation has nothing to do with monasticism or renunciation. During the period of classical meditation, when the Hindu Spiritual texts, the Upanishads, were written, the sages who meditated and revealed transcendental truths were house-holders, some of them with two wives!

Now meditation has entered ordinary homes. It is as it should be.

It is while meditating as a house-holder that a new definition of renunciation emerges. It is the further awakening of the I, from the soporific embrace of impulses, thoughts, desires and cravings. When the I becomes the observer, and thoughts and desires become the observed, an act of disidentification and renunciation is already accomplished. The I has refused to be lost in impulses and cravings The I wakes up in the middle of the river in spate, swims across to the other bank and starts watching the flood. This is the only renunciation there is.

What is Meditation?

Meditation is Conscious Evolution.

Most of us are acquainted with the broad concept of Darwinian evolution, in which struggle for survival and accident play a big part. This evolution has no purpose, at least of reaching a higher state. If man is produced from a unicellular organism, it is a series of accidents. It is a blind movement. However, it is not technically correct to maintain that Darwinian evolution has no purpose as maintained by evolutionary biologists. There is a powerful purpose, and that is survival and reproducing one's kind. Obviously, such an evolution is blind, involuntary and unconscious. Apart from survival of the individual and the species, it has no other higher purpose, nor is it driven by any underlying higher evolutionary urge.

In this presentation, such blind Darwinian evolution is accepted. It is a typical example of blind non-self awarenessprocesses. As we shall see later, non-self-awareness is the prime force in the manifested universe, operating from the physical to the physiological, to the instinctual, to the psychological, to the psycho-spiritual (excluding the spiritual component of this stage). Darwinian evolution is just one phase in this unfolding.

Actually, this evolution is part of a much wider movement — the cosmic evolution, which starts from the inorganic evolution at the physical level, then becomes organic or Darwinian evolution at the physiological (plant) level, instinctual (animal) level and psychological (human) level. This Darwinian evolution wanes and a cultural evolution sets in, which is the current psycho-spiritual man. (In the cultural evolutions, which is part non-self-aware and part self-aware, survival of the fittest is no more the prime force. The weak and the ailing are also accommodated unlike in the Darwinian evolution).

But the cosmic evolution envisages one more stage beyond the psycho-spiritual, which is the pure spiritual stage. The current psycho-spiritual man is only a transition stage between the psychological and the spiritual man.

This evolution from the psycho-spiritual to the spiritual is an altogether new kind of process. It is awakened, voluntary and self-aware. Voluntary means by choice. As far as the psycho-spiritual goes, nature produced the movement. From here onwards, the self-aware man has to produce further movement himself. This self-aware, voluntary process of developing the psycho-spiritual into the spiritual is called meditation. This is the basic definition.

Meditation is building the higher self

There is quite a common belief in meditation circles from ancient times that if the body and mind are somehow set aside, one will come face to face with a readymade already existing higher self, spirit or atma. It is believed that the higher self is masked by the body and mind. The truth is, there is no readymade higher self awaiting our vision. When the physical came into existence, there was no plant. When the plant came into existence, there was no animal. When the animal came into existence, there was no man.

Certain natural processes extracted the plant from the physical, the animal from the plant and man from the animal. Similarly, a certain process will extract the spirit from the physical, physiological, instinctual, psychological and psycho-spiritual man. The spirit was lying latent and potential in the earlier stages, which extended from 15 to 18 billion years, (or whatever is today's scientific computation). This process of extracting the latent spirit from the body and mind is called meditation. (It may please be noted that the birth of the spirit is from the body/

mind complex. It is only after it is born that it attains an independent existence, with its own dynamics). This process of extracting the higher self is the same as conscious evolution, envisaged earlier. The same concept is worded differently.

Meditation is awakening

There is a lot of talk about awakening and self-awareness, but without ever coming to brass tacks. Those who cannot concretise, awakening and self-awareness have no business to talk about meditation.

In deep sleep, man is unconscious or non-self-aware of everything, including the external world, the body and the mind. The I itself is lost in sleep. When he wakes up in the morning, he first becomes conscious of the mind then the body and then the external world. But then there are vast stretches of body and mind, of which he is totally non-self-aware. No doubt, he has awakened in the morning, but only partially to his body, mind and even the external world. Someday, by a process of progressive self-awareness, he will awaken more and more to the body, mind and the external world. In other words, the awakening in the morning is just the beginning. A lot of 'sleep', in the form of non-self-awareness of the unknown regions of the body, mind and the external world, still continues. This process of further awakening by self-awareness is called meditation. This will culminate in the sighting of the higher self buried in the mind, which in turn is buried in the body. This activity is also the same as conscious evolution mentioned earlier. The concept is the same, the presentation is different.

Meditation is Self-analysis

There are further corollaries to the act of awakening. Awakening to the internal world of thoughts and feelings can be carried a step further, by consciously and voluntarily observing more and more of the internal world. As we shall see later, this process of self-observation, i.e. observation by the I of the non-I (impulses, thoughts, feelings), leads to the enlargement of the "I" and its self-awareness, And shrinking of the non-I and its non-self-awareness.

56

In cognitive meditation, the act of self-observation is followed by analysis of impulses, thoughts, and feelings. In the meditative process, we note that impulses, thoughts, feelings are constantly moving by themselves. They are powered by their respective energies (we shall deal with these energies later). Analysis means identifying the particular specific energy moving the impulse, thought, feeling. It could be anger, love, greed, fear, sex and so on. Observation is becoming aware of the particular impulse. Analysis is becoming aware of the specific propellant moving the impulse, thought, feeling. It is this 'analysis' which results into transmutation of the non-I into the I, or the non-self-awareness into self-awareness. The vehicle of routine self-awareness is the current I, and that of advanced self-awareness, the higher I or higher self. Self-observation and self-analysis are the ultimate procedures for developing self-awareness and the higher self. Self-analysis, as also hetero-analysis, has transmutative and curative power. Self-observation when combined with self-analysis makes the reaching of the equipoise, the stillness, much faster.

Freud, whose psycho-analysis is based on hetero-analysis (analysis by another i.e. an analyst or therapist), does not approve of self-analysis. Paradoxically, the birth of psycho-analysis took place, in Freud's own self-analysis, considered a great heroic act by his biographer Jones (Ernest Jones, 1964).

But for reasons not quite clear, Freud denies this possibility to others. To complicate the issue further, Freud continued to carry out mini self-analysis every night before going to sleep (Ernest Jones 1964). This practice is remarkably similar to that followed in certain esoteric schools.

Another attempt at self-analysis (E. Pickworth Farrow, 1948), was graced by a forward by Freud without warming up to the enterprise. However, a psychoanalyst like Karen Horney has accepted the possibility of self-analysis. (Karen Horney, 1942).

The process of cognitive meditation resembles Vipassana, the Buddhist meditation, in so far as 'mindfulness' or self-observation is concerned. But no 'analysis' is permitted in Vipassana. I have not come across any reasons for prohibiting analysis. However, quite a bit of self-observation automatically involves analysis, and I believe it is this component, rather than mere observation, which produces results for Vipassana.

Though the term 'analysis may be common to psychoanalysis and cognitive meditation, procedure and objectives are different, in both the cases. As far as procedure is concerned, self-observation is carried out by the analysed or the patient by following the free-association method, and the analysis is carried out by the analyst. The activity is split between two persons. In the case of cognitive meditation, the analysed and the analyser are one and the same person.

Further, in psycho-analysis, the objective of much of the analytical investigation is devoted to the childhood period. The past is considered to be the cause of the present neurotic difficulties. The objective of self-analysis in cognitive meditation is the analysis of current events, of the 'here and now' leading to the building of the higher self with all its powers.

Self-observation without self-analysis is a job half done. An examined life and cognitive meditation call for both. Meditation is coming across the stranger within, making friends with him, however repugnant and difficult it may be, and persuading him to transmute and be absorbed with his energies into us, leading to the building of the higher self. This is conscious creative evolution. Only those who can love and tolerate the stranger within, can love and tolerate the stranger without.

Meditation is Transmutation

The most common belief about meditation is that it is 'control' of the mind. When elaborated, it means stillness of the mind. This is obviously an act of suppression of various thoughts, desires, cravings, which are constantly on the move. It is now a scientifically admitted position that all suppression and repression cause pathology. Another way of life is expression. Modern thinking is giving way to one's instincts and passions, leading to mental health and happiness.

A suppressive way of life is called asceticism. An expressive way hedonism. It will be news to many that neither asceticism nor hedonism are meditation-friendly. In fact, excess of either can seriously jeopardise a genuine meditative enterprise. These issues will be dealt with elsewhere.

What really is called for is transmutation. Transmutation is not sublimation. Sublimation means refining a cruder state. Aggression is one of our cruder energies but when sublimated could become sports. Sports continue to be an aggressive activity but in a refined way.

Transmutation is not refinement. It is leap into an opposite and higher state — what is called the dialectical leap. When dung is changed into a fragrant rose, it is transmutation. In the area of meditation, transmutation means changing of non-self-awareness and its energies like aggression, fear, greed, love, empathy into self-awareness with its energy of free colourless consciousness. We shall be dealing with these issues in greater detail later. Transmutation is spiritual alchemy and the method of producing it is cognitive meditation.

Meditation Is Therapy And Managerial Efficiency

The Buddha declared that this life is suffering and the cure for this disorder is vipassana — a specialized meditation. Others have also maintained that life is a fever and its cure, meditation. Meditation was supposed to be a treatment for spiritual disorders, chief amongst which is 'agnan', ignorance of our spiritual potential.

There are psychological disorders like greed, fear, partiality, indecisiveness, lack of promptness, favoritism, groupism, manipulativeness, duplicity, incapacity to reach solutions, poor interpersonal relations, lack of objectivity, intellectual dishonesty, neuroticism, mental blocks, immaturity, lack of concentration, vindictiveness and so on. These affect our family and professional lives. They would be serious obstacles to a managerial position. Meditation is an ideal therapy for these ills. Management development books emphasize decisiveness ', 'creativeness, 'successful inter-personal relations' and so on. But how does one cultivate 'decisiveness', impartiality', 'empathy'? These could be boring themes of management texts. But they can hardly be differentiated from sermons. Sermons benefit the 'preacher', never the audience.

It is in this area of personal and managerial inadequacies that meditation will be found most useful. Hence, it is very surprising that there is hardly any literature directly linking meditation to managerial efficiency. I came across couple of titles, which are hardly worth mentioning.

Meditation is basically concerned with developing self-awareness. And self-awareness has a number of allotropes or facets, which have a direct impact on psychological health and managerial skills. These will be dealt with when we come to the dynamics of self-awareness.

I may mention here, in passing, that there are no separate independent skills like concentration, good interpersonal relations, assertiveness, objectivity, creativity, etc. requiring separate training program's These are all different facets of self-awareness and what is necessary is the single skill of meditation, which generates self-awareness. All that is required is a single training program for meditation. The various apparently disparate skills will automatically follow.

Meditation can be prime therapy for stress and stress disorders like ulcers and hypertension. In fact, there are so many papers establishing the role of meditation in lowering blood pressure that one might think that meditation means anti-hypertensive therapy. There is an element of exaggeration here. For example, there is a paper which demonstrates that sitting alone quietly for some time, brings down blood-pressure. (Holmes A.S. 1985, quoted in 'Michael A. West Ed, 1991). Much more impressive is the use of meditation along with diet and exercise in reversing heart conditions and avoiding heart surgeries (Dean Ornish, 1991).

Meditation is perhaps the only therapy which acts on several levels of the human being – physiological, instinctual psychological and psycho-spiritual. The therapeutic cleansing action of meditation is dealt with separately below.

Meditation is Cleansing

Our times are prolific in a phenomenon I have christened the 'vertical wound'. Vertical because it simultaneously cuts the surface of the conscious, the preconscious and the unconscious, which are situated one above the other, by a vertical gash. For example, in the case of an insult, the victim suffers a vertical wound. Part of this wound injures the conscious surface and part of it the unconscious surface. The latter is much bigger in size (man is much more sensitive in the unconscious). The injury to the unconscious surface is much deeper, much sharper, long lasting, at times permanent, very intense and far more damaging. The irony of it all is that the I knows only about the conscious wound and has no idea what an upheaval is going on in the unconscious.

The ill effects at the conscious level are much lighter and palliated by the I in its self-awareness. The situation in the unconscious is serious. Being in the unconscious, even the victim is not aware of the wound's existence. And there is no hope of relief as the curative action of self-awareness of the I does not reach there.

Besides insults, slights and indignities, man has to face other vertical wounds like irritations, threats, non-co-operation, treachery, rejections, disappointments, failures, anxieties, fears...

It is the fate of man in this age to daily suffer such vertical wounds at home, on the streets, in the office, in society....

Unless the victim hits back in retaliation or undergoes cognitive measures like analysis or cognition-oriented meditation, the unconscious portion of the vertical wound is likely to become chronic. In the unconscious, everything tends to be perpetuated. Such wounds may continue to fester. And when other such wounds are inflicted, the mess coagulates within a man. Such pathology is bad for both body and mind. Psychotherapists do not take such pathologies seriously. But those who meditate and build a connection with the unconscious immediately recognise the seriousness of the problem.

The only solution is to get rid of the muck on daily basis, just as we get rid of physiological waste. This is possible only through meditation. A daily session of cognitive meditation simultaneously acts as a deep cleansing agent. At the physiological level the waste is only thrown out. At the psychological level, the vertical wounds are not only healed, but are also transmuted into self-awareness. The destructive energy of the wound is transmuted into the constructive energy of self-awareness.

Even if meditation had no other advantages, its cleansing and purifying action would make investment in it several-fold profitable.

Meditation is a shift in the Balance of Power:

A new way of life beyond asceticism and hedonism

Until now, balance of power has been in favour of non-self-awareness. This has been continuing from the moment of the big bang, supposed to have taken place 15 to 18 billions of years ago. All these years, non-self-awareness has reigned supreme. Thus, the physical elements, the plants and animals are non-self-aware. Even man is predominantly non-self-aware. It seems in the last hundred thousand years, self-awareness has made its appearance. Being of such recent origin, compared to non-self-awareness, it is extremely fragile and weak.

But the future evolutionary development is in favour of self-awareness. Non-self-awareness will wane and self-awareness will take over. The balance of power will shift in favour of self-awareness. This will happen through meditation.

Non-self-awareness and self-awareness, to a certain extent, are abstract terms. When concretised, as we shall see in the section dealing with dynamics, non-self-awareness means unconsciousness, 'blindness', contamination of pure consciousness by thoughts and feelings, fragmentation, life of tension and discharge, life of stress, chaos, bondage, conventional morality, becoming, involuntary flux, stagnancy..

And self-awareness when concretised means awakening, insight, pure uncontaminated consciousness, wholeness, freedom, higher morality, equipoise, being, transcendence...

Non-self-awareness is the non-spiritual way of life. Self-awareness is the spiritual way of life. Meditation is that process which brings about the shift in the balance of power from the non-self-aware, the non-spiritual to the self-aware, the spiritual way of life.

Meditation and Goodness

This may appear to be an uncalled for theme. It is taken for granted that a meditator is by definition a good human being. But the issue is more complicated.

Goodness is of two types —compulsive and free. The former in turn can be segmented into goodness for the sake of goodness and goodness out of fear, weakness, non-assertiveness, and ulterior motives or as a means for securing a place in heaven. The latter variety is obviously pseudo-goodness. But then, those who are good for the sake of goodness, in a compulsive way, are also practicing, an inferior goodness. Good behavior could also be drive-oriented and as such belongs to non-self-awareness. It causes bondage and has no spiritual status. Deviation from such goodness causes discomfort and even guilt, thus proving its drive origin.

Only those who are good for the sake of goodness, unconditioned by considerations of punishment or reward and without being driven to be good, and practice goodness in a free and self-aware way, know what true and spiritual goodness really is. Only meditation can help in attaining such goodness.

Meditation is the ultimate experiment

Man has been experimenting with meditation for at least five thousand years. All kinds of objectives and all kinds of techniques have been tried out. The last century has already yoked meditation to unexpected uses. In the years to come, meditation will undergo extraordinary developments — both objective-wise and technique-wise. However most books on meditation are not at all concerned with theory. It is possible that this work of mine will be treated as an attempt in this direction. I have, maybe presumptuously, attempted a story beginning with the big bang and ending with the big mergence with a focus on the role that non-meditation and meditation play in this. I believe it is not possible to understand what meditation is without scripting a cosmic evolutionary scheme and meditation's place therein.

In all experimental work, practice precedes theory. In actual life, the same has happened to me. But for purposes of communication here, practice follows theory. And I make no claim that all theory is deduced from practice. Certain gaps in practice and realisation have been filled by informed speculation to round off the theoretical framework. Even though theory follows practice, a well-rounded theory of meditation can only be of immense help in the actual practice of meditation.

Meditation is an extraordinary experiment. It is an experiment in which the investigator (the I) and the investigated (the non-I) are both modified. The experimenter is the laboratory, the experiment and the discovery. It is the only experiment in which physics, chemistry, biology, physiology, psychology, all are involved, leading to the spiritual. It is the ultimate experiment.

Words of Caution

For me the term 'spiritual' does not mean taking of vows, self-abnegation, fasting, visiting temples, going on pilgrimages, giving and listening to sermons, contorting the body, suppressing breath and the thought stream, or even virtuous acts. These are acts of asceticism as opposed to hedonism. As we shall see later, both asceticism and hedonism, being driven and compulsive, spring from non-self-awareness. At times, they are pathological. The authentic spiritual is beyond asceticism and hedonism, a state with which, even concept-wise, we are far from familiar. Meditation is going beyond asceticism and hedonism, to the land of equipoise.

If you are a career person, a professional, or an intellectual, you are likely to be put off by my constant use of the term 'spiritual'. You would be right if this term meant what theologians and priests have made of it. But as pointed out earlier, my idea of the spiritual (along with some of the greatest minds) is altogether different. For me, any act carried out through self-awareness is spiritual, be it in the family, on the street, at the office, on the shop floor or in the boardroom. And even if an act takes place in a temple, if fuelled by some non-self-aware drive, however exalted, like pity or compassion, it is still a non-spiritual act. All action arising from a drive that is from non-self- awareness is compulsiveness and bondage. It is non-spiritual, if not anti-spiritual. Even Marxists avail of the term spiritual, though with specific reference to the culture accomplishments of man. I hope, henceforth you will be better able to receive this term 'spiritual'

Above all, meditation is work. For X turns of the hand pump on the Indian well, one bucket is filled with water. For 2 X turns, two buckets will be filled. More work, more results. Similarly, for every round of procedure carried out in meditation, so much self-awareness is generated. For twice the number of rounds, twice the 'quantity' of self-awareness would be generated. Of course, as of today, it is not possible to 'measure' the 'quantity' of self-awareness. Perhaps it never will be. But the fact remains that more meditation will produce more Self-awareness. Meditation is not a conservation piece or reading matter. It is regular, systematic, hard work.

The Objectives of Meditation

In a way, the objectives of meditation have already been discussed while dealing with what is meditation. From this, it transpires that the objectives of meditation are 'conscious evolution', 'building of a higher self', 'transmutation' and so on. Here, I shall consider some issues related to these objectives.

One of the objectives of meditation is investigating the inner reality by self-observation and self-analysis. As one progresses deeper one can reach some of the most puzzling realities concerning our existence. These are actually experiment in inner exploration. Three of the greatest such experimenters are the Buddha, Shankara and Patanjali.

Some seminal conclusion arrived at by them are

1. **The Buddha**
   a. The birth of the universe. There is no such birth. The universe always existed and will continue to exist, similar to the steady state theory.

b. The external world, though in a state of flux, is real. In Buddhism, even a blade of grass will one day attain nirvana. This would not be possible if the blade of grass were an illusion rather than a real structure.

c. What we call the I is not a stable and enduring structure. It is only an empirical construction. There is nothing like the I, in the sense usually understood by us.

d. The final reality is nirvana. Also called the 'Shunya', the 'Zero' or the 'void'. It is beyond descripition. It harbours and is at the same time beyond all dualities. It is paradoxical. It is and is not.

e. The human unit (not the I or the atma) attains nirvana. It is not clear whether it is a merger or something else.

f. Nirvana, the ultimate Reality, is neither one nor many. It is beyond both.

2. Shankara – Vedanta

a. The universe comes into existence by a birth at some point of time. Similar to the big bang theory.

b. The external world, i.e. the universe, whose birth we just mentioned is an illusion.

c. The I is a stable and evolving structure, one day becoming the 'atma', the highest individual Spiritual Reality.

d. The final Reality is the Brahman. It is the source of all physical, mental and spiritual existence. It is beyond description. Having asserted that the Brahman is beyond all description and qualities, in the next breath it is revealed that it is 'Satchitananda', i.e. having qualities of existence, consciousness, and bliss.

    It is pure, stainless and effulgent. If Brahman were really beyond dualities, it would also be beyond existence and non-existence, consciousness and non-consciousness, bliss and distress, purity and impurity, tainted and untainted, effulgence and darkness.

e. The atma when fully enlightened merges in the Brahman. In fact, atma and Brahman were always one and the same, only apparently separate.

f. Brahman, the ultimate reality is one. This is the monistic view of Shankara. (those who believe in matter only are also monistic but of a materialistic nature.)

3. **Patanjali – Patanjali Yoga.**
   a. The universe was never born and will never end. Similar to the steady state theory.
   b. The final reality is dual, consisting of Prakarti and Purusha. Prakarti is nature and Purusha, individual consciousness. The external world is a part of Prakarti and therefore real.
   c. The self-aware self- the Purusha – is independent of 'Prakarti' and is also real. Purusha is also incapable of any action, though cognition is permitted. (one would have thought that cognition is also a kind of action).
   d. Purusha is contaminated by the pressure of Prakarti. (since both belong to altogether independent categories, it is not clear how they can interact, contaminate and get contaminated.)
   e. At the moment of enlightenment, Prakarti withdraws, leaving Purusha liberated. The final event of liberation is called Kaivalya. (since Purusha is incapable of action and since Prakarti is bent on causing contamination, it is not understood who brings about liberation).
   f. There is no merger of the liberated Purusha into any higher Reality. It continues to live independently. Accordingly, the number of liberated Purushas would go on increasing as more and more liberations take place. (incidentally, this thinking is similar to the Jain doctrine).
   g. Purusha and Prakarti are two ultimate Realities. This is a dualistic view.

Contradictory Conclusion of the Great Meditators

The Buddha, Shankara and Patanjali have arrived at their views, not by philosophical arguments but by experimental meditations. From my highly condensed and even controversial outlines, you must have noted that all the three accounts of Reality contradict each other. This should not dampen the budding meditator. It only means that there are more areas still to be explored, which may reconcile and sort out the contradictions.

Physics furnishes an unusual example. It has the most advanced equipment for 'objective' study and also the support of the most advanced mathematics. Still, Einstein and Bohr came to contradictory conclusions. For the former, the universe is determined and predictable, both at the macro and micro levels. For the latter, at the micro or sub-atomic level, the universe is indeterminate and unpredictable. For Einstein, 'God does not play dice; Bohr is supposed to have replied: 'Albert, stop telling God what to do' (Hozen and Trepid, 1996). If contradictory conclusions can be arrived at in the 'hardest' of sciences, i.e. physics, it would be much more so in the 'softest' of sciences – meditation. And scientists do not differ only on matters related to quantum physics. One set of astronomers 'scientifically' believes that the universe was born at a particular moment with a big bang. Another set, equally 'scientific', believes that the universe was never born and will never end. This is the steady state theory.

The staples of science are facts, observations, experiments, repeatability, reproducibility, testability, falsifiability. None of these are applied or can be applied to the issue of the birth of the universe. One can only speculate. Such speculations are considered science. And the current 'science' believes in the big bang and not the steady state theory. But if there is a down to earth successful experiment in telepathy, it is not science. All such experiments by definition are sloppy, shoddy, when not fraudulent!

To return to our theme, if the exploration of inner realities is the serious objective of meditation, then the next objective can only be experimentation. Do not take anyone for granted including myself. Find out for yourself the truth or at least your truth. If nothing else, it will improve the efficiency and quality of your life.

Change in the objectives of meditation

In ancient times, the main objective of meditation was investigation into the spiritual and attainment of liberation. In the modern world, this objective of meditation is bound to recede into the background. In any case, it is not a project of one lifetime. It will easily involve several lifetimes. Whether one believes in reincarnation or not, for most of us, one lifetime will only be a beginning, as far as the meditation project is concerned.

But the last century, ridden by tension and anxiety, has discovered altogether new uses for meditation. It seems the whole world is seeking mental peace and all kinds of devices are resorted to, And peace, which is only a byproduct of meditation, becomes its main objective. Because of its capacity for dissolving stress, another scourge of the twentieth century, meditation restores psychosomatic health. One brand of meditation specialises in lowering blood pressure.

But it is still not realized that meditation can develop faculties which are inestimable in the development of interpersonal relations, such as creativity, organizing ability, maturity, which are so essential in professional and business careers. For all these skills, nowadays there are separate unconnected training programs. Later, I shall make the rather radical assertion that these are not different skills but sub-skills of the basic skill, i.e. self-awareness. And self-awareness is developed by meditation. He who meditates acquires the basic skill, from which all sub-skills automatically follow.

Then there are skills like decisiveness, objectivity, judgment with which either one is born or which can be cultivated by meditation only. No seminar can teach these. It is true that these can also be acquired over a long period by sheer experience and no meditation. Such maturity is also based on self-awareness, as in meditation. But it is inordinately extended and slow-moving. Besides, it is sporadic and unsystematic, with uneven results. What the mediocre can achieve in a lifetime by experience, the intelligent can achieve in a shorter time by meditation.

I have dealt with the meditations of the Buddha, Shankara and Patanjali and the conclusions arrived at by them. There is absolutely no need to believe that one of them or a combination of these could be the last word on the subject. As you read further, you will see that different conclusions could be arrived at, which will not be self-contradicting or much less so. Before concluding the objectives, I would like to introduce to you a special meditation.

A Special Meditation

The circumstances of my life demand that to pursue my deeper and non-professional interests, I have to work late hours every night. If one is serious about such work, one has to be fresh and energetic, as in the morning. To make this possible, I started experimenting. By accident, by trial and error, through curiosity, because of some luck, by what some might call serendipity, I landed upon a meditative procedure, which met my expectations. This meditation literally gives me a second morning when others go to sleep. It wipes out the days fatigue, makes me fresh and bright, ready to tackle the night's task. Now my day consists of twenty six hours.

But this was not all. By and by I also found that this meditation enhanced my immunity, made me resistant to disease and helped in preventing the ageing of the mind and to some extent of the body. It might even confer a certain youthful look.

We are conversant with the relaxation response of the muscular system. In this meditation, the brain itself is relaxed, which in turn produces muscular relaxation.

Elsewhere, I have argued that in the long run, direct, 'effortful' muscular relaxation, being a kind of suppression of tension, is harmful as any other suppression is. But in this meditation, both the brain and in turn the muscles get relaxed without making any direct effort. By relaxation of the brain, I mean that area, which is just behind the forehead, most likely the frontal lobes, which perhaps bear all the burden of the day-to-day stresses and strains.

The main meditation in this book works on the psychological self (the thoughts, desires and cravings) and produces equipoise, which is a facet of the higher self. The meditation I am now talking of works on the physiological self (the brain) and produce its own equipoise, at the physiological level: a truly fantastic experience.

This heightened physiological bliss is produced without any drugs, or music or any other external resource. It is purely self-generated. A sine qua non of authentic meditation.

I will not be surprised if some readers opt for this meditation instead of the main one. The actual procedure is dealt with later.

Who is the meditator?

There is a lot of talk about meditation. There is no talk about the meditator. Indeed, who is the meditator? None of the classical systems of meditation, be it that of the Buddha, Patanjali or Shankara, raise the question.

The classical Meditators and their antipathy for the I.

There must be a reason. Frankly, the very systems are such that they do not contain the answer. The Buddha is not supposed to have believed in the existence of the I. And no other entity is projected who can undertake meditation. Patanjali's Purusha, the conscious principle, is incapable of action. And Prakarti, nature, whose mission is to ensnare Purusha cannot be expected to undertake meditation. No other entity is projected. For

Shankara the body and mind (including the I), are illusions. How illusions lead us to Reality, for which the process is meditation?

I am also sure apologists have instant replies refuting my above queries. Someday, I shall engage them.

Meanwhile, for an ordinary human being who intends to undertake meditation, words like 'soul', 'spirit', 'divine element', 'atma' strike no experiential chord. At the most, he can indulge in parroting these terms to ensure that he appears to be on the side of the 'spiritual'. Meaninglessness piled upon meaninglessness.

The I is the Meditator

The truth is, we honestly do not know any entity other than the I who can undertake either a worldly or a spiritual enterprise. But for reasons best known to them, perhaps to emphasize their close connection with the 'spirit', the 'spiritual' always run down the I. For them I means pride and self-interest, which are considered to be anti-spiritual. But it does not occur to them that the entity which practices humility and charity is also the same I.

The obvious truth is the meditator is the I. The I hears about meditation, the initiates meditation and the I reaps the benefit of meditation. It is the same I, the which becomes the higher self or the spirit in the course of time through meditation. The paradox is that the meditator, the I, himself undergoes change during meditation. And one can speak of the spirit only after this change has taken place. And this can happen only in a specialised meditation. For other kinds of meditation, the term 'spirit' will be so much jargon.

In the beginning is the current I, and in the end the purified I, and, in between, the meditation.

Who are interested in Meditation?

It is a fact that most people are not interested in meditation. They do not feel any need to meditate. That may even deride it.

The Not Interested

The householder, comfortable in his creature comforts, the bookworm in his reading, the critic in contemplating aesthetics, the philosopher in building his theories, the tycoon busy making his next fortune – none of them see any need for meditation. The scientists and the artists, involved in investigating, interpreting and creating the external and internal worlds, may also not find any need for meditation.

To some extent, I may excuse the scientists and the artist, but the rest, I am afraid, have just fallen in a rut, a groove or even a hole. Even their curiosity is not aroused. It is a typical state of what I have elsewhere called 'Stagnance'.

The Interested

It has not struck people that there is something like growth. Or their 'growth' appears to be just more knowledge or more money. The executive corroded by a fast business life or a family member unbalanced by interpersonal strains may look out for therapy. And meditation is one of the known options.

There are also those disillusioned by religion who are looking around for another approach to satisfy their spiritual hunger. If he escapes the psychedelic trap, he, may turn towards meditation. Though current scientists do not admit the possibility that there could be scientists of the soul, they exist. For them meditation is the most appropriate technique. There are others who meditate most probably as a pursuit from their previous lives. A rare breed perhaps, but there are adventurers who prefer to explore the spirit, the route being meditation. Unfortunately, in certain quarters meditation could become a fashion, attracting large flocks.

Who are competent for meditation and what are the obstacles?

At least as far as meditative capacity is concerned, all men are not born equal. Some are incompetent and some are competent. And even those who are competent may be hindered by obstacles.

Incompetence

The following are incompetent:

1. Those with crippling physiological disease.
2. Those who have schizophrenic or psychotic tendencies. It is very interesting that these types have a fascination for meditation and bring a bad name to it by their bizarre conduct.

71

3. Those who have serious neurotic problems. However, there is hope for them, if they undergo psychotherapy.
4. Those who are overzealous in religious matters or belong to cults. This is because the meditation I am promoting is non-religious and follows no cult. I believe genuine meditation is secular. It is spiritual, even mystical, but not religious. As we proceed further, we shall notice the chasm between the spiritual and the religious.
5. Those who are puritanical or hedonistic. Both the tendencies, which are neurotic, make a person incompetent to practice meditation. Perhaps psychotherapy can help them. It is a myth that the puritanical are spiritual and are especially suited for meditation.
6. Those who are highly introverted or highly extroverted are also unsuitable for meditation. There is also another myth that introverts are natural Meditators, because they are accustomed to look within. Introversion is a compulsive phenomenon and therefore an expression of non-self awareness. It reduces the competence of the meditator. There is a good chance of overcoming either introversion or extroversion if meditation is practiced for a good period.

Competence

The following are competent to undertake the meditative enterprise:

1. Those who are 'normal'. The objective of psychotherapy is to make the sub-normal and the abnormal, normal. The objective of meditation is to make the normal, super-normal.
   Normality is no more an absolute concept. There are degrees of normality. Those who are reasonably normal are good material as meditators.
2. Those who earn their livelihood and face the problems of life reasonably well.
3. Those who are well adapted to their family members as well as their business professional and office colleagues.
4. Those who have got extracurricular activities.
5. Those who are particularly interested in self-improvement.
6. Most important, those who are capable of voluntarily (not compulsively as in the case of introversion) watching their own thought stream.

Obstacles

Mere competence is not enough. The circumstances of life should also be favourable.

1. Persons highly competent in worldly pursuits suffer from an unsuspected obstacle. Such a person already had qualities of the head and heart, which could further be developed by meditation. However, he does not feel any need for meditation. Still, the most competent person someday will start feeling that he is missing something he cannot pinpoint. A vague restlessness develops. It is at this stage that he will productively introduce himself to meditation. Such meditation will not only further develop his existing faculties but also open out new avenues of which he was not even aware.

2. There are two other serious obstacles. One of them is the time factor. The lopsided development of the technological society is responsible for consuming all his time in the pursuit of livelihood and 'advancement'. There is no time for self-improvement or meditation. It does not serve the purpose if one artificially gets up early. This will affect the freshness of the brain, which is a prime requisite for practicing meditation. The stresses of modern 'civilization' impose a strain, which require full sleep. Any tampering with natural sleep is absolutely counter-productive. The evenings too are not ideal when a man is fatigued. At the most, one can practise the physiological meditation in the evening for health and for arresting the ageing process and senility.

   Except for a few lucky ones who can spare half an hour to one hour in the morning, I do not see much hope for others. Today's technological society is cruel. In the past, it deprived children of their childhood (it is still happening in the developing and underdeveloped countries). Today, it robs adults of their opportunity to undertake spiritual development by depriving them of their most important asset-time in the morning when they are fresh and energetic. Any society which encroaches upon man's morning hours for the sake of his survival is basically barbaric.

   The solution foolishly seems to be not less technology but more. Now it is technology alone which can bring man leisure. Only the perverse would believe that leisure is the devil's workshop.

3. The other serious obstacle is poverty, which is contraindicated for meditation. Poverty is the mother of all obstacles. It is a paradox that those who take the oath of poverty are better fed, better clothed, better housed and better looked after than most others, particularly in the developing and underdeveloped countries.

   Wealth and riches create their own obstacles. But unlike in the case of poverty, it is within the capacity of the individual to overcome them.

Meditations and Meditations

All meditations are not congruent. A peculiar universal ignorance prevails about meditation. All meditations are considered to be the same. The truth is, there are meditations and meditations. Each meditation has its own basic mode, its own objective, its own technique and its own results. There is nothing common between these various meditations except the nomenclature.

Three kinds of meditations

Broadly, there are three kinds of meditations. They can be introduced by a chart.

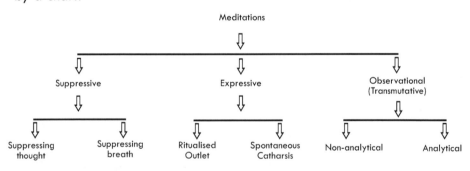

The three modes, suppressive, expressive and observational, are dominant characteristics only. None of the modes can be 100 percent. Such things do not happen amongst humans. If a mode is predominantly suppressive, it can have a thread of the observational too. The observational mode also can have a thread of the suppressive. This will be clear when we come to the examples. We now come to the characteristics of the three modes.

The suppressive way

This refers to all kinds of suppressions, particularly the thought stream and its accompaniments – the thoughts, impulses, desires, cravings, etc. A classic example is the Patanjali Yoga. 'Yoga is the suppression of the mind stuff'. (Aphorism 2, Book 1, Woods, 1927).

Suppression can be of two types. Of the thought stream (Patanjali Yoga proper) or suppression of the spontaneous breath movement (Hatha Yoga). This is technically known as Pranayam – disciplining the breath.

Suppressive techniques are widespread. They are expressions of ascetic drives (and to that extent 'expressive'). They command respect and acceptance. The practitioner of austerities is an object of great wonder, awe and reverence to the lay man.

Whatever the respective yogic texts might say, it is doubtful whether suppression and repression can produce any spiritual results. That they can produce stunting and neurosis and abnormal states of mind is the accepted post-Freudian wisdom. All those who enter the field of meditation see themselves as conquerors of the mind and, in the beginning, conquest is considered to be synonymous with suppression.

The truth is that suppression and repression push the objectionable element back into the unconscious, where they petrify or where they constantly simmer. In any case, instead of being conquered they go underground, where they are perpetuated.

Sensing the havoc the repressed can play, the technique of 'prati-prasava' was also recommended by Patanjali Yoga (Aphorism 10, book 11). 'Prati' means towards and 'Prasava' means birth. To go to the root of the problem. To reach the root of the objectionable element, 'by digging into the subtle', i.e. by investigating the unconscious. Thus, realising the futility of the purely suppressive approach, the 'insight technique' is also provided, which is the way of self-awareness.

But the predominant note of Patanjali is suppression. Shankara is quite explicit. Neither 'Sankhye' (Patanjali Yoga) nor 'yoga' (yoga of postures and breath control) can lead to liberation. (Shloka 58 of Shankara's Vivek Chudamani').

The Expressive Way

This is the opposite of suppression. Letting go and giving vent to thoughts, impulses, desires, cravings, etc.

The classical example is Tantra, the left hand path — the vamachar (the way associated with the woman). Its 'expressive' ritual is based on indulging in the five Ms, which when translated stand for alcohol, drink, flesh, fish, rice and sexual intercourse (which could be promiscuous). This ritual propbably came into existence to circumvent strict social conventions of an anti-permissive society. No wonder, it was held in secret. But this is only one part of Tantra, which otherwise calls for strenuous mental exercises, particularly recitation of mantras.

These days, there is a lot of unhealthy interest in tantra because of its association with sex. This aspect of tantra loses its significance in a permissive society. And nobody seems to have heard of the more serious and strenuous aspects of tantra. A modern godman was particularly responsible for reducing tantra to a farce.

But along with the expressive aspect, tantra also has a suppressive one. The practice of mantra recitations thousands of times in one session serves as a powerful suppressive for the thought stream and its accompaniments.

The Bengali tantric master admonishes
'Eat and drink, indulge the senses,
Fill the mandala (with offerings) again and again
By things like these, you'll gain the world beyond,
Tread upon the head of the foolish worldling and proceed'
(Conze, 1964).

'Eat and drink' has a much deeper significance than imagined by those who mistake profound spiritual endeavour for fun and games. One of the deepest practices of tantra is the technique of 'making the very obstacle a stepping stone to success'. We shall try to understand this when we deal with the encounter between self-awareness and non-self-awareness, between the I and the non-I, between the conscious and the unconscious, between insight and darkness in another chapter.

These days, some celebrate the expressive way by undergoing encounter therapy or indulging in a session of howling, screaming, shouting, gesticulating, moving, shaking or in a prolonged session of loud laughter(without any provocation). These practices are supposed to unclutter the mind and prepare it for some serious meditation.

Few may realize the similarity between this pompous moving and shaking and its informal clone – the disco dance. Both serve the same purpose – releasing a feeling of exhilaration. Such exuberance can be treated as examples of spontaneous catharsis or outlet.

If the suppressive way leads to bottling up, neurosis and stunting, the expressive way leads to dissipation, draining and frittering away of lowly but potentially exalted energies. (This observation does not apply to tantra, whose expressive strategies are followed by transmutation and transcendence). Cheap exhilarations and 'highs' are not objectives of any kind of meditation, excepting those of some modern godmen.

There is a technique of the expressive way, which is of great importance to the highest form of meditation, with which we will deal now. It is letting the 'mind run'. To allow the thought stream indiscriminate movement, to allow the good and evil, pleasant and unpleasant, acceptable and non-acceptable elements of the thought stream 'to rise to the surface', to become conscious, to subject themselves to self-awareness. It is generally accepted that one must not judge others. In this exercise one has not to judge oneself. This is the basis of observational meditation which is thousands of years old. Incidentally, it is the same practice as 'free association' of psychoanalysis, which the genius of Freud tumbled upon. The difference between the two is, in the 'free association' technique, two people are involved – the analysand and the analyst. The analysand is supposed to blurt out – express – whatever comes to his lips. In the former, only one person is involved, the meditator, who temporarily, bifurcates himself into the observer (analyst) and the observed (analysand).

In both cases, meditation and psychoanalysis, insight brings about certain transformation. (in psychoanalysis, transference also plays a very important part). But in meditation, the objectives are much more advanced. If psychoanalysis makes you a 'normal' person, restoring all his miseries, meditation can make you a god.

The Observational Way

Observation implies self-observation. And self-observation implies the observer and the observed. The observer is the I, its self-awareness and its insight. The observed is the non-I, its non-self-awareness and its thoughts, desires, impulses, cravings, etc.

Before we proceed further, we need to understand the I and particularly, the non-I. We all know what we mean by the term I. but the term non-I requires elaboration. The non-I, unlike the I, is a conglomerate composed of the physical, physiological, instinctual and psychological selves. In other words, food and water in our system (physical or 'mineral level'), the growing and decaying body (physiological or vegetative or 'plant level') the instincts (instinctual or a specialised physiological or 'animal level') and drives, desires, cravings, passions (the psychological or 'primitive human level') — these four levels constitute the non-I. It is a conglomerate because it involves four levels. (the 'I' or more accurately the 'current I', is a single level).

The psychological level in turn has three sub-levels — the unconscious, the pre-conscious, and the thought spray (generally called the 'thought stream', as christened by William James). Remember, there is no conscious or self-aware level in the non-I.

In modern psychology, the thought spray (or the thought stream) is considered to be conscious. At times, thoughts, desires, etc. are considered to be contents of consciousness. Rarely, but correctly, they are considered to be objects of consciousness (of self-awareness in my terminology).

According to me and certain other meditators, consciousness (self-awareness) is restricted to the I. The thought spray is the last extension of the non-I and thereafter begins the land of the I. In other words, the non-I at the level of the thought spray is contiguous to the I. It is because of this proximity that the I is capable of taking cognizance of the thought spray. This creates the mistaken impression that the thought spray and its contents are conscious. In meditation, this mistake is completely removed.

I repeat, thoughts, impulses, desires, cravings, passions are 'blind'. They have no self-awareness or consciousness and hence no I-hood. They are merely objects of self-awareness or the I. They belong to the non-I. The following 'ladder' will graphically summarize the position.

The 'Pure' I	The Spiritual Self	The fully self-aware I.
The Incipient I (the ego) and the current I	The Psycho-spiritual Self.	The current I, partly psychological, partly spiritual (preceded by the ego, the incipient I).
	The Psychological Self	The Unconscious' (The psychological instincts (drives) i.e. the id. (also super ego)
The Non – I		The Preconscious (contains the outflow from the Unconscious and back flow from the thought spray).
		The Thought Spray or the Thought Stream of which the I is conscious
	The Instinctual Self	The Instinctual (Instincts at the Physiological level).
	The Physiological Self	The Physiological (vegetative processes of growth and decay.)
	The Physical Self	The Physical (air, food, water, etc. ingested in the body, but still not absorbed).

With the clarification of the terms 'I' and the 'non-I', we can now proceed further.

What is the observational or self-observation way? It is the observation or cognition by the I of the non-I, i.e. thought spray, which is the most proximate constituent of the non-I to the I.

Self-observation is considered to be something like introspection. But if somebody thinks that self-observation is a mere cataloguing of the various thoughts, rising and falling in the thought spray, he is sadly mistaken. Self-observation turns out to be a dynamic process in which both the observed (non-self-awareness or the non-I) and the observer (self-awareness with I), get modified. This is a process in which non-self-awareness, the non-I or the observed, shrinks and the self-awareness, the I of the observer, expands. (The reverse can also happen if the observed is more powerful). And, along with the growth of self-awareness, a number of its allotropes like Purity, Wholeness, Equipoise, etc. also grow. This self-observation or cognition itself is the process of meditation. To meditate means to observe oneself, transmute oneself and take to a new way of life, which relates to, as far as worldly goals are concerned, efficiency, progress, achievement, happiness. As this meditation leads to the development of the pure-I, the higher self or the spirit, it can also be called the spiritual way (which concept incidentally is altogether different from that presented by priests and theologians and the religious).

How this encounter between non-self-awareness and self-awareness takes place and with what consequences will be dealt with in some detail later.

Actually, there are two observational ways. The non-analytic and the analytic Vipassana belongs to the former, and cognitive meditation to the latter. In Vipassana, only the rise and fall of thoughts is observed, without any judgment. But there is no thought-wise analysis as this. What does the particular thought signify? How is it fuelled? Why did it originate? In cognitive meditation, each thought is analysed, the fuel or the energy which propels it is identified and resolved then and there into self-awareness. I firmly believe that the analytic way produces results much faster.

In Vipassana, it is observation only, and in cognitive meditation, it is observation plus analysis.

The Overlapping of the Three Ways

Earlier I mentioned that each of the three ways, being predominantly themselves, partake, though in a smaller degree, of other ways also. Thus, the suppressive way of Patanjali meditation resorts to prati-prasava, which is a cognitive process.

The expressive way also resorts to the cognitive process by converting the obstacle into a stepping stone to success, which is possible only through cognition. Similarly, the observational or the cognitive ways resorts to the expressive way by allowing the thought spray to rise and express itself. The basis of this meditation is to allow the thoughts to run, i.e. to allow the preconscious and even the unconscious to express themselves. If the thoughts do not 'run', there would be a blank, which is an obstacle. Incidentally, this process of allowing thoughts to run is thousands of years old. Most interestingly, it has been independently discovered by Freud, who called it 'free association'.

The pure suppressive way can only lead to choking of energies, neurosis and fanaticism. The pure expressive way can only lead to squandering and dissipation of energies. Only the observational way-based on self-observation or self-awareness, can generate worldly and spiritual progress.

If the suppressive and expressive ways do show some results, it is because they are contributed to, more or less by an element of the observational method. In the suppressive way such contribution is minimal, in the expressive, it is greater.

The very act of suppression or expression has a cognitive shade, which to some extent contributes to understanding, meaning, self-awareness, transmutation and realization.

Of the three ways, the observational way is supreme and amongst its two sub-divisions, the analytic way – cognitive meditation is more creative and fruitful.

Summary of Cognitive Meditation

After having some idea of the three great methods of meditations, you may be curious about my conclusions. Nobody who is intensely involved in meditation can help coming to one or the other conclusion. I am no exception. Frequently it is a mix of observation with informed speculation, to round off the lacunae in the observations. My ideas and conclusions are presented in the theoretical sections of this work. For a bald summary, please read on.

1. The ultimate Reality is THAT, which is beyond name and description. It harbours all the dualities of the manifested universe and is at the same time beyond them. It is beyond existence and non-existence, beginning and end, manifestation and non-manifestation, real and unreal, consciousness and matter and at a more domestic level, beyond birth and death, non-self-awareness and self-awareness, non-I and I, evil and good, demonic and angelic and so on. (This is nearer to Buddhist thinking than that of Shankara).
2. The manifested universe was born with a big bang from THAT, about 12, 15 or 20 billion years ago.

3. The manifested universe, including the 'internal' and 'external' worlds, is real. It is not an illusion. (This differs from Shankara's theory).

4. From the big bang onwards, a cosmic evolution starts (of which the Darwinian evolution is a valid but limited phase). The stages of the cosmic evolution are:

   a. Physical (Physical entities level)
   b. Physiological (Plant level)
   c. Instinctual (Animal level)
   d. Psychological (Early man level)
   e. Psycho-spiritual (Current man level)
   f. Spiritual (Future fully self-aware man level)

5. The entire universe including its physical level is aware. This awareness manifests either as non-self-awareness or self-awareness.

   Non-self-awareness means awareness without the presence and help of the I. There is no I at the physical, psychological, instinctual and psychological levels. But awareness is there at all these four levels. Due to the absence of the I, such awareness is called non-self-awareness.

   At the psycho-spiritual level, the I is partially present and at the spiritual level, it is present as fully developed self-awareness. Awareness, through the partial I of the psycho-spiritual level (current man) or through the fully developed I of the spiritual level (of the future man), is called self-awareness.

6. The cosmic evolution from the physical to the psychological is non-self-aware, there being no I at these levels. From the psycho-spiritual to the spiritual, the cosmic evolution is self-aware, because it takes place through the agency of the I.

   The non-self-aware cosmic evolution is blind and involuntary. The self-aware cosmic evolution, which is a continuation of the non-self-aware evolution by a dialectic leap at the end of the psychological level, is 'awakened' insightful and voluntary.

7. At the end of the non-self-aware cosmic evolution, i.e. the psychological level, due to certain factors, which could be pain or mutation and survival advantage, non-self-awareness turns upon itself and is transmuted into self-awareness. Self-awareness is a restructured non-self-awareness by transmutation through a dialectic leap from the non-self-awareness. Thus, there is a common

Reality behind both non-self-awareness and self-awareness, because of which one can pass into another (both ways) and also interact.

When the first nucleus of such self-awareness is crystallized, it is called the ego. The ego, the current I and the future spiritual I are three stages of the I.

The ego is largely non-self-aware, with a speck of self-awareness. It is the incipient I.

The current I is much more self-aware than the ego, but is still weighed down by non-self-awareness.

The spiritual I is theoretically fully developed self-awareness, without a tinge of non-self-awareness.

8. The ego is the spiritual seed capital with the help of which further self-awareness is developed. Only self-awareness can generate further self-awareness. That the ego is the spiritual seed capital, contributed by nature, without any conscious exertion on man's part, will be met with incredulity by conventional experts in spirituality, who prefer to wallow in concepts like God, grace, or anything which runs man down.

This becomes clearer in the current man, who has a larger self-awareness. Further, progress from the psycho-spiritual level is entirely dependent on man, for whom it is a matter of voluntary choice. No God or grace can help him. To attain the higher spiritual, man has to exert himself. It is a lonely undertaking. If this journey is embarked upon, bliss awaits man. Otherwise, sooner or later there will be misery, the unavoidable fruit of non-self-awareness.

One parameter of the spiritual is freedom. Therefore, if one has to attain to the spiritual, it can only be done on the basis of free choice. The spiritual is its own reward.

9. Before proceeding further, we need to define the term 'spiritual', a term used by theists like saints and atheists like the communists. For the communists, 'spiritual' appears to be synonymous with the cultural. For the religious, this term has references to God, heaven, saintliness, theology, asceticism, religious rituals and services, virtue, good deeds, vows, observances, etc.. To me, the term spiritual does not mean either the cultural or the religious. It specially means concepts, meanings, activities connected with self-awareness. Any self-aware act is a spiritual act. It may be

eating, running or an advanced state of self-aware meditation. I have conceived of three I selves, the ego (the incipient I), the psycho-spiritual I (the current I) and the spiritual I(the future fully self-aware I). The ego is the beginning, however miserable, of the spiritual. The psycho-spiritual is the middle of the spiritual progress. The future I is the fulfillment of the spiritual journey, (though this 'spirit' which is pure self-awareness has nothing to do with the spirit of theologians)

10. Another issue which requires clarification is that man is not born with the spirit as it is generally understood. There is a conventional division of man in body, mind and spirit. I do not believe in any such spirit, much less its constant presence along with body and mind. As pointed out above, from the stage of the ego man has to work consciously and voluntarily for his spiritual progress. This 'work' is meditation. It is meditation which generates more and more self-awareness, which, when a critical mass is attained, crystallizes as the higher self or the spirit. Thus, each man has to 'build' his own spirit. And it is only when this is done that man can be said to have body, mind and spirit. Till such time the spirit is 'built', it is only in a potential state, invisibly contained within non-self-awareness, i.e. the psychological, the instinctual, the physiological and the physical.

Not only is the spirit potentially present in man, but also in animal, plant and stone. But it is only at the level of man, who has been gifted by nature with the seed capital of self-awareness- the ego, that the possibility of the potential spirit being built into manifested spirit arises. Everything connected with this spirit and self-awareness is spiritual.

Another way of describing 'spirit' is to call it a pool of pure self-awareness.

11. There is another aspect to the entity 'spirit' as I understand it.

For certain philosophers, theologians and meditators, existence is divided between matter and consciousness, body and spirit. It is believed that:

A. The sources of the birth of matter and spirit are entirely different.

B. Matter and spirit are different categories, they have nothing to do with each other.

C. Matter is something to be frowned upon, and spirit, something to be adored.

I believe all these three conventional views are untenable. Each standpoint is dealt with separately.

A. I believe that the spirit is the end product of a long chain of cosmic evolution starting with the physical. A fraction of the physical becomes the physiological. A fraction of the physiological becomes instinctual. A fraction of the instinctual becomes the psycho-spiritual. A fraction of the psycho-spiritual becomes the spiritual. Thus, the ultimate source of the spiritual is the physical.

Similarly, steam is produced from ice. However, water and steam have different and even contrary properties and independent entities. In the same way, the spirit has not only properties contrary to matter but also is a separate, independent entity. Once the spirit is 'fractionated' from the physical, through intermediate levels, it leads its own life.

B. Matter and spirit may be separate entities but in a way are not different categories. This is because there is a common underlying reality behind the physical, the physiological, the instinctual, the psychological, the psycho-spiritual and the spiritual.

Because of the common underlying Reality, all levels from the physical to the spiritual can interact with each other. This clears the confusion that theologians create for themselves. They believe that the spirit is 'pure' and has nothing to do with the body and the passions, and in the same breath suggest that is is 'contaminated' by the body and the passions. It is not understood how the pure spirit, which has nothing to do with the body and passions, can ever get 'contaminated' by them. The same difficulty arises in the Samkhya Darshan (philosophy). In what way does the 'pure' Purusha (pure consciousness principle) get contaminated by Prakarti (nature/matter)?

C. Because of the common underlying Reality, from an independent point of view, all the levels, from the physical to the spiritual, have the same value. 'Matter' is in no way inferior to 'spirit'. Both, including the intermediate levels are wondrous expressions of the same underlying Reality. Manifestation is monistic, dualistic and pluralistic.

12. There is no I and no self-awareness until the psychological level which consists of impulses, desires, cravings, passions, storms.

As we saw earlier, under certain circumstances, the birth of the ego, with its incipient I-hood and incipient self-awareness, takes place, followed by the stage of the psycho-spiritual level. It is psycho-spiritual because it is an association of the psychological (desires) and the spiritual — the ego, later on evolving into the current I.

Thus, at the psycho-spiritual level now, there are two centres of power — the existing non-self-awareness of the psychological, and the newly developed self-awareness of the current I. One can also say the non-I and the I.

Although self-awareness (the ego and the current I) is born from non-self-awareness (desires, cravings....), both have contrary dynamics. And because of this, encounters start taking place between the two.

Non- self-awareness is billions of years old and well-entrenched. Self-awareness is a recent growth and comparatively fragile. But it all depends on the particular encounter. If, in a particular case, self-awareness is more massive than non-self-awareness, the former transmutes contending non-self-awareness into self-awareness, thus increasing the overall mass of self-awareness and decreasing that of non-self-awareness (positive transmutation). If it is otherwise, non-self-awareness transmutes contending self-awareness into non-self—awareness (negative transmutation). In this case, non-self-awareness increases and self-awareness diminishes.

The dynamics of such encounters are complex and cannot be dealt with in a summary. They will be dealt with in the appropriate chapter.

13. Such encounters, when placed in a designed strategic format in which self-awareness has an advantage over non-self-awareness, thus predictably leading to positive transmutations and incremental enhancement of self-awareness, is called cognitive meditation. The function of cognitive meditation is to continuously enlarge self-awareness and diminish non-self-awareness.

14. Non-self-awareness being highly massive and well-entrenched over billions of years, takes time to yield to the fledgling self-awareness. But, by a continuous process of cognitive meditation

over a period, a critical mass of self-awareness develops, which becomes the nucleus of the higher self or the higher I, or the self-aware self. Theoretically, the nucleus can develop into a pool of pure self-aware consciousness. This is the ultimate and highest level of cosmic evolution.

15. Since self-awareness is the current buzz word, everyone talks about it. But I wonder what conversationalists make of it. Come to think of it, self-awareness is a fairly abstract term and any number of references evoke no genuine concrete response in the listener or the reader. I have also been guilty of this, but only to serve a purpose in this book.

    Both non-self-awareness and self-awareness are the final realities of our existence and they express themselves in infinite ways. As infinite as existence itself. These diverse expressions can be broadly grouped under six facets or categories. I have called these allotropes of non-self-awareness and self-awareness. Thus, the allotropes of non-self-awareness are blindness (or sleep), drivenness (or subject to drives), fragmentation, tension and discharge and so on. Similarly, the allotropes of self-awareness are awakening, insight, purity (from all drives, good and bad), wholeness, equipoise and so on.

    These allotropes are dealt with in some detail in another chapter. They are concretised non-self-awareness and self-awareness, which we can relate to experientially. There is no scope for abstractions in meditation theory. These allotropes enable one to understand how non-self-awareness and self-awareness operate in our lives and what they do to us.

16. The final allotrope of self-awareness is 'transcendence' (as opposed to 'stagnance' of non-self-awareness). Transcendence is the final stage of self-awareness as well as the final stage of the manifested universe, which started with the physical from the moment of the big bang. At some point in the future, this transcendence will fly off into THAT and become one with IT. The physical is nearest to THAT, being born directly from IT, and the spiritual (the transcendence facet) is also nearest to THAT, getting directly merged into IT.

The Journey

With this act of mergence into THAT, the physical and the spiritual (and the intermediate states) non-self-awareness and self-awareness and their allotropes, the non-I and the I, all disappear into THAT. The journey which started with the big-bang ends with the big mergence. That which left its home at the moment of the big-bang returns home. This journey entails sorrow and joy. Till we reach the psycho-spiritual level, we have no say in the matter, there being no I. But after this level, it is for the I to opt for non-self-awareness and its eventual sorrow, or for self-awareness and its eventual joy. The latter means opting for meditation.

CHAPTER II

THAT AND THE COSMIC EVOLUTION

Everyone has his own concept of the Ultimate Reality. For some it is God, for some, Brahman, for some the Void. For some it is the Manifest Universe itself. For me it is THAT.

I will not try to show how THAT is distinguished from God, Brahman or the Void. It is perhaps nearest to the Buddhist concept of the Void.

From THAT arises the cosmic evolution and it also subsides into THAT. In order to understand meditation, we should understand cosmic evolution, and in order to understand cosmic evolution we should understand THAT. We shall begin with THAT.

THAT

THAT by definition is indefinable. It is a paradox. It is the beginning and the end of the end. It contains everything and nothing. It is and it isn't. For some, it is the ultimate Reality, and for some, the Ultimate Unreality.

The truth is, one can approach THAT and make intelligent guesses about its nature. However, one cannot experience it and come back to narrate it. As the great sage Ramkrishna, teacher of Vivekananda said, the salt doll went into the ocean to be dissolved and lost, never to come back. Perhaps a man who dies can come back, but not one who is dissolved into THAT. And if he cannot come back he cannot personally narrate his experience of THAT. All those who talk of God, Brahman, Nirvana, as if they are connected with them on the hotline are to be taken with a hand full of salt.

> Modifying a Tibetan proverb
> "Those who know cannot speak
> And those who speak do not know"
> (For the original read "do not" for "cannot").

For all of us THAT can remain only an intellectual concept.

Keeping the subject of meditation in mind, I would like to attempt a working description of THAT.

THAT is the source of the ENTIRE manifested universe. And if one honestly believes this, THAT harbours ALL the dualities without exception. The following tentative list of dualities gives you some idea of what I mean.

Non-existence and existence, finitude and infinitude, material and spiritual, immorality, and morality unrighteousness and righteousness, evil and good, non-consciousness and consciousness, non-selfawareness ans self-awareness, non-I and I, illusion and reality, illogic and logic, void and fullness, darkness and light, time and timelessness, falsehood and truth, the demon and the angel, infidelity and fidelity, mortality and immortality, hard and soft, black and white, continuity and peaks, anti-spiritual and spiritual, depression and exhilaration, the hunter and the hunted, the exploiter and the exploited, miserliness and generosity, vice and virtue, inspiration and craft, chaos and order, turmoil and stillness, change and no change, the spontaneous and the deliberate, accident and design, chance and calculation, and so on.

THAT not only harbours these dualities but is at the same time beyond them, totally unaffected by them.

Like the endless dualities, THAT also harbours coiling and uncoiling, which leads to equilibrium and non-equilibrium. When the manifest universe is born from THAT, the energies are in the highest coiled state. And this produces the highest state of non-equilibrium. With the uncoiling of the energies, the universe starts evolving. One day, some fractions of it will be completely uncoiled. The lack of equilibrium, which accompanied the coiled state, becomes equilibrium. It is this coiled and imbalanced state of ours that is responsible, at a much later stage, for our tension and restlessness.

When we are completely "uncoiled" and completely in 'equilibrium', we reach the door-steps of our home, THAT from where we started. This is the prototype of all home-coming and all the happiness, bliss and ananda it brings. As we shall see later, meditation is the only route to this home-coming. I repeat, the only route.

It may be mentioned here that meditation is a spiritual activity and has nothing to do with philosophy, religion, theology, cults, ritual, prayer, asceticism, hedonism, vows, fasts, self-abasement, etc. it is a technology of the spirit. And the spirit is the higher self, the pool of self-awareness of which one never hears in religious places or philosophy classes.

It can be very validly argued that by involving concepts like THAT, which are admittedly intellectual, I am already indulging in philosophy, even religion. My reply is simple. The concept of THAT is not purely intellectual. It is a deduction from advanced meditative experience. Meditation, particularly cognitive meditation, is based on observation, investigation and transmutation. These are neither philosophical nor religious processes. They are more akin to science. They are not speculative but experiential. THAT is validated by meditative experience, where intellectual lends a helping hand.

Beginning of the Cosmic Evolution

Meditation is the story of THAT. The manifested universe came into existence with the big bang from THAT and the cosmic evolution was initiated. It comprises six stages. The first four stages are 'natural', unconscious, non-self-aware. The fifth stage is partially non-self-aware and partially self-aware, an intermediate stage. The sixth stage is a spiritual one, which is fully self-aware. The first four stages are compulsive, the fifth stage part compulsive and part free. The need for meditation arises at the fifth stage or the psycho-spiritual stages, which is that of the current man. Its birth is in the spiritual component of the psyco-spiritual level. Its mission is to transmute the psycho-spiritual into the sixth stage, the spiritual. Meditation Is the quickest and most efficient route to the spiritual. Even if meditation is not practiced, the spiritual can be attained, but only after innumerable births, by the tedious and painful process of 'learning from life'.

The Moral Dilemma

I am sure the acute reader must have started wondering where and how the spiritual component of the psycho-spiritual is derived. The psychological level of drives and appetites which just precedes the psycho-spiritual level is incapable of meditation. Still, a part of the psychological is transmuted into the spiritual, giving rise to the psycho-spiritual level. This process, in which nature itself endows man with the seed-capital of the spiritual, will be discussed later. But once this happens, nature leaves us to our fate, and man to struggle to establish the spiritual, a freely chosen activity. Until we establish the spiritual, we shall not reach the doorstep of our HOME, i.e. THAT, and will continue to suffer from tension and restlessness, which is built into the manifested universe.

Before I conclude this section, I will have to deal with an issue, which must have disturbed you considerably. According to me (and some others) THAT is a repository, where falsehood and truth, evil and good, amongst other equally provocative dualities, reside. If this is really so, why should I not pursue falsehood and evil, which have an attraction of their own?

The issue is not all that simple. In the first instance, as of today, we are the residents of the manifested universe and not of THAT.

Further, though the dualities are present both in THAT and the manifested universe, the local situation is quite different. I have already stated that THAT harbours not only the dualities but is also beyond the manifested universe which is in the grip of dualities. THAT is not tainted by the dualities but the manifested universe is completely contaminated by them. THAT is not disturbed by the dualities, while the manifested universe constantly suffers from the turbulence of the dualities.

Falsehood, evil and other similar components of the dualities eventually arise from non-self-awareness, as we shall see later. Amongst other pathologies, non-self-awareness also causes tension and restlessness. No amount of progressive relaxation is really going to overcome these disturbances.

The first knee-jerk reaction to this situation is the conventional morality taught by religions, which is of a suppressive nature. When man ultimately found out that suppression and repression only add to the pathology, the need for a new morality become evident. This is the higher morality of the spiritual. It works through insight, self-awareness and self-knowledge. It does not suppress the lower but transmutes it into the higher. Then, and only then, does man become free of tension and restlessness.

The moral dynamics of THAT and the manifested universe are altogether different. We start being in the grip of the lower, but our salvation lies more in our release from this grip and not greater involvement in the lower. The only way to free ourselves from the lower or rather transmute the lower itself is meditation; the only route to self-awareness, besides the painful 'lessons of life'

The concept of THAT does not disturb the higher moral vision of the manifested universe.

We inherit from THAT both foolishness and wisdom. It is not enough to be foolish. It is not enough even to be wise. Nor is it enough to be both foolish and wise. One has to ultimately go beyond foolishness and wisdom via meditation, and return to THAT.

The substances and states that were released from THAT at the moment of the big bang are present in my system at this very moment. Conversely, I was also present, though potentially, at the moment of the big bang. I am the creature and the creator, from THAT to THAT.

From the creature to the creator is a long haul. I have called it cosmic evolution. Today, we are in its fifth, the psycho-spiritual stage.

I now come to the cosmic evolution as related to meditation.

The Cosmic Evolution

Cosmic evolution is a process which has already been dealt with, partly by scientists and partly by spiritual investigators. The study involves astrophysicists, chemists, biologists, psychologists and eventually, meditators. Where the biologists and psychologists leave off, the meditator takes over.

The Six Stages

Excluding the birth of the cosmic evolution from THAT and its mergence into THAT, cosmic evolution consists of six stages or levels.

Though eventually all the six stages are incorporated in the human being, to start with, three stages evolved without man.

To anticipate, these are the 'physical', the 'plant' and the 'animal' stages. When man appears on the scene, he 'recapitulates' these three stages and on his own develops three more stages, the 'psychological', the 'psycho-spiritual' and the 'spiritual'. Though man appeared later on the scene, he represents all the six stages, i.e. the entire gamut of the cosmic evolution.

All the six stages evolve successively, the first stage being the physical and the last one being the spiritual.

Further Development of the Cosmic Evolution

According to scientists, the beginning of the cosmic evolution is supposed to have taken place with the big bang, twelve to eighteen billion years ago. The figure varies, with the latest advances and refinements. According to scientists, we are not supposed to speculate about what preceded the big bang.

As usual, scientists have their differences and, according to some, the universe was always there as a 'steady state', there being no big bang. But it seems the big bang theory is the current favourite. Meditative experience and theories arising from it also chime in with the big bang. But with one difference.

According to the meditators, at least like me, there is a Reality antecedent to the big bang. I have called it simply 'THAT'. To use this term itself is an intellectual hazard, but to coin any term more concrete could be an intellectual disaster. The cosmic evolution is born from THAT, with a big bang. As we saw earlier, THAT is beyond description. It harbours all the dualities narrated above and is at the same time beyond them. Not very logical. But logic is a part of existence; existence is not a part of logic. THAT also harbours all the stages of cosmic evolution.

With the big bang comes the first stage of cosmic evolution – the 'physical' stage. It is the domain of the physicist and the chemist. It is supposed to be inorganic or lifeless. It consists of 'inert' matter with its atomic and sub-atomic particles.

From the physical, at some stage of the cosmic evolution, is 'born' the 'physiological' stage. It makes its first appearance as bacteria-like organisms that eventually evolve into plants. The main phenomena of the physiological stage are birth, growth, decay and death. Some call it the vegetative formations. I have designated this stage as the 'plant' stage. The plant stage incorporates within it the physical stage also, in the form of air, water, nutrients, etc.

The plant stage is succeeded by the animal level. To some extent, it could be a parallel movement. In addition to the physical and physiological stages, the 'animal' stage has a diversified instinctual life. Stretching the term, we may say that the 'plant' has two 'instincts'- life and death. The animal also has these two instincts, but in addition has many others – fear, anger, aggression, hunger, sex, being some of them. I am afraid the classification and enumeration of instincts, from the point of view of science, is still an unfinished task. I doubt if finality will ever be reached. Life is too complex and overlapping to be neatly parceled out.

Instincts are driving forces of life and death, as well as of many other functions. The animal life can be interpreted as a dynamic play of instinctual forces. The animal is a creature of instinctual forces. The animal level can be called the instinctual stage.

Though both the plant and the animal are physiological entities, the former is designated as the physiological and the latter as instinctual. This does not mean that instincts are not physiological. They are as much physiological as the vegetative functions of the plant. But the sheer variety, intensity and display of instincts is so powerful that the animal has to be distinguished. The instinctual is variegated and intensified physiology.

The 'animal' has three layers, the physical, the physiological and the instinctual. From the physical level, the animal draws its air, water, food, etc. From the physiological level, it draws the vegetative functions, and from the instinctual level, its own characteristic stage.

The animal stage is succeeded by the human stage. Everyone is familiar with the Darwinian concept. From ape-like ancestors developed the primitive man. As the animal has instincts, the primitive human has drives. However, while instincts belong to the physiological level, drives belong to the psychological level. Drives also have the same terminology like hunger, sex, aggression, fear and so on. (with further evolution, more drives like altruism, cooperation, compassion also evolve). The nomenclature for the instincts and drives may be the same but, as stated above, the former belong to the physiological level and the latter to the psychological. In other words, drives are psychologised instincts. This kind of thinking implies two distinct categories – the physiological and psychological. It eventually leads to the so-called insoluble problem of the brain and mind. I fully appreciate I am making a very controversial statement. The psychological level, distinct and independent of the physiological, is unacceptable to current science. The common scientific view today is that psychology is just another name for physiology, and what passes off as the mind is just another dimension of the brain. When physiology ceases, so also does psychology, and when the brain dies, so also does the mind.

Obviously, I do not subscribe to this view. For me, psychology and mind are distinct from physiology and the brain. I shall try to justify myself later.

Meanwhile for me drives are transmuted instincts.

Thus, the primitive man has four levels – the physical, the physiological, the instinctual, the drive or the psychological. (The primitive and current man both carry the animal heritage of instincts in addition to the drives).

The Darwinian evolution is supposed to have slowed down with the emergence of the primitive/psychological man. With further development, the biological evolution is substituted by a cultural evolution. This is still a continuation of the Darwinian evolution. The skills and talents of the primitive man evolve into the arts, sciences and technology of today. The primitive, the psychological man, once propelled by instincts and drives, becomes today's psycho-cultural man. Though still not recognized by scientists, a part of this cultural component has also evolved into the spiritual. Perhaps, some scientists may accept the spiritual if they follow my definition of it.

If the primitive man was psychological, the 'current' man is psycho-cultural or better still, psycho-spiritual.

The psycho-spiritual stage evolves from the psychological. It harbours the physical, the physiological, the instinctual, the psychological and a component of the spiritual.

Emergence of the spiritual

I would like to introduce you to my concept of the 'spiritual'.

The inorganic evolution (a phase of the cosmic evolution) deals with the changes that take place in the physical elements from the moment of the big bang to the formation of the earth's crust. It is something during this period that the inorganic 'leaps' into the organic bacteria-like organisms, which is the beginning of the physiological stage. From this organic evolution (which is also a phase of the cosmic evolution) has come the 'current' man. Both the inorganic and organic evolutions are scientific property. Even the cultural evolution of man following the fading out of the biological evolution is scientific property. Thus, conservative science plays a role till the stage of psycho-cultural man. Some daring biologist might even accept a sprinkling of the spiritual and consider the current man as psycho-spiritual.

The very heart of cosmic evolution is the emergence of the 'spiritual' from the psycho-cultural or the psycho-spiritual. The 'spiritual' is the sixth and last phase of the cosmic evolution. But, unlike the preceding stages, current science does not recognize any such 'spiritual' stage. Perhaps rightly so. Such an evolution till now is not a mass or general phenomenon.

However, unknown to science, such evolution has already taken place in advanced individuals and will continue to do so.

Perhaps, in the distant future, it might become a mass phenomenon, which science will not be able to ignore.

What exactly is spiritual evolution? It might surprise and even annoy you to learn that it has nothing to do with religion, cults, theology, asceticism, virtue, merit, self-abasement and so on.

Positively speaking, the 'spiritual' is a state of self-awareness. The next question would be: what is self-awareness. Since it is the central theme of meditation, the issue will be discussed at the appropriate place. Self-awareness expresses itself in various ways like 'purity', 'power', 'higher morality', 'being', 'transcendence'. All these are highly loaded terms and are not going to easily explain the nature of the spiritual. Had I the capacity to coin new and beautiful Greek or Sanskrit terms, I would not use the existing ones. Half the charm of Freud is in his terminology.

I could use other terms which are functionally derived from the present ones, like 'wholeness', 'equipoise', 'freedom', 'perfection', 'immorality', but these are no less loaded and as ineffective as the earlier ones in conveying what exactly the 'spiritual' is. For example, everyone talks of 'wholeness' and forgets to explain what it means. 'self-awareness is today's buzz word, but how many can proceed beyond it? The chapter on the 'Dynamics of Non-self-awareness and Self-awareness' explains what I mean by the 'spiritual'. Meanwhile, I will have to pay the price of poaching upon the terms evolved by others.

To return to the theme of cosmic evolution, the psycho-spiritual stage is followed by the 'spiritual' stage. It is the sixth and final stage. The last phase of the 'spiritual' is transcendence, after which the spiritual merges back into THAT. The cosmic evolution started with the physical from THAT, passed through the physiological (the 'plant'), the instinctual (the 'animal'), the psychological (the 'primitive man'), the psycho-spiritual (the 'current man') and reached the spiritual (the 'higher man'). And the spiritual in its last stage leaps back into THAT. It is a cyclic movement from THAT to THAT.

The spiritual stage carries with it the earlier stages of the psycho-spiritual, psychological, instinctual, physiological and physical. Of course, these components attenuate as the spiritual develops more and more.

Thus, excluding THAT, the cosmic evolution passes through six stages or levels as follows. Later on, I have referred to the six stages as six selves.

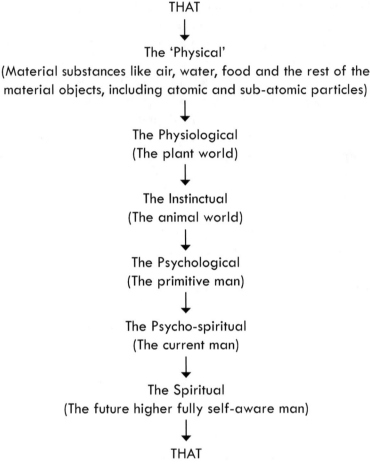

THAT

↓

The 'Physical'
(Material substances like air, water, food and the rest of the
material objects, including atomic and sub-atomic particles)

↓

The Physiological
(The plant world)

↓

The Instinctual
(The animal world)

↓

The Psychological
(The primitive man)

↓

The Psycho-spiritual
(The current man)

↓

The Spiritual
(The future higher fully self-aware man)

↓

THAT

It is only natural that a number of questions by now are flooding your mind. Perhaps some will be clarified in the related topics ahead.

Acceptance of the Darwinian Evolution

Darwinian evolution is one of the most accepted theories of modern science. Except for details, all biological scientists embrace it, in spite of the fact that there are big holes in its factual evidence. Evidence or no evidence, it is one of the modern Kuhnian scientific paradigms believed implicitly despite the warning of the greatest philosopher of science of the twentieth century, Sir Karl Popper, who said, "I have come to the conclusion that Darwinism is not a testable scientific theory but a metaphysical research program, a possible framework for testable scientific theories" (Poppers, 1976). Still, all scientists continue to believe in Darwin. Such is the power of any scientific paradigm (Kuhn, 1970). Even Popper believes in Darwinian evolution as a fact, though he does not accept it as scientific theory. (Come to think of it, the factual evidence for extra-sensory perception or ESP is much stronger than that for Darwinian evolution. But current scientists accept Darwinian evolution and reject ESP!)

I also believe in Darwinism. Not so much because of the current paradigm but because of the fact that its concepts mesh in very well with a Meditator's overview. Darwin illustrates scientifically the presence of the animal, the plant and the physical within me. It explains the dark, the repulsive, the gory, the ugly, the inert, the hyperactive, the unconscious, the non-self-aware that we constantly witness within and without. Darwinism not only dispenses with God but also with the devil.

I, as a meditator, am no exceptional believer in the cosmic evolution, including Darwinism.

But Darwin is anathema to the religious and the pseudo-spiritual. For them man is 'divine'. Obviously animals, particularly apes, are not 'divine'. Much less the physical substances from which we are derived after the big bang. (That the big bang itself is derived from THAT is another matter).

To the religious, only the 'spirit' which they never experienced is 'divine'. In their hatred of the physical, the physiological and the instinctual, they opt for an illusion called 'spirit'. This is not the first time pathology passes off as the spiritual. This cheap concept of the 'spirit' is one of the main obstacles in reaching the genuine entity, also termed 'spirit'. Being authentic, it can be experienced and lived, not endlessly parroted about.

The Cosmic Evolution a Succession of Stages — The Dialectical Leaps

Between THAT and THAT stretches the cosmic evolution, with its six stages.

To start with, the physiological — the plant and plant-like organisms evolve from the physical. The physical is inert and lifeless. It is supposed to have no sensation, perception, cognition, whereas the plant is a living entity, with birth, growth, decay and death. It has sensation-like activity. How can the living emerge from the inert? The fact is it does happen. The only conclusion could be that the 'inert' and the 'living' are an expression of an underlying and continuing Reality. The 'inert' is restructured and it becomes the 'living'. If we consider the living stage higher than the inert one, then the succeeding stage is higher and opposite. Such a leap into the higher and the opposite is what I have called a dialectical leap.

Then comes the restructuring of the physiological into the instinctual. Here, the dialectical leap consists of the physiological fanning out into numerous instincts which were not present in the plant.

Next comes the much more important leap – from the instinctual to the psychological, in the primitive human. Here exists real category change. The instinctual may be akin to the physiological, but the psychological is a much more subtle world of thoughts, desires, cravings, appetites. Unlike instincts which are ultimately chemical substances, the psychological is ultimately 'thought substance'. Desires and cravings arise from instincts, but in the process are 'psychologised'. The dialectical leap is from the crude material of instincts to the subtle material of thoughts. The instinctual and the psychological are not two sides of the same coin. They are two different coins. I am fully aware that the current scientific paradigm curtly rejects this kind of thinking. Steam may arise from water, but it is still an independent entity. And, I believe, like steam, thought can leave its original container, the physiological body, and move about in space. I mean telepathy.

The next dialectical leap is from the psychological to the spiritual. In fact, there are two leaps. First to the psycho-spiritual, an intermediate stage, and then to the spiritual.

The main differences between the psychological and the spiritual are:

The psychological, like the previous stages, is non-self-aware. It has no sense of the I, (therefore, described as non- I). It is subject, (again like the previous stages) to the law of inertia. Being inert it is involuntary, bound and compulsive. It is also subject to tension and discharge and therefore to psychosomatic disorders.

The spiritual is self-aware and therefore has the sense of the I. It is not subject to the law of inertia and therefore is voluntary and free. It is in a constant state of equipoise and therefore beyond tension and discharge. Therefore, also free from psychosomatic diseases. The spiritual constantly assures psychological health.

The main difference between the psychological and the spiritual is the non-self-awareness of the former and the self-awareness of the latter. From these two basic antagonistic states are derived a number of other antagonistic states. This theme will be considered in some detail in the chapter on the 'Dynamics of non-self-awareness and self-awareness'. From the psychological to the spiritual is the greatest leap a man can take.

The current man is part psychological, part spiritual, i.e. psycho-spiritual. His destiny is to transmute the psychological component and become entirely spiritual. This dialectical leap can be taken with the help of meditation alone. There is no other route, whatever some may imagine otherwise.

The Non-human and Human Levels of the Cosmic Evolution

You must have noted that three levels of the cosmic evolution are non-human-the physical (physical entities), the physiological (the plant) and the instinctual (the animal). The remaining three levels, i.e., the psychological, the psycho-spiritual and the spiritual take place in the human being. However, by 'recapitulation', man acquires the first three levels too.

Of the six levels, four (three from the non-human phase and one from the human) – are 'natural', bound, compulsive, inert. In one word, non-self-aware, having all the characteristics as described in the chapter on 'The Dynamics of Non-self-awareness and Self-awareness'. The fifth level, the psycho-spiritual is part bound, part free, part non-self-aware and part self-aware. It is an intermediate stage between the psychological and the spiritual, in which the current man finds himself. The sixth level - which is obviously human – the spiritual level is theoretically fully free and self-aware.

Thus, non-self-awareness is not only the characteristic of physical entities, plants and animals, but also of human beings. This theme recurs in philosophers like Hartman – 'Philosophy of the Unconscious' (1950), Nietzsche, finally culminating in the celebrated concept of the unconscious of Freud. Somewhere, I shall deal with the issue, why I prefer the term 'non-self-awareness' to the 'unconscious'.

Their Spiritual and My Spiritual

I have termed the last stage of the cosmic evolution – spiritual. Spiritual is obviously from the noun- the spirit. I am not at all happy with this term, with its entrenched theological meanings. And the first thing that a meditator would like to shun is theology. Instead, I prefer to use the term the higher self. Unfortunately, I cannot derive a suitable adjectival term from 'higher self' like the 'spiritual'. Hence, I fall back upon the 'Spiritual', with all its confusions.

So my spiritual is not their spiritual. Their spiritual is heaven, hell, virtue, merit, fasting, austerities, asceticism, prayers, vows, self-abasement, rituals, attending temples, reading scriptures, saying the rosary and so on. In my view, all or most of the above is anti-spiritual. A compulsive super-ego, instinctual or neurotic or even psychotic activity — products of non-self-awareness. For me, the spiritual is the self-aware, the non-compulsive, the non-driven, the 'free', the equipoised, the transcended.

This issue will be examined in some detail in 'Dynamics of Non-self-awareness and Self-awareness'.

It is not possible to understand the anti-spiritual and the spiritual without realizing the true significance of non-self-awareness and self-awareness. This realization happens only through meditation.

CHAPTER III

THE VARIOUS SELVES OF THE HUMAN UNIT

We saw that cosmic evolution unfolds at three levels.

> Physical (material objects),
> Physiological (plant),
> Instinctual (animal).

When man emerges from the animal, three levels repeat in him as recapitulation. From there on, only in man do the further three levels unfold, they being the psychological, the psycho-spiritual and the spiritual. Thus, man has six levels in all. Each of these levels constitutes a 'self'.

From the physical self emerges the rest of the selves, right up to the spiritual. However, this does not mean that all the emerging selves are also physical. The physical harbours within itself the rest of the five selves which emerge dialectically. Because of these dialectical leaps, eventually, the spiritual self begins to have characteristics opposed to those of the physical. A crude example would be, ice, water and steam placed in one container. Though water and steam 'emerge' from ice, the first (ice) and last (steam) stages have opposing characteristics.

Since all the six selves have THAT as the common ground, i.e. Reality, they are connected with each other and thus become interdependent and interactive.

Interdependence of the Selves

The Physical Self

The effect of the physical self are studied via nutrition, biochemistry, pharmacology and ecology.

The physical self also has considerable influence on meditation. A man is literally what he eats, not only physiologically but also psychologically. To take an extreme example, drugs, which belong to the physical self, extend their influence all the way to the psychological self, which is the basis of the dreaded drug culture. A lot of false information is peddled regarding the use of drugs. Some hace taken for granted that the 'chemical' Samadhi produced by the drugs is the same as the one produced by prolonged meditation. Nothing can be more nonsensical. Drugs destroy the body and the mind. Meditation builds them.

There is no way a drug addict can have any idea of the higher states of consciousness produced by meditation. This fact has been known for the last several thousand years in meditation circles. More subtle is the effect of inertia proceeding from the physical self. This also extends to the psychological self. Sloth, hyperactivity, conservatism, grooved non-creative thinking, absence of initiative, incapacity to change direction, incapacity to change speed, incapacity to start, if at rest, incapacity to rest, if in movement. Inertia is one of the biggest obstacles to understanding and undertaking meditation.

The Physiological And Instinctual Selves

These are subjects for physiology and ethology.

The physiological self is very intimately related to meditation. If one has to succeed in meditation, apart from health, a specialized maintenance of the body or physiological self is very essential. This is the middle path. One shall not eat too much or too less. One should not sleep to much or too less. One should not overwork or underwork. One should not be over involved or under involved in the world and so on. This principle of moderation applies to all physiological activities. Observing the middle path greatly facilitates the building of the spiritual self.

Actually, as the practice of meditation progresses, moderation becomes more and more a way of life. Moderation facilitates meditation and meditation leads to moderation. Such is this gracious circle.

The instinctual self basically is the physiological self. But it has been given an independent identity as (i) it is a highly specialised and complex segment of the physiological and (ii) it does not occur in the plant kingdom, but appears for the first time in the animal kingdom.

By considerably stretching the term, one may say that the plant has two instincts, that of life and death. This explains the physiological phenomena of birth, growth, decay and death. By comparison, the animal has a large and indefinite number of regular instincts — hunger, sex, fear, aggression to name a few. They may in all probability be hormone-based, which are physiological substances.

The aggregate of the instincts constitutes the instinctual self and it appears at both the animal and human levels.

Instincts are to be distinguished from drives. 'Drives' occur on the psychological level, which belongs to humans. Unlike instincts, which are physiological entities, drives are psychological entities. Actually, drives are 'psychologised' instincts. There are as many drives as there are instincts and a few more, which arise for the first time in humans at the psychological level. Thus, in the human being, the same 'substance' occurs in two forms — instinct and drive. For example, sex occurs both as instinct and drive, the former at the physiological level and the latter at the psychological.

The drive is a transmuted instinct. When such transmutation takes place, the drive augments and the instinct diminishes. Man becomes less physiological and more psychological.

Meditation

Of the physical, physiological, instinctual and psychological, the last one is the most influential. Hence, cognitive meditation is concerned with the encounters between the psychological energies and the I and its self-awareness principle. Between the psychological and the spiritual is the intermediate transition stage — the psycho-spiritual self. Meditation is initiated here.

The Psycho-spiritual Self

The psycho-spiritual self is our current evolutionary and predominant self. It is partly non-I, in the form of psychological drives, and partly I, with its limited share of naturally gifted self-awareness.

As already noted earlier, the psycho-spiritual self is in intimate interdependence with the nether, psychological self. In future, it will also develop intimate interdependence with the spiritual self, when it is built.

As far as interdependence is concerned, the psychological self with its drives, desires, cravings could be toxic to both the physiological self (psychosomatic disease) and to the psycho-spiritual self (psychological disorders – neuroses). Not to mention emotional blizzards blowing from the psychological over the psycho-spiritual. (However, the psychological self has its plus points also. It is the source of the arts springing from inspiration. Also the source of noble sentiments like sympathy and compassion).

With the development of the psycho-spiritual self, there is a turnaround in the human condition for the better. It is for the first time that the non-self-awareness of the psychological is countered by the self-awareness of the spiritual. (interestingly, the spiritual, as we see later, is a dialectical transmutation and restructuring of the psychological.) Thus, the spiritual, though an offspring of the psychological, has diametrically opposite characteristics. Like the fragrant rose from foul manure.

Psychosomatic and Psychological Health

People seem to have heard only of psychosomatic disease and neuroses and seem to be quite unaware of psychosomatic and psychological health. These are results of self-awareness and insight of the psycho-spiritual self. Though the effect has always been known to the meditators, it was Freud who put in on the scientific map with his research in conversion, hysteria and treatment of neuroses. What we have termed as non-self-awareness is the unconscious in the Freudian system. An important aspect of Freudian treatment lies in making the unconscious, conscious. The Freudian conscious is the equivalent of our self-awareness and its insight. In our language, the cure lies in making the non-self-aware, self-aware. (Of course, transference is an additional lever in Freudian treatment.) Though Freud seems to have become a pessimist, due to an over-exposure to the pathological, he never lost his faith in reason, a spiritual energy, which will someday improve the lot of mankind.

The spiritual component of the psycho-spiritual self also helps in attenuating the emotional storms blowing from the psychological.

Thus, for the first time, we find that interdependence plays a benign role; in fact a curative one. All this with the help of nature – gifted self-awareness of the psycho-spiritual. With the help of the same self-awareness, meditation is undertaken, man sets out on a wondrous journey of self-cultivated self-awareness and its extraordinary accompaniments.

Inter-self Interdependence in the Psycho-spiritual Self

We have been considering interdependence and its consequences between the various selves. In the case of the psycho-spiritual self, exceptionally, there are two components – the psychological and the spiritual. One of them is a spillover from the receding psychological self and the other from the budding spiritual. The two components of the same self being interdependent, continue to interact ceaselessly. And one more problem is generated.

As you may be aware, some philosophers and psychologists believe that man is determined, i.e. bound and not free. In his thinking and actions, he can be only involuntary. He has no free will. One of the major exponents of this stand in the 20th century is Freud. Philosophers in the opposite camp believe that man has free will and is capable of voluntary thought and action. They are in the majority these days. This has been an age-old and fierce controversy. Most interestingly, according to both schools man is either completely bound or completely free. To the non-philosophers this could be a strange conflict. They know from personal experience that man is partly bound and partly free. Partly involuntary and partly voluntary. In this case, the non-philosopher is closer to the truth.

When we come to the dynamics of non-self-awareness and self-awareness, we shall find that the psychological is fuelled by non-self-awareness and the spiritual by self-awareness. Further, we shall find that non-self-awareness is the source of bondage and self-awareness, freedom. As the name indicates, the psycho-spiritual self, the evolutionary, current dominant self, is composed of both the psychological (non-self-aware) and the spiritual (self-aware). In other words, we are partly bound and partly free, depending upon the physiological and psychological areas concerned. Philosophers addicted to controversies and having penchant for endless arguments will find this solution anti-climactic and disappointing.

From the cosmic evolutionary view, the solution is quite clear. It needs no argument to establish that the physiological (with some exceptions) and the psychological selves are non-self-aware and bound. Those who have experienced it or are theoretically prepared to accept the possibility of the spiritual self will find it self-aware and free. The psycho-spiritual self is a transition stage between the psychological and the spiritual and therefore partakes of the characteristics of both. Thus, current man is both non-self-aware and self-aware and therefore both bound and free. Part bound and part free. It is as simple as that. Even freud tacitly accepted the principle freedom in man by acknowledging the prospect of getting relieved of neuroses (bondage), by the unconscious becoming conscious and being cured. (Freedom through insight the self-aware, spiritual, principle).

Earlier, up to the psychological level, man was fully bound. In future, when the spiritual self evolves, at least theoretically, he will be free. In between, at the psycho-spiritual level, he is partly bound and partly free.

And the above dual nature of the psycho-spiritual self becomes evident in other areas also. Thus, man is part impure and part pure; part fragmented and part whole' part tense and part equipoised. And so on, as we shall see later.

A popular derivation of the above is that, at the present level of cosmic evolution, i.e. the psycho-spiritual, man is neither wholly evil, nor wholly good.

In the psycho-spiritual self, the psychological component belongs to the past and the spiritual to the future. It is the mission and task of meditation to dissolve the psychological and dialectically restructure or transmute it into the spiritual. Till this happens, man will remain, perpetually and inexplicably, restless. The divine discontent. It is only after many and varied but unsuccessful efforts to overcome this restlessness that man becomes ready to take to the path of meditation. Till then, he may even ridicule it.

The Spiritual Self

The manifest universe begins with the physical and ends with the spiritual. In the case of the human unit, history begins with the physical self and ends with the spiritual self. Both of these are nearest to THAT, but from opposing directions. The physical self is the highest of non-self-awareness and its consequences. The spiritual self is the highest of self-awareness and its accompaniments.

As of today, of all the selves we know the psycho-spiritual the best, because we are it, at the present stage of evolution. We are most conscious at the psycho-spiritual level. The earlier selves belonged to the 'unconscious' of which we were only partially conscious. Reference to the spiritual self does not arise as it is still not manifested. It has still to be built up.

All those who talk of the spirit, the atma, the Purusha, do so, as if these entities already exist and they are in direct contact with them. We know that the use of these terms is mere parroting and there is no direct experiential knowledge. These words are just the stock-in-trade of theologians and preachers. When pressed harder, they invoke the concepts of maya, avidya, etc. to explain away the absence of verifiable experience. The spirit or atman is masked by maya or evil and hence inaccessible!! In my experience, the truth is something altogether different. There are no self-existing entities like the spirit or the atman. What I am trying to drive at is that spirit, (words like atman, Purusha, do not figure in my technical vocabulary), as I understand it, is just a potentiality, which has to be concretized. And the difference between being masked and being a potentiality is not just semantic. Masked means it is already in existence but cannot be seen or experienced. Potentiality means it has still not come into existence.

The builder of the spiritual self is the spiritual component of the psycho-spiritual self. Only the spiritual can build the spiritual. Unless of course, one wants to wander on the deceptive paths of unrelieved pain and frustration, which may someday suddenly wake you up to behold the spiritual. A very uneven and uncertain way, meant for the unfortunate. Thus, the spiritual component is a gift of nature, in the sense that man has not worked for it. We shall see later how this one-time gift of nature comes across man's way. But the full-fledged spiritual self is no gift. It has to be built by hard work. And this hard work is called meditation.

Another erroneous concept concerning the spirit is about its origin. The most common division of the human unit is between body, mind and spirit. In other words, the spirit has nothing to do with the body and mind. It is supposed to be an independent category, having descended directly from God or Brahman. For me, the spirit has descended from the psychological, which in turn has descended from the physiological, which in turn has descended from the physical. If one does not like the term 'descend', we can say, the physical ascends to the physiological and so on until the spiritual is reached. In a way, the ancestry of the spirit is of very humble origin and the posterity of the physical, the most aristocratic. Of course, all of them, in turn, have manifested from THAT, which does not exactly coincide with Brahman, much less with God. It is nearer to the Buddhist VOID, which is full of the entire manifested universe!

The spiritual self, being the last part of the chain of various selves, is obviously interdependent and interacting with them. Particularly so with the psychological self, which is its immediate source.

Those who derive the spirit or atman directly from God or Brahman have never explained its relation to the body or mind. As a matter of fact, they never tire of maligning the body and mind for the shadow they cast.

All this does not mean that the spirit shares any of the characteristics of the psychological or any of the previous selves. In fact it is the very opposite, like coal and diamond, who though different have the same underlying reality — carbon.

The spirit can and does interact with the other selves, even though diametrically opposed to the psychological, like ice and steam. This is because all the selves, including the spiritual, have a common underlying Reality — THAT.

The first consequence is that the spirit is a variable quantity. After all, the spiritual self is a pool of pure self-aware energy. If this energy is augmented by meditation, the spirit component enlarges. In antagonistic conditions, it may shrink. Theoretically, as meditation advances, the spirit will go on enlarging from the transmuted energies of the preceding selves.

Interdependence, which leads to the interaction of the spiritual with the other selves, leads to the most important phenomena in a man's life. Essentially, they are encounters between the self-awareness of the spiritual and non-self-awareness of the non-spiritual selves. They bring about a complete turnaround in man's life.

The interaction of the spiritual self with the other selves enhances self-awareness, substitutes 'impurity' by 'purity', 'fragmentation' by 'wholeness', 'tension' by 'equipoise', 'stagnance' by 'transcendence' and so on. These have been discussed in some detail, under the 'Dynamics of Non-self-awareness and Self-awareness'.

The constant gnawing, the endless wanting, consumerism, workaholism, drug addiction, religious involvements, spurious spiritual paths, escapism of all sorts, will be healed only when the spiritual self is established. Had there been no interdependence and interaction of the selves, the spiritual would not have operated on the non-spiritual. The exclusive spirit or atman of the theologians and priests not only cannot interact with the body and mind, it holds them in great disdain. The spirit of which I am talking embraces the non-spiritual and elevates it to its own spiritual level. This is the story of encounters between non-self-awareness and self-awareness, between the non-I and the I. Al those who meditate will be able to learn about this enchanting journey.

The Anatomy of the Selves

We are aware of five levels of the cosmic evolution — (1) the physical, (2) the physiological, (3) the instinctual, (4) the psychological and (5) the psycho-spiritual. All these levels were produced in the course of 'involuntary', 'natural' cosmic evolution. Eventually, one more level was produced by voluntary action — the sixth or the spiritual level. We have also noted that all these levels were embedded as discrete layers in the human being. This is the beginning of the concept of several selves in a single human being, which also happens to be age old. Of course, there are two schools which believe only in a single self.

Modern Scientist

We may start with modern scientists, particularly neuroscientists. They believe in only one self — the physiological or the brain. If at all they concede entities like mind, spirit, etc., they are to be treated as just variegated expressions of the brain. With the death of the brain, these will disappear; not having any independent existence.

The Vedantin

The Vedantin, who belongs to the school of Shankaracharya, also believes in the one self — the atma (very roughly, the spirit). It does recognize the physiological, the psychological and psycho-spiritual levels, but only as transient illusory entities.

Thus, both the modern scientists and the vedantin are monists — one material, the other spiritual.

Patanjali

The author of the celebrated work, 'Yoga-system of Patanjali', a highly respected text on meditation, seems to combine both the scientists' and the vedantin's point of view. He talks of the 'purusha,' an immaterial entity, having some similarity with the atma and the 'prakarti' or nature, which

111

incorporates the body and mind. Patanjali is a dualist, both 'purusha' and 'prakarti' being real.

The Philosophical And Scientific Dualists

Nowadays, this is a rare and dying breed. Illustrious examples are Sir Karl Popper, the great philosopher of science and Nobel Laureate Sir John Eccles. They have jointly authored 'The Self and Its Brain' (1977). The title is highly suggestive. Other similar works by Eccles, 'The Human Mystery' (1979) and 'The Human Psyche' (1980), are simply ignored by cognitive and neuroscientists. Both of these, one a great philosopher and the other a Nobel Laureate in neuroscience, are dualists. This means, they believe both in body (brain) and the mind as independent entities and also in their interaction.

Christian Theologians

Their division of the human unit in body, mind and spirit is quite famous.

The Freudian Scheme

Freud's division of the human unit, with the ego, the superego and the id, is now common knowledge. In fact, such is the universal influence of Freud that these terms have become colloquial. Though I have not come across specific remarks, he must have taken for granted the independent existence of the body. In a stray remark, he even talked of a future possibility of reducing all psychological entities to cerebral structures. Meanwhile, he developed the psychoanalytic theory of personality as if the brain did not exist.

Upanishads

One of the most celebrated theories is that of five 'Koshas' or sheaths or selves as I would put it simply. It is propounded in the Taittiriya Upanishad. They are summarized in one sentence in the Paingale Upanishad. 'Then the five sheaths made of food, vital air, mind, understanding and bliss'(Radhakrisnan, 1996). The 'annamaya kosha', the physiological sheath or self is the one produced by food. The 'Pranamaya kosha', the vital sheath or self is produced by breath and life currents. 'Manomaya

112

kosha' the psychological sheath or self is produced by desires, purpose, drives, etc. 'Vijnanamaya kosha', the intellectual sheath or self is produced by the intellect. 'Anandmaya kosha' the blissful sheath or self is produced by ananda or bliss. (Of course, none of these sheaths is the final reality or the atma).

Buddhism

The Buddhist scheme of selves may not be so well-known as the Upanishadic one. The term 'self' is out of bound for the Buddhists, as they do not believe in the existence of any self. Instead, they talk of 'skandhas', 'aggregates' or 'heaps'. They are five and are as follows:

1. 'Rupa' The bundle or aggregate of physiological components consisting the body.
2. 'Vedana' The bundle or aggregate of sensations and feelings – pleasant and unpleasant.
3. 'Sanna' The bundle or aggregate of perceptions.
4. 'Sankhara' The bundle or aggregate of tendencies, drives.
5. 'Vinnane' Consciousness.

The Occult Classification of Selves

1. The physiological body.
2. The ethereal body.
3. The astral body.
4. The mental body.
5. The casual body in which all the previous bodies retreat during deep dreamless sleep.

The Classification of Selves as per Cognitive Meditation

1. The Physical Self – Air, water, food and other substances, ingested by the physiological body but not absorbed.
2. The Physiological Self – The body with all its organs, tissues and vegetative processes, subject to birth, growth, decay and death.
3. The Instinctual Self – a specialised further diversification of the instincts of birth and death. (These 'instincts' appear for the first time in the 'plant'. This simple pair gets sub-divided and diversified

into a number of instincts in the 'animal'. The animal heritage is carried over into man, constituting his instinctual self).

4. The Psychological Self — Here, the physiological instincts are 'psychologised and become 'drives'. It is the self, consisting of impulses, desires, cravings, passions.... The appetitive self is on both the levels — physiological and the psychological. For example, on the physiological, it is sex, whereas on the psychological level, it is love. The difference between the two is that of structure. The psychological is distinct from the instinctual by virtue of being structurally more refined. The sublimation of the physiological into the psychological is also the beginning of an independent proliferation of the psychological without any relation to the physiological.

   The psychological self came into existence with the very primitive man, who must have just emerged, from the animal stage. In addition to being a bundle of instincts, he is also a bundle of drives.

5. The Psycho-Spiritual Self — This brings us to a hybrid. It is a bridge. It is part psychological and part spiritual. We have understood the psychological and we shall soon see, at least partially, what the spiritual is. Suffice to say that the spiritual is the self-aware. All the four selves upto the psychological are non-self-aware. Thus, the psycho-spiritual self is partly non-self-aware and partly self-aware. The non-self-aware is non-I and the self-aware is the I. Therefore, the psycho-spiritual is partly non-I and partly I. The physical, the physiological and the instinctual belonged to the physical objects, the plant and the animal. (That they are also incorporated in the human, by way of recapitulation, is another matter). The psychological self of desires, impulses, cravings, etc. only belongs to the most primitive man. Theoretically, he is non-self-aware and has no sense of the I, as in the case of the animal stage from where he has just emerged. In the course of evolution, self-awareness and its vehicle, the I, slowly develop till we reach the current man, who has added a psycho-spiritual self.

6. The Spiritual Self — the sixth self that man acquires is the spiritual self. The first five selves are 'contributed' by nature. The spiritual self has to be built by man himself. This enterprise is undertaken by the spiritual component gifted to man by nature at the time of formation of the psycho-spiritual self.

Most human beings have only five selves. The spiritual self is known only to those who have built it. Hence, most human beings have no experience of this self. No doubt, the whole world speaks of the spirit. But it is nothing more than a word and they understand it as much as a parrot would. One of the immediate objectives of the cosmic evolution is developing the spiritual self. And the way to do so is through meditation. Today, man is not body, mind and spirit. He is body and mind only. The spirit is only a potentiality, which has to be concretised. Had the man been really body, mind and spirit today, this world would not be what it is, but a paradise. The spiritual component of the psycho-spiritual self is only an incipient spiritual self. Only a nucleus. It is because of this nucleus that civilization exists, with its arts and science. But the full-fledged spiritual is much more, as we will see in the chapter, 'Dynamics of non-self-awareness and Self-Awareness'.

General Comments on the Selves

My scheme regarding the selves is the conclusion arrived at, after taking into account the unfolding of the cosmic evolution on the one hand and the unfolding of the individual on the other, who is undergoing meditation of the cognitive type. It has a certain relationship to physics, biochemistry, biology, physiology, psychology, depth psychology, transpersonal psychology and the farther reaches of the human consciousness. My scheme may be acceptable or non-acceptable, but certainly not opaque or ambiguous.

Above all, it establishes a rational relationship with the phenomenon of meditation. It is the understanding of the psycho-spiritual self of the current man, which explains the need for meditation, the best process that should be followed and its crowning achievement – the Spiritual Self.

I am quite aware that modern man and cognitive scientists will find some of my concepts untenable. I am an unabashed dualist, in fact a multiplicist with six selves. This flows from my conclusion that the psychological is distinct from the physiological. In fact, I am going beyond the usual dualist. I find that the spiritual in turn is a category distinct from the psychological. If telescoped, my six selves would match the three selves of St. Paul – body, mind and spirit. But then, when we reach the spirit, we completely part ways. For the theologians the spirit already exists as the body and the mind. In my case, the spirit is only a potentiality that has to be concretised and built. Further, my spirit is not inflexible and immortal. For me, from matter onwards, everything is immortal or mortal, as you look at them. The spirit is also mortal in two ways. It may regress to the psychological or take a leap and progress into THAT — the big mergence.

Unlike the theologians, I believe in the essential underlying unity of all the selves. From the physical to the spiritual or, if you like, from the spiritual to the physical is all one 'Substance'. The different selves are merely the restructuring of this 'Substance' into different kinds of expressions. And paradoxically, even if there is a common underlying 'Substance', it can assume contrary forms, like the physical and the spiritual.

The psychological and the spiritual being distinct from the physiological, I believe in survival after death. I even believe in reincarnation. There is already some evidence for these. But I am certain that more compelling and undeniable evidence will become available in the centuries to come.

The Reality of the Selves

Varying schools have varying number of selves. They also differ with respect to the reality status.

The Vedanta School talks of five selves from the 'anna maya' to the 'ananda maya'. But they are all apart from the 'atma', which alone is real. All the five selves and even the external world are illusory and unreal.

For the Buddhist too, all the five 'aggregates' are unreal because they are constantly changing. For the Buddhist, even the 'I' is unreal. (Ironically, it is the 'I', which is supposed to say that the 'I' is unreal. How can the unreal know that it is unreal. If such knowing were real, then the knower also becomes real!) For the Buddhist, the final category is the 'shunya' or the 'void', which is beyond description and therefore, cannot be categorized as unreal or real.

Patanjali in his yoga sutras is nearer the earth. He is a dualist, his 'purusha' being the consciousness principle and 'prakarti' being the material principle. Both are real for him.

For the Christian theologian, all the three —body, mind and spirit are real. However, body and mind are mortal, while the spirit is immortal. On Vedantic and Buddhist logic, one can argue that the Christian concept of body and mind, which are mortal and subject to change, also indirectly accepts the unreality of the body and mind.

For me, all six selves from the physical to the spiritual are real. I find that all the six are subject to change. But merely being subject to change does not impose unreality. As already noted, all six are outward expressions of an underlying reality — THAT. So essentially, all the six are real. For me, even a dream, an illusion or a delusion is real, since it produces objective physiological and psychological changes. And whatever produces a change is real.

To the unsuspecting reader, this discussion on the unreality or reality of selves, may appear to be an academic excess and luxury. It is far from being so. Meditation is too serious a business. Logically, unless the I is real, the non-I is real, the body and mind are real, the good and evil are real, the external and internal worlds are real, the entire meditative enterprise loses its meaning.

The Vedantist and the Buddhist, having announced the unreality and non-existence of the body and mind, strenuously and persistently set to work, as if these two were the most real entities in the world. They are never tired of singing paeans to asceticism, which is wholly dependent on the existence of body and mind. This is the beginning of a psychosis, which passes off as spiritual accomplishment.

The value of the selves

Apart from the issue of the reality of selves, equally important is the issue of the value of selves.

Even those who do not believe in body and mind do not cease denigrating them. The body, particularly the female body, is the object of hatred and condemnation by many who profess to be on the spiritual path. They divide the selves into lower and higher from a moral angle.

The genuine meditator tends to go beyond likes and dislikes. He is not only non-judgmental towards others, but also towards himself. For him, the physical, the physiological and the psychological are as wonderful and as divine as the spiritual. Neither loving nor hating them, he beholds their true splendor.

I am also guilty of using the term higher self and by reference, the lower and middle selves. The physical, the physiological and the psychological are lower selves. The psycho-spiritual is the middle self and the spiritual the higher self. My difficulty is, I am still in search of better terminology. In any case, the parameters I have applied are not moral and theological but purely evolutionary. Come to think of it, both the physical and the spiritual are equidistant from THAT. The physical is the first entity emerging from THAT and the spiritual, the last one merging into THAT.

Excessive involvement in the body and mind, either by way of love or hatred, is a discouraging scenario for the meditator. The objective of the meditator is to go beyond the body and mind. And the more one is involved in them, either in love or hatred, the more difficult becomes the task of meditation. And one goes beyond the body and mind, not because there is anything bad about them, but because the spiritual is the unavoidable destination of cosmic evolution. The body and mind are intermediate stations on the cosmic journey, where the terminal destination is the spiritual. Meditation is the map of this journey.

Inter-independence of Selves

If the Selves are mostly interdependent, they could occasionally become inter-independent also. I shall deal with three situations.

The first situation is concerned with the independence of the spiritual self, even when the meditator is alive, i.e. with his psychological and physiological selves intact.

When the meditator succeeds in establishing the spiritual self, it becomes independent of the psychological and physiological selves, at least for a limited period.

On the psychological level, all thoughts, desires, cravings become effortlessly still. Latent and inactive desires and cravings are in any case still. Similarly, on the physiological level, there are no sensations and no awareness of the body. The only sign is faint breath.

When both the psychological and physiological selves are stilled, the spiritual manifests in all its brightness, in all its aspects.

There are claims that meditators can make their spiritual selves permanently independent of the psychological and physiological selves. They become – jivan mukta – liberated while alive. This may be treated only as a theoretical possibility. Ramkrishna, the teacher of Vivekananda and a genuine sage of modern India, says 'Ornaments cannot be made of pure gold. Some alloy must be mixed with it. A man totally devoid of maya (read desires and cravings), will not survive more then twenty-one days. So long as man has a body, he must have some maya, however small it may be, to carry on the functions of the body.

But even the temporary independence from the psychological and physiological is sheer ecstasy. Incidentally, ecstasy comes from the Greek 'ecstasys' – to make to stand aside. In other context, it means aside from the body and mind.

The second situation concerns death. Unfortunately, death has more to do with religion and emotion than with science. For science, death is the end of the entire story. Along with the death of the brain, the psychological and, if ever there was such a thing, the spiritual, also die. In other words, the psychological and the spiritual, are not independent of the physiological. In fact, they are only physiological, though in different modes.

For me, death is not a religious issue. Whether man survives death or not should be a purely scientific problem. As of today, current science has decided against survival. I believe, and am sure, there are a number of intellectuals, scientists, psychologists, psychiatrists, doctors and philosophers, who will agree that this conclusion of modern science is premature. The psychological and the spiritual selves are highly subtle and today's science is just not equipped to follow their fate after death. But, as we shall see later, the phenomenon of telepathy can enable us to formulate a reasonable hypothesis in favour of survival.

The capacity of the psychological and the spiritual to survive death displays their independence from the physiological.

We frequently come across two terms – survival and immortality. For most of us, they are synonymous. But spiritual literature distinguishes between the two. Immortality is in some a reward for high spiritual accomplishment. Survival does not require any spiritual accomplishment. In fact, all the spiritual, the non-spiritual and the anti-spiritual continue to survive.

So then, what is the difference between survival and immortality? Survival refers to the persistence of the psychological after death. The spiritual is not in the picture because, in most cases, it has not been established and continues to be latent in the psychological. But in case the spiritual self is established, not only will the psychological survive but also the spiritual. Both of them being independent of each other will go their own ways. The psychological can reincarnate, but the spiritual need not. It becomes 'immortal'. It either merges in THAT or voluntarily reincarnates on a special spiritual mission.

The third situation concerns us most in our day-to-day life. When, due to meditation over a period, the spiritual becomes more and more established, it starts becoming independent of the psychological and to some extent of the physiological also. We leave behind our anger, hatred, fear, jealousy, revenge, aggression....

They are not suppressed but have been transmuted into the spiritual. There is change in the balance of power, with the spiritual expanding and the psychological contracting. The spiritual becoming more powerful to an extent becomes independent of the wantings and 'not-wantings', likes and dislikes, inclinations and disinclinations, partialities and prejudices, involvements and withdrawals elations and depressions and similar phenomena of the psychological. A new life dawns for the meditator.

Dynamics And Energies of Selves

The six selves can be divided into three groups. (1) Non-self-aware (2) Partly non-self-aware and partly self-aware and (3) self-aware.

The physical, the physiological, the instinctual and the psychological selves are non-self-aware. This does not mean that they are not aware, but that they have the awareness of the non-I or non-self-awareness. A common example would be swotting a mosquito in deep sleep. The I knows nothing about this, but the physiological self, the body, is aware of the bite. Non-self-awareness is knowing, but without knowing that one knows.

The spiritual self when established is self-aware. It is the awareness of the I. The I knows that it knows.

The psycho-spiritual self which is the current dominant self is partially non-self-aware and partially self-aware. It is the transition stage between the psychological and the spiritual.

Meditation is undertaken by the psycho-spiritual self. To be more exact, by its spiritual component.

Today, everyone talks of self-awareness. Nobody defines it or elaborates upon it. It is assumed that everyone understands it. The fact is the exact opposite. Today, to talk of self-awareness is more fashion then experience.

To start with, nobody is involved in tracing the source of self-awareness. The way people talk and write, it seems as if self-awareness is falling from the skies. Even though it can bring about radical behavioural changes, nobody seems to suspect that it is an energy. For only energy can bring about change. It is as simple as that. Similarly, non-self-awareness also has energy dimensions. Self-awareness is a single energy, whereas non-self-awareness is a conglomerate of energies. Self-aware energy is 'awake'. Non-self-aware energies are 'blind'.

Only two kinds of energies can generate self-awareness. Either pain or existing self-awareness. The source of self-awareness is the psychological self and its non-self-aware energies — the drives of hunger, sex, fear, aggression and so on. At some time, these drives come under pressure, are blocked and start experiencing pain. It is in this moment of pain that the psychological 'turns upon itself' and what is non-self-aware becomes self-aware. To give the crudest analogy, the pain of the mosquito bite 'wakes up' a 'sleeping' man. This is how the first nucleus of self-awareness is formed. It can be treated as a gift of nature of which man is deserving, by virtue of his having undergone pain.

Not only are the energies of self-awareness and non-self-awareness different, their dynamics, their ways are also different and opposite. The ways of the psychological are indulgence, suppression, repression, tension, stress, inertia, repetition, fragmentation, conflict, turbulence, bondage and so on. The ways of the spiritual are neither indulgence nor suppression/ repression. The psychological is transmuted into equipoise and its bliss. Fragmentation and conflict of the psychological are transmuted into integration and wholeness (another buzz word, without any accompanying specific meaning). Bondage is transmuted into freedom, repetition into creativity. Inertia and stagnance into transcendence.

My idea of the spiritual is entirely different from that of theologians and priests. It has nothing to do with virtue, merit, compassion, sacrifice, fasting, vows, rosaries, asceticisms, etc. it has also nothing to do with divinity (another meaningless term). Talking of virtues and ascetic practices, they are as compulsive and binding as vices. In fact, the source of virtues, like vices, is the psychological self. Virtues are as much drives as vices.

Man's cosmic evolutionary destiny is to move from non-self-awareness to self-awareness. Till this happens, he will be in a state of constant restlessness. No consumerism, no drugs, no cults, no religions, no escapism, no science, no philosophy, can ever save him. And beside pain and 'lesson of life', the only way to self-awareness is meditation. It is for the wise to choose. And closing the eyes, listening to soothing music in a state of relaxation is not meditation. It is just another variety of sleep. Meditation is self-awareness encountering non-self-awareness along with its grip, the bondage, the compulsiveness, the turbulence, the conflicts, the tensions, the psychosomatic diseases, the divisiveness, the dead ends, the meaninglessness, the unending repetition − compulsions, the stagnance. Meditation is a war declared by Zarathrushtra, three thousand years ago between Vohuman (the awakened, good self) and Akoman (the blind, evil self). Meditators are warriors, fighting the cause of spiritualizing the cosmos, starting with their own minds and bodies

CHAPTER IV

THE THREE 'I'S

'The I is hateful,' says Blaise Pascal (Pensees). I came across a book running into couple of hundred pages, which put 'I' in its place by replacing the capital letter with the small 'i'. i am sure, with this profound act of humility, the record was set right. But then Emerson creates doubts. 'I am the doubter and the doubt'. As if this sudden inflation of the I were not enough, Shankara, the founder of his Vedanta School announces, 'I am the Final Reality'. No wonder Satan was mighty perplexed. He visited Hallaj, one of the greatest Sufi Saints, at his execution block. Hallaj was being executed for heresy; his heresy being 'I am the Truth! Such self-elevation is not permissible in orthodox Islam. So Satan asked Hallaj, "you said 'I' and I said 'I'. Why is it you received God's eternal mercy and I eternal damnation?" (Mojdah Bayat and Mohammad Ali, Jamnia, 1994).

Could there be two 'I's? in fact, there are three

Before we proceed, let us understand the three terms (1) the ego, (2) the current I, and (3) the pure I or the higher I or the spiritual I or the spirit.

All three have the basic identifying characteristic — self-awareness. In fact, wherever there is self-awareness, there is I and vice-versa. The only difference among the three is the varying intensity of self-awareness. The self-awareness of the ego is very dim almost non-existence. The self-awareness of the current I is partial and that of the pure I, full.

The term 'ego' has two connotations. Popularly, it is a despicable kind of I. In psychoanalysis and other disciplines, the ego is what we commonly mean by the term I. This common I is what I call the 'current I'. 'Current' because the I is an evolving structure. Earlier, this current I was the ego and in the future, it is going to become the pure I. Today's 'I' is the 'current I'. The psychoanalytical 'ego' is the same entity as the 'current I'.

In my formulation, the 'ego' is the primitive I, similar to popular conception. It is not recognized by psychoanalysis. But if a place is to be found for it, it could be a tiny globule between the id and the psychoanalytical ego. The pure 'I' is also not known to psychoanalysis. One life was just enough to investigate the id and that is what Freud did. He hardly had time to develop ego-psychology or the advanced stages of the ego.

The 'Pure I' is known to the meditators only. For others, it is a future objective.

Thus, there are three 'I's. the ego, evolving from the psychological self, the current I, evolving from the ego, and the pure I, evolving from the current I.

The ego is associated with the psychological self. It is time for a small academic correction. The psychological self is supposed to be totally non-self-aware. Then how can the ego, which is an I structure having self-awareness be associated with it? In the first instance, the self-awareness of the ego is very dim, tentative, shifting between the existent and non-existent. It grows as a bud, on the fag end of the psychological self, the thought spray, which is about to unfold the psycho-spiritual self. Most of the ego is non-self-aware.

The current I is associated with the psycho-spiritual self, which is partially non-self-aware and partially self-aware.

The pure I is associated with the spiritual self, which is fully self-aware. In fact, the pure I and the spiritual self are one and the same.

The ego is the most contaminated I. Contaminated with the drives of non-self-awareness. Drives of aggression, anger, sex, fear, greed.... The current I is partially contaminated by the same drives of non-self-awareness. It has also an identifiable component of self-awareness. The pure I is not contaminated at all. Theoretically, it has no non-self-awareness or drives. It is not the same, but similar to the 'purusha' of Patanjali,'atma' of Shankara or 'spirit' of Christianity.

When somebody says, 'I am angry', it is ego speaking, where the current I is completely contaminated by anger. It has lost its identity to anger. It has regressed to the stage of the ego, which can hardly be distinguished from anger. The current I has become ego-cum-anger.

When a person explodes into anger and does not remember that he is bursting with anger, when he is beside himself with anger, when he is drowned in anger, when he cannot even say 'I am angry', it means even the ego and its incipient self-awareness are wiped out. Such eruption of anger is pre-ego arising from the deep psychological self.

When somebody says I am overcome with anger, it is the current I speaking. Here the I distinctly retains its identity but acknowledges that it has been penetrated by anger. It just maintains its head above the flood of anger.

The pure I, by definition remains untouched by anger or any other drive of non-self-awareness.

The goal of meditation is to prevent regression to the ego and achieve progression to the pure or higher I. This enterprise is undertaken by the current I.

Birth of the ego and the current I

The first four selves from the physical to the psychological are non-self-aware and without the I, i.e. they are the non-I. the ego has incipient I, the psycho-spiritual self, partial I, and the spiritual self, full I. Each has its corresponding self-awareness.

The obvious question is: How does the I arise from the non-I?

We are not concerned with the birth of the physical, the physiological, the instinctual and even the psychological in this book. Here, we shall deal with the births of the ego, the current I and the pure I. All three are most intimately connected with meditation.

First, we shall deal with the birth of the ego and the current I and thereafter, that of the pure I.

Even in the case of the ego and the I, we shall be dealing only with the birth of the current I because the process of birth for both the entities is the same. The only difference between the two is in the degree of self-awareness. The ego is of much more incipient structure, whereas the current I is better developed and more visible.

To fall in line with popular usage, it will be more convenient to use the term 'I' instead of the 'current I', in this particular discussion.

It is seen that there are three possible routes for the formation of the I.

(1) Mutation

During the evolutionary process, a mutation may have taken place adding the 'I' to the already existing 'non-I'. Because of its survival value, this mutation must have perpetuated itself, becoming hereditary.

(2) Demarcation

Not only do all stages upto the animal stage have the non-I, even the human infant has non-I. In the course of its growth and development, a demarcation between the non-self, the external world and the self sets in.

The external world becomes the non-I and the self becomes the I. (Only later on, it is realized that even in the self, i.e. the human unit, there are large areas which are non-I, the actual I being a very small component).

(3) Pain

Perhaps the most important and effective route from the non-I to the I is pain.

In the foetal stage there is no pain or frustration. It is uninterrupted, blissful sleep. All the requirements of the foetus are effortlessly and automatically met. It feeds, excretes, grows without knowing that all these processes are going on. It is a state of sweet non-self-awareness. It is obvious the foetus is non-I. If it were possible to continue to remain in the foetus stage indefinitely, it will never develop the I.

But the trauma of birth takes place, suddenly depriving the foetus of its paradise forever. Henceforth, the newborn has to face its physiological awakening to 'life's difficulties'. Now, it will have to face discomforts and pain of disturbed sleep, unattended hunger, excretion, inconvenient posture, etc. The pain of a mosquito bite awakens the sleeping man. The growing pains of existence 'awaken' the infant from its blissful sleep. The non-self-awareness 'turns upon itself' and becomes self-aware. And wherever there is self-awareness, the I exists. ('I', in this case is the ego, the most primitive of all Is, which in course of time will become the current I). Pain is the mother of the I and not vice versa, as many mistakenly think.

The birth of the I has an incidental but enormously important aspect. The ego and the current I were not acquired by choice or voluntary effort. It is an involuntary growth. One may say, a gift from nature. It is the last involuntary product of cosmic evolution.

The story is altogether different at the birth of the pure or higher I. The pure I can be acquired only by choice and voluntary effort. Choice, voluntariness, free decision are the hallmarks of the higher I. The higher I or self has to be consciously built. There are no more gifts of nature. In fact, from here on one can only expect obstructions from nature. The building of the pure I or spirit is a complicated, long drawn process. There is still one more aspect to be considered. How does the non-I or non-self-awareness become its opposite, the I or self-awareness? This is a dialectical leap, a restructuring, into the opposite and the higher.

The current I or the self-aware component of the psycho-spiritual self, which was a gift of nature, is the agent which undertakes the enchanting enterprise of building the pure I, the higher self or the spirit. This process is called meditation.

It is not that without meditation the higher I cannot be developed. It can also be done by 'learning' from the excruciating experiences, knocks, blows, sufferings of life. Such growth is more commonly known as maturity. But this is a haphazard, inefficient, uncertain process. The results are bound to be uneven. And for all one knows, it may, in any case, lead to the undertaking of meditation in this or the future birth. So why not now?

Birth of the Higher Self or the Pure I

We have dealt with the birth of the ego and the current I. In this sense, there is nothing like the birth of the higher self or the pure I.

This is simply because the higher self or the pure I is to be actually built brick by brick.

Acquaintance with the Higher Self

All of us are on familiar ground with the lower self, consisting of the physical, the physiological, the instinctual and the psychological selves. We are also well acquainted with the middle self, i.e. the psycho-spiritual self or the current I. in fact, we are predominantly the current I. But when it comes to the higher self, we know nothing about it, except a lot of dubious information circulating in religious circles. For most people, the higher self or its nearby equivalents are just empty terms. There is no dearth of people who parrot, day in day out, words like higher self, spirit, atma, which when analysed, boil down to high sounding verbiage, a transaction between the spiritually conceited and the spiritually gullible. This introductory section is meant to offer a broad conceptual notion of what the higher self, as understood in this presentation, is supposed to be.

Similar Terms

When it comes to terminology, the world of meditation offers a fertile ground. Soul, psyche, spirit of the dead, spirit of the Shaman, spirit of Christian theology, I, atma of Vedanta, atma of the Jains, Purusha of Patanjali, Buddha-nature, Buddha-self, self, mind, consciousness, mindfulness, self-awareness are some terms on offer in the spiritual market. Each of these has a distinct connotation. Very few may be aware that the term 'atma' in Vedanta is altogether different from the term 'atma' in Jainism. In modern popular spiritual literature, these terms are used indiscriminately, particularly by western writers. No wonder the scientifically-oriented, accustomed to well-defined terms, develop a distaste for sloppy, sentimental, spiritual stuff.

There is another greater difficulty. Experience beyond the physiological and psychological selves is not too common, and so on standard terms and vocabulary have developed. Each one has floated his own terminology. The wiser sages of the Upanishads have described this experience negatively — 'neti, neti' — 'not this, not this' (Brihad — Aranyaka Upanishad; S. Radhakrishnan, 1996).

I have opted for a simple term: 'higher self'. I am talking of the lower self and the middle self and now of the higher self, to satisfy terminological symmetry. The other terms mentioned above are overloaded with varying meanings, becoming meaningless. For me 'pure I' and 'spirit' are synonymous with the 'higher self'. I am sorry for using the term 'spirit' in yet another sense, that's different from the theological. But as I have to use the term 'spiritual', the occasional use of the term 'spirit', of course in my sense, is convenient and inevitable.

It would be a rewarding exercise for someone intellectually honest to bring out the distinct and at times contradictory meanings and implications of the various spiritual terms mentioned above.

Higher Self is a Creation by Transmutation

It is an unstated belief with most of us that entities like the spirit or atma are not an integral part of the human unit. They are supposed to have nothing to do with the body and mind, and trace their lineage to sources like God or Brahman.

The stand taken here is altogether different. The higher self is creation within the human unit from the psychological self by a process of transmutation. It is an intrinsic component of the human unit. We shall try to understand what transmutation is, and later, how it produces the higher self.

Transmutation

Manure is stinking and the flower is fragrant. We can say that the stinking manure is transmuted into the fragrant flower. Transmutation is a structural change from the lower to the higher into the opposite.

Such transmutations are critical stages in the cosmic evolution, as well as human development.

In the cosmic evolution, the non-living (the physical) is transmuted into the living (the physiological). Next, the non-hormonal (the physiological) is transmuted into the hormonal (the instinctual).

In the human development, the same phenomena are recapitulated. Air, water, food (the physical) are transmuted into living tissues (the physiological). Next, the living tissues are transmuted into hormones/ instincts (the instinctual). Next, the instincts are transmuted into drives, desires, cravings, passions (the psychological). The material instincts are transmuted into ultra-material drives and desires.

It is common experience in cognitive meditation that drives and desires are transmuted into 'purity', 'power', 'equipoise', etc. (the higher self).

In the non-human cosmic evolution, transmutations start with the physical to the physiological to the instinctual. In the human cosmic evolution also, transmutations start with the physical but proceed beyond the instinctual, to the psychological, to the spiritual. (The psycho-spiritual in between is only a hybrid transition stage).

A more fundamental presentation would be non-self-awareness or the non-I (spread from the physical to the psychological) being transmuted into self-awareness or the I (the spiritual).

There is another aspect of transmutation in the cosmic evolution. Transmutations from the physical to the instinctual at the non-human stages to the psychological and the psycho-spiritual at the human level are involuntary, which is another facet of non-self-awareness. The transmutation from the psycho-spiritual to the spiritual is voluntary and by choice, which are facets of self-awareness.

Simply put, the four lower selves are transmuted into one higher self.

Negative Transmutation

When lower selves are transmuted into the higher self, it is positive transmutation, simply called transmutation. But the higher self is susceptible of regressing to the lower selves due to their onslaught. This is quite a common phenomenon in meditation experience. The upward progress is not linear, but zigzag.

Contrary Characteristics, Common 'substance' and Continuity

Another interesting aspect of transmutation is that, though it is a restructuring of the same 'substance', the transmuted version can have contrary characteristics. Steam is a transmutation of ice. But the latter is cold and solid, while the former scalding and vaporous. Manure stinks while the rose is fragrant. Coal is black, but a diamond, sparkling. Our lower selves are non-self-aware, 'impure', bound, tense, etc. The higher self is self-aware, 'pure', free, equipoised, etc.

This brings us to the realisation that the 'substance' underlying ice, water and steam is common, even if its various expressions are contrary. Similarly, the 'substance' underlying the various selves from the physical to the spiritual is common, even though its expressions, i.e. the selves, may have contrary characteristics.

The spiritual is made from the psycho-spiritual, which in turn is made from the psychological, which is made from the instinctual, which is made from the physiological, which is made from the physical. Thus, the physical can become the spiritual (positive transmutation), and the spiritual can become the physical (negative transmutation). This goes to show there is an organic continuity between all the selves. The entire universe is one and many at the same time. Both monistic and pluralistic; unity in diversity and diversity in unity.

Transmutation is not sublimation

When aggression is transformed into competitive sport, it is sublimation. But when it is transformed into love, it is transmutation.

Sublimation is a refinement of the crude drive. Transmutation is a restructuring into the higher and the opposite, a dialectical leap. From the physical to the psychological level, both sublimation and transmutation are non-self-aware (unconscious in Freudian terminology) and involuntary. Transmutation from the psycho-spiritual to the spiritual can only be self-aware and voluntary.

Transmutation Agent

The agent transmuting ice into steam is fire. That transmuting manure to rose is light. The transmutation of the psychological into the spiritual is carried out by self-awareness. Thus, fire and light are synonymous with self-awareness.

Spiritual Alchemy

The raw material of the higher self is the psychological, i.e. the drives, the desires, the cravings, the passions... in alchemy, base metals like lead are transmuted into a noble metal — gold. In spiritual alchemy, 'base' material like desire and cravings is transmuted into 'noble' material like the higher self. No wonder alchemists are vague, evasive, secretive about the raw materials they use, lest the ignorant misunderstand. Denigrators of body (physical self) and desires (psychological self) will have to reconsider their notions. What is lower is potentially higher, if only we knew the alchemist's secret. The alchemist's secret is the fire of self-awareness, which cooks desires into the higher self.

An Intellectual (non-experiential) Understanding of the Higher Self

The higher self is also one of the realities of the universe. And, like all realities, has to be experienced. For most of us, this may not be possible, as our higher self has not yet been built. The only other way of understanding the higher self is by an intellectual exercise. The higher self is an antagonist of the lower. If the lower selves are non-self-aware, the higher self is self-aware. Experientially too, we know the dynamics of the lower selves (or non-self-awareness), and this helps us in preparing a table on the following lines.

Dynamics of the Lower Selves and the Higher Self

<u>Lower selves</u>	<u>Higher Self</u>
1. Non-self-awareness	1. Self-Awareness
2. 'Impurity'	2. 'Purity'
3. 'Impotence'	3. 'power'
4. Conventional Morality'	4. Higher Morality
5. Becoming	5. Being
6. Stagnance	6. Transcendence

The apparently common terms used above are technical, having specific and even uncommon meanings. They will be elaborated in the chapter 'Dynamics of Non-Self-Awareness and Self-Awareness'. Meanwhile, the right hand column serves as a vague idea about the higher self.

The dynamics bring out the following:

a. The characteristics of the lower and the higher are antagonistic because the higher self is a consequence of transmutation, which causes the leap into the higher and the opposite.

b. There is an organic continuity from the physical to the spiritual and vice versa.

c. Though the lower and higher selves are antagonistic, the underlying Reality is the same, as in the case of ice and steam.

The Energy of the Higher Self

To understand the energy of the higher self, it is essential to understand the energies of the lower or psychological self. This topic is dealt with at some length in 'Energics'. The lower self is a bundle of different drives, like hunger, sex, aggression, greed and so on. Each of these drives constitutes a distinct energy. It is called energy because it brings about change. Hence, the lower or the psychological self has many energies. When the psychological self is transmuted into the spiritual or higher self, the energies are also transmuted, both in number and dynamics. On transmutation, the many energies of the psychological-self become one energy of the spiritual self. When different colours are passed through the prism, they become one. Similarly, when many psychological energies are passed through the prism of self-awareness, they are transmuted into one energy of the spiritual self.

Apart from numbers, the energies of the lower self and the energy of the higher self have different and opposing dynamics. For example, the energies of the lower self are 'blind' and bound. The energy of the higher self is awakened and 'free'. The various dynamics of both kinds of energies will be dealt with in 'The Dynamics of Non-self-awareness and Self-Awareness'.

I, the Spiritual Entrepreneur

The actual building of the higher self is undertaken by the current I. The spiritual component of the psycho-spiritual self is the current I. It is not built by us, but is gifted by nature. It is the transmutation of a part of the psychological self, by pain, into awakening, self-awareness. It is this gifted self-awareness, the seed capital, which produces self-earned self-awareness, which when it reaches a critical mass becomes the higher self. This is done by the process of cognitive meditation.

The Eventual Independence of the Higher Self

It has been maintained all along that the higher self is the fifth generation issue of the physical self. And because of this, in the earlier stages, it is under the control and influence of the physical and the psychological. It has also been clarified that this does not make the higher self a physical or psychological entity. In fact, its characteristics are contrary to those of the physical and the psychological. To once again refer to the crude but effective analogy, steam not only has characteristics contrary to those of ice but also becomes independent of ice.

The higher self is capable of becoming and does one day become independent of not only the physical but also the psychological.

I believe with good reason that the psycho-spiritual complex, at the time of death outlives the physical. This is called survival. Similarly, at a later stage, the spiritual gets separated from the psychological of the psycho-spiritual and continues as an independent self, beyond both the physical and the psychological. This is called immortality and should not be confused with survival. What survives the psycho-spiritual complex is an individuality. What becomes immortal is pure consciousness, the higher self, which does not have an individuality.

It is for the liberated higher self or pure consciousness to decide, voluntarily and by choice, whether to incarnate again or to merge into THAT.

The Higher Self and the Business Executive

There is no walk of life in which the higher self established by meditation is not active. From time immemorial, the higher self is associated with other-worldly activities. Of late, the function of the higher self and the meditation that produces it is being recognized in the field of psychotherapy. We do not realize it but the higher self, if we understand its dynamics correctly, is active in our family, social and professional lives. It is even intimately involved in the daily chores of our personal life.

For those who have bizarre notions about the higher self, it will be news that it can and does play a very important role in the business executive's life.

By now people have become quite familiar with the process of relaxation, which has been dubbed as a cure-all for all the stresses and psychosomatic disorders of executive life. Meditative procedures based on relaxation, soothing music, dim lights have also come into vogue. None of them, however refreshing, have anything to do with the dynamics of awakening, of self-awareness. They just constitute another variety of sleep and the recuperation it offers. But that is all. They offer no further potential growth. In fact, they are stultifying.

When I talk of meditation and the higher self entering the executive's life, I refer to cognitive meditation and the higher self produced by it. In 'The Dynamics of 'Non-self-awareness and Self-awareness', this issue will become clearer.

Whatever the management texts might maintain, I consider the highest skill of a business executive to be self-awareness. As explained in the dynamics of non-self-awareness and self-awareness, from the skill of self-awareness follow all other skills, including executive skills like effortless concentration, creativity, freedom from prejudices and partialities, tolerance, interpersonal accord, team-work, magnanimity, freedom from stress and psychosomatic disorders, judgment, sensitivity, character assessment, productivity, maturity .... Above all, access to the unique energy of self-awareness which is non-specific, unbound, free, having no likes and dislikes, no inclinations and disinclinations, susceptible to being bent to any task however repulsive and boring.

All successful executives have these characteristics, which are acquired (painfully) by experience, meditation, like processes or are just inborn.

Executive action is not the preserve of business and industry. It pervades the entire range of life activities. The most systematic way of cultivating it is cognitive meditation.

The Story of Skills Continued

A business executive, or for that matter everyone, requires skills of self-management and other management. I have maintained that in the case of the business executive, these apparently heterogeneous skills flow from one source - self-awareness. Self-awareness is the skill of skills. If self-awareness is not present, the specific trainings for specific skills will just not take root. When there is self-awareness, one can as well do without these specific trainings.

These days there is an avalanche of 'how to' books: 'How to Manage Business', 'How to Relax', 'How to be Assertive', 'How to Improve Interpersonal relations', 'How to Develop Creativity', 'How to Stop Frowning', 'How to Manage Anxiety', 'How to become a Better Manager' .... There are some weird titles like 'How to close a deal in Half-a-Minute'.

This variety of titles creates an impression that they are dealing with a variety of disparate and specific skills. And that they require differing specific trainings. It is also implied that the acquisition of one skill has nothing to do with another.

My submission is that there is only one basic skill — the skill of self-awareness from which all other specific skills are derived. This theme is taken up more systematically in 'The Dynamics of Non-self-awareness and Self-awareness'. And these 'Dynamics' are experienced through the practice of cognitive meditation.

Building an advanced higher self is a job of a lifetime or several lifetimes. The purely spiritual objectives of 'Being' and 'Transcendence' are very long term projects. But even a budding higher self can cope with the skill requirements of executive function. One does not have to undergo so many differing courses. Only one seminar on 'How to Build the Higher Self' is enough.

Return Journey

As we have already seen, cosmic evolution is non-self-aware up to the psychological phase. From there on begins the psycho-spiritual phase, when the self-aware cosmic evolution begins. This is the moment self-awareness makes its first appearance in the universe. It is the spiritual or self-aware component of the psycho-spiritual self which contributes to self-awareness. This component also happens to be a gift of nature for which man has not consciously worked, but which he has paid for in pain.

With the establishment of the psycho-spiritual self, which is also the current I, the possibility of the conscious self-aware cosmic evolution begins.

When, with the help of meditation, the higher self or the pure I is established, the cosmic evolution comes to an end. The higher self is the last station, after which it is purely a matter of choice for the higher self either to reincarnate or to merge into **THAT**. The beginning of the higher self took place by choice and its end also depends on choice.

The final resolution of the higher self can only be dissolving into **THAT**. Till such time as this happens, a mysterious restlessness continues to nag and trouble. No drugs, morality, religion, philosophy, workaholism, entertainment can ever remedy this restlessness. The way back **HOME** is meditation.

CHAPTER V

THE REALMS OF NON-SELF-AWARENESS AND SELF-AWARENESS

The cosmic evolution yields six selves. The last three, the psychological, the psycho-spiritual and the spiritual are added at the human level. The psychological self is non-self-aware and has no I. The psycho-spiritual self is in two stages, incipient self-awareness (practically non-self-awareness) and part self-awareness. The former is associated with the ego, with all its psychological involvements and the latter with the current I. The higher self will be fully self-aware. It is associated with the pure I. Earlier, we have already dealt with the three 'I's – the ego, the current I, and the pure I. All the three 'I's are, in various degrees, the vehicles of self-awareness.

Now it is time to consider self-awareness and the spiritual (both mean the same), which are the final objectives of meditation. To do this, we shall need to understand non-self-awareness too.

The Term 'Consciousness'

By tradition, the theme of this chapter involves the use of the term 'consciousness' and in order to accommodate readers familiar with this area, I am going to lapse into using the term 'consciousness' instead of 'self-awareness'. The intention is to reduce terminological dissonance. Like despots, terms also have a proclivity to perpetuate themselves.

A Very Brief History of the Existence Status of Non-self-awareness and Self-awareness

Some scientists called behaviourists arrived at the conclusion that no entity called 'consciousness' exists. J B Watson, the founder of behaviourism, published his lectures in 1913. For him, the human being, a biological machine, worked by stimuli and responses.

When in the '70s cognitive scientists appeared, the extreme and rather absurd denial of consciousness was given up. The existence of consciousness was accepted, but on one condition – that it has no independent existence apart from the brain and its neural network. In other words, consciousness exists, but only as an expression of the working of the physiological brain. When the brain is dead, so also is its consciousness.

The Three Positions

Some believe that it was in 1913 that J. B. Watson 'discovered' that there is nothing like 'consciousness'. Not true. The problem of existence or non-existence of consciousness is several thousand years old. If we over-simplify and telescope the history of this problem, it can be abstracted into three positions, dealt with below.

Position 1

There is only the physiological brain. The mind, consciousness, self-consciousness, self-awareness have no independent existence. They are only an expression of brain function. When the brain dies, these also simultaneously cease for good. Terms like 'mind' are loose and redundant, creating a false impression of being an independent entity. All these terms should be dropped and the term 'brain' substituted. 'Mind language' should be replaced with 'brain language'.

This is the materialistic monistic position. Matter alone exists. Monism, with matter as the base and final reality.

Position 2

The second position believes in the existence of two entities, the brain and the mind (or consciousness/self-consciousness/self-awareness). This position can easily slide into the concept of a body, harbouring a soul.

I don't have to emphasize that the current scientific paradigm is inexorably hostile to any such concept granting an independent existence to mind/consciousness/self-awareness/soul, etc. Basically, all cognitive scientists opt for position one (even though, otherwise, their individual concepts may be at total variance with each other).

I can mention only one great contemporary science philosopher, Sir Karl Popper (1977), who propounds the existence of an independent 'self' (mind, etc.). Similarly, Sir John C. Eccles, neuroscientist and nobel laureate, also emphasizes the independent existence of the 'psyche'. But two of his works (1984,1992) have been resolutely ignored in bibliographies on the literature on consciousness.

While Popper is silent on the fate of the 'self' on death, avoiding the issue by calling it the 'ultimate question', Eccles is much less inhibited, almost bestowing Christian scriptural immorality on the 'psyche'.

The second position recognises both 'matter' and 'consciousness'. This position involving the existence of two entities, body and mind or brain and consciousness (self-awareness, etc.), each being independent and real, is called dualism. Incidentally, today dualism has become a pejorative term. A very strong wind is blowing in favour of the first position. This, in my opinion, is just a passing phase, a 'scientific paradigm' conceptualised by Thomas Kuhn in 'The Structure of Scientific Revolutions'.

The 'scientific paradigm' may be stable over a period but is eventually changeable. In simpler language, one can call it 'Scientific Fashion', which can and will change like any other fashion.

Meanwhile, if any scientist or philosopher is to be abused, you only have to call him a 'dualist'. If you want to pat him on the back, you have to assert that he is not a dualist. This attitude has now become quite sharp, even abusive. I get the impression on reading certain authors that they are inclined towards dualism, but are afraid to frankly acknowledge it. This eventually leads to circumlocution.

Position 3

For the common man, this is a bizarre position. It is the reverse of position one, where consciousness is matter. Here, matter is consciousness. In the former matter is the final reality, whereas in the latter consciousness is the final reality. Let me introduce you to a couple of quotations:

'Man has no Body distinct from his soul'; (William Blake from 'The Voice of the Devil').

'Some truths there are so near and obvious to the mind, that a man need only to open his eyes to see them. Such I take this important one to be, to wit, that all the choir of heaven and furniture of the earth, in a word all those bodies which compose the mighty frame of the world, have not any subsistence without a mind, that their being is to be perceived or known'. (Bishop George Berkeley in 'A Treatise concerning the Principles of Human Knowledge').

Though it is not necessary for us to pursue this concept further, it would be interesting to note that logically it is considered to be irrefutable.

The great Indian philosopher Shankaracharya's celebrated proposition is 'The world is unreal, the only Reality is Brahman'. Brahman is the highest kind of consciousness, which produces this world or the mundane existence. The world is just a dream from which we shall one day awaken to realise its reality.

Consciousness is Consciousness

As per position one, cognitive scientists and neuroscientists accept the existence of consciousness (unlike behaviourists), but only as an expression of cerebral working. When the brain dies, consciousness also dies, it having no dependent existence beyond the brain.

However, the meaning of the term 'consciousness' as used by cognitive scientists and neuroscientists is different from that understood by meditators. For the former, impulses, thoughts, ideas, desires, passions are example of consciousness. If these are absent, the person is supposed to be unconscious or non-conscious. This is grave and fundamental error. Like tables and chairs, thoughts, desires also are objects of consciousness. The former belong to the external world and the latter to the internal world. As tables and chairs have no 'consciousness', thoughts, ideas, desires and passion also have no consciousness. Both physical objects like tables and chairs and psychological ones like thoughts, ideas, desires are aware in a non-self-aware way. They can never be self-aware or have consciousness. Consciousness or self-awareness is something altogether different from thoughts and desires. Consciousness is consciousness. It is a pool of self-aware energy, a function of which is cognition of the external and the internal worlds. Consciousness or self-awareness or the I is the cogniser, and the tables, chairs, thoughts, desires are cognised. Cognitive scientists and neuroscientists will also come to the same conclusion after a few decades, earlier if they care to meditate. An extraordinary implication (to the cognitive scientists and neuroscientists) of this thinking is that it is perfectly and completely possible to remain conscious or self-aware without any sensation, perception, impulse, thought, idea, concept, desire, passion. Meditators call it 'manokshaya', destruction of the mind, i.e. the psychological. It is also loosely called the 'still mind'. In fact, in this state, there is no mind but only a realisation of one of the characteristics of consciousness self-awareness — stillness or equipoise.

Consciousness or self-awareness is essentially non-material. However, at our level of evolution, it is still emerging from the brain and to that extent is dependent on the brain. When self-awareness is fully evolved, it will have left the brain behind and become fully independent.

Fully developed self-awareness is not only independent of the brain but also of thoughts and desires, i.e. the psychological (or the mind). Cognitive and neuroscientists have caused lots of confusion by equating 'mind' with consciousness.

Further Remarks on the Three Position

Position 1:

Currently, among cognitive scientists and neuroscientists, this is the hypothesis of choice. However, being thousands of year old (e.g. Charvaka Darshan of Hindu philosophy), there is nothing astonishing about it.

All the ingenious experimentation that has been going on for decades hardly yields any significant conclusion regarding consciousness. No amount of tinkering with the physiological and psychological will ever throw any light on consciousness. The only epoch-making discovery that scientists can make is there is no consciousness! Back to Watson, though in a more sophisticated way. Dennet (1991), after labouring over five hundred pages, ultimately wonders whether it is 'Consciousness Explained' or 'Consciousness Explained Away'!

The only way to investigate the investigator I self-investigation. Consciousness/self-awareness can be understood by consciousness/self-awareness only. There are only two ways of realizing this:

1) By spending millions of dollars in the laboratory with no success or,
2) By practising cognitive meditation.

Position 2:

The dualistic position basically belongs to theologians, philosophers, mystics and the common man, who believe in the body and something like a 'soul'. But merely because something appears to be true, does not make it so. The sun may appear to be going round the earth. The fact is otherwise.

With today's extremely limited or non-existent scientific knowledge about consciousness, it would be very difficult to scientifically establish the dualistic position. But then it is equally difficult to establish position one as well. The whole situation is summed up in one sentence by Nobel laureate Francis Crick (1994), a confirmed position one holder, that the neural correlate for consciousness, which is the fundamental basis of position one is still not found. Today, hardly any philosopher, cognitive scientist or neuroscientist holds a dualistic position, excepting Popper and Eccles. (There could be a few more, whom I have not come across).

There are two main objectives against dualism (1) Until now, nobody has demonstrated the existence of consciousness, independent of the brain. (for example, Marcel Kinsbourne, 1995) and (2) the brain and consciousness if they are independent, would belong to two different categories and as such could not interact. However, interaction between the psyche (mind, consciousness) and the soma (brain, body) is of everyday experience, of which psychosomatic disease is but one special case. Since there is interaction between mind and body, they must belong to the same category. And since the body (brain) is the category known to us, the mind is nothing else than the brain. In other words, the mind is only the brain. (one can conveniently drop the term mind, consciousness, self-awareness, etc.) This is reverting to position one.

However irrefutable these philosophical and scientific arguments may appear, they are susceptible to being breached.

To take up the first argument — thoughts and desires cannot exist independent of the brain. The well-known phenomenon of telepathy throws light on this issue. This is one para-psychological phenomenon which has widespread support, both in the lay and scientific community. I am a believer in telepathy, not only because of extensive laboratory and episodic favourable findings, but also because of extensive personal experience based on a specialised experimental experience.

It is true, at the current level of evolution; it is very difficult but not impossible to give an on-demand scientific demonstration of telepathy. (the standard statistical experiments, running into thousands of readings, may prove telepathy but without retaining its natural flavour.) But there is extensive and imposing evidence of involuntary and sporadic telepathy with which the public and scientists are quite familiar. Even the materialistic Russian scientists believe in telepathy. This is an engrossing story. It is an irony of history that a communist state whose philosophy is dialectical materialism should come to accept an 'occult' phenomenon like telepathy. Telepathy was intensively studied by Russian academicians, who are supposed to be the highest scientific authorities of the country. These were led by Dr. Leonid L. Vasiliev, Head of Physiology at the University of Leningrad, Corresponding Member of the Soviet Academy of Medicine and holder of the Lenin Prize. A special laboratory for studying telepathy was established with Vasiliev as the head at the Institute of Physiology of Leningrad University. Vasiliev became famous for inducing long-distance hypnosis by mental suggestion. According to Vasiliev, thought transference was transference of some kind of energy, at present unknown to science.

All that he could prove was that such energy does not belong to the electromagnetic spectrum.

Such unabashed and unembarrassed acceptance of telepathy suggests that Russian physiologists and neuroscientists were not interested in facts rather than their blind spots. (Refer K. Platanov, 1965 and Sheila Ostrander, 1970). Of course, apart from Russia, extensive work on telepathy is being carried out practically all over the world, but in sheer convincing power, the Russian work is outstanding and compelling.

Even if we accept the materialistic theory of Russian academicians, that telepathy is due to waves of some unknown but material energy, generated by one brain and picked by another one conclusion becomes crystal clear. This means that the 'thought wave', while transiting from one brain to another, was able to survive without any brain. In other words, thought can live without a brain. If this is so, it cannot be maintained that existence of thought has not been demonstrated apart from the brain. This belief in dualism, in which brain and mind are believed to be two independent entities, is justified. This disposes of the first objection to dualism.

As for the second objection regarding the impossibility of interaction between different categories, we have already seen that the cosmic evolution from the physical to the spiritual is a continuum. All the six levels, even though apparently differing or even contrary (like ice and steam) are variegated expressions of a common underlying Reality — THAT. The apparently differing categories are one ultimately. If this is so, there is no problem of philosophical difficulty of interaction between two differing categories. (To prolong the ice/steam analogy, even though they appear to be two contrary categories, they still can and do interact). This disposes of the second objection.

Position 3

Practically all cognitive scientists and neuroscientists approve of position one. Exceptionally, a neuroscientist might support position two. But it would be impossible to find one, who will stand by position three, according to which pure consciousness can maintain itself without body, brain or mind.

Interestingly, in ancient India, the subject of consciousness was one of the hottest pursuits. Brihad — Aranyaka Upanishad asks, 'Lo, whereby would one understand the understander?' (Hume, 1995). How to know the knower?

The method of investigating consciousness was meditation. Various investigators arrived at different conclusions (This continues to happen even today, even in the most rigorous of scientific disciplines, the most celebrated example being Einstein's refusal to accept quantum mechanics, otherwise accepted by most physicists.)

These conclusions were crystallised in the six 'darshans' or systems of philosophy. Of this, Charvak's materialistic system coincides with position one. All body and brain and no independent consciousness. Another darshan, the Samkhya system, supports position two. The dualism of Purusha (consciousness) and Prakarti (nature including body and mind). The Vedanta darshan corresponds to position three, wherein consciousness is the only Reality; body and mind (and also the world) being illusions.

India has produced many celebrated systems of meditation. They appear to be applied aspects of the various darshans. Thus, the most celebrated text on meditation 'The Yoga System of Patanjali' (J H Woods, 1927), is the applied side of Samkhaya darshan. It is based on suppression of all mental activity, which is the representative of Prakarti. 'Yoga is the restriction of the fluctuations of mind-stuff' (the second sutra or aphorism). The objective is to salvage consciousness from the contamination of Prakarti — in the form of thoughts, ideas, feelings, desires, likes, dislikes, fears, hopes, emotions — the entire thought stream.

Not so well-known is 'Vivek Chudamani' by Shankaracharya, which can be considered the applied aspect of Vedanta darshan. In this system of meditation, the illusion of body, mind and the world is dissolved by gnana — knowledge of an insightful type. Shankaracharya's views are revolutionary. Liberation is not possible by Yoga, by Samkhya, by work, by learning and by no other means except a realisation of one's true nature. (Swami Madhavananda, 1926, Shloka 56.) Liberation is also not possible by bathing in sacred waters nor by gifts, nor by a hundred pranayamas — controlled breathing (Shloka 13).

These are frightening concepts for most of those nurtured in goody, goody ideas of spiritual life. Even more serious aspirants, like practitioners of Patanjali Yoga, get short shrift.

The Buddha also goes beyond body and mind to reach Buddha-nature — an exalted consciousness. Here also the tool is Vipassana, i.e. mindfulness or insight.

It is a paradox that the modern cognitive neuroscientist does not believe in the independent existence of consciousness, whereas, in ancient India, one of the main objectives was to reach consciousness, unconditioned by body or mind.

As far as cognitive meditation is concerned, position three, i.e. pure consciousness, is one of the segments of cosmic evolution, being the third and ultimate one. (For cognitive meditation, all three segments are equally valid and real, being parts of a continuum).

If position one is proximate to THAT by virtue of being born from THAT, position three is also proximate to THAT by virtue of being about to merge in it.

Birth of Non-self-awareness and Self-awareness

As mentioned earlier, there are meditations and meditations – some suppressive, some expressive, and still others, observational (transmutative). I recognize only the last category as genuine meditation. Transmutative meditation is based on cognition (and therefore 'cognitive meditation') and cognition is based on self-awareness.

Earlier, we developed some acquaintance with self-awareness. This could be deepened if we could understand the origin or birth of self-awareness.

THAT

According to me, the ultimate Reality is THAT, which is beyond all words, description, concepts, dualities. One such duality is non-self-awareness, and self-awareness and its source is also THAT. Of course, THAT not only harbours this duality but is at the same time beyond it.

Big Bang

This universe was born, at the moment of the big bang, as nuclear particles followed by hydrogen and helium. With further developments came the galaxies. Our galaxy is supposed to have been formed about half a billion years after the big bang. Our solar system, composed of nine planets including our earth revolving around the sun, is part of this galaxy. (There could be accounts with other time frames and sequences. Such details are not germane to our issues).

The immense temperatures and pressures developed by the supernovae, extraordinarily bright stars in the galaxy, resulted in the production of other elements besides hydrogen and helium. These developments, till the advent of life, can be called inorganic evolution

Origin of Life

With the cooling of earth, life developed, perhaps 3.5 billion years ago, in the form of a unicellular organism – perhaps a bacterium. First land plants appeared 440 million years ago. And animals took to land 395 million years ago.

We are not concerned here with the complex details of the organic or Darwinian evolution. An extremely broad outline could be, that with the big bang were 'born' the physical entities. These were followed by plant-like organisms and plants. These in turn were succeeded by animals. The animal world ultimately evolved into homo sapiens. The modern man appeared on the evolutionary scene some 40,000 years ago.

Cognitive meditation has no quarrel with Darwinian evolution, which is unconscious, accidental, and survival-oriented. It is of course not all that purposeless as it is made out to be. To survive is one of the two greatest purpose known to man. (The other, as we shall see later, is to free oneself from the strangulation and diminution that the compulsion for survival causes). At the same time it must be realized that Darwinian evolution is only a fraction of a much wider cosmic evolution.

Recapitulation

Each phase of the inorganic and organic (Darwinian) evolution has got precipitated, embedded and perpetuated in the form of traces or layers, even in the modern man. So the physical level is represented by food, water, air, etc. which we have imbibed but not absorbed. The plant level is represented by the physiological system. The animal level by the instinctual system. There is a wide consensus that an animal is lurking all the while in humans. It is not so well understood that man harbours plants and minerals too. When somebody is in deep slumber, he is a 'log of wood'. When someone becomes comatose, he becomes a 'vegetable'. And when man dies he is 'reduced to dust', regressing to the physical level from which he started.

As a continuation of Darwinian evolution, in addition to the physical, physiological and instinctual levels, man acquires one more level — the psychological, which we have already dealt with in an earlier chapter.

Post-Darwinian Evolution

Any mature meditation, particularly of the cognitive persuasion, finds that Darwinian evolution is followed by another kind of evolution, which is cultural, intellectual and spiritual. Inorganic and organic evolutions were involuntary, while the post-Darwinian evolution is semi-voluntary and eventually voluntary. Darwinian evolution precipitated four selves right up to the psychological. The psychological self gives rise to the psycho-spiritual which in turn gives rise to the spiritual self. The story of the psycho-spiritual and spiritual evolution is the story of meditation. The cosmic evolution from the big bang to the modern man, from the physical to the spiritual, is also the story of the birth of self-awareness and self-awareness with which we are concerned here.

The Universe and its Awareness

The submission here is that the entire universe from the physical to spiritual is pulsating with some kind of awareness. The awareness of the physical (physical entities), the physiological (the plant), the instinctual (the animal) and the psychological (part of the human) is of the non-self-aware variety. The psycho-spiritual (human) is partly non-self-aware and partly self-aware. The spiritual (advanced human) is fully self-aware. Another way of putting this is, the first four levels or selves are the non-I, the psycho-spiritual is part non-I and part I, and the spiritual is all I.

The Birth of Non-Self-Awareness!

Now we come to the birth of non-self-awareness (and also self-awareness).

It is one of the basic assumptions of cognitive meditation that the entire universe with all its components: physical, physiological, instinctual, psychological, psycho-spiritual and spiritual are aware either as non-self-awareness or self-awareness. We see that THAT harbours both non-self-awareness and self-awareness and is at the same time beyond it. At the moment of the big bang, non-self-awareness and self-awareness are born with the universe.

However, there is a difference between the birth of both kinds of awareness. Non-self-awareness manifests overtly, whereas self-awareness is born as a potentiality. It is sort of 'hidden' or 'imprisoned' in non-self-awareness. There is nothing unusual about such a potentiality. The entire universe, which in the course of time evolves as physical entities, plants, animals, humans, is originally held as potentialities in the nuclear particles that are generated at the moment of the big bang.

The undisputed reign of non-self-awareness continues for about fifteen to eighteen billion years. (those who undertake any kind of meditation, where non-self-awareness is to be replaced by self-awareness, may kindly keep this in mind. Non-self-awareness is the most formidable foe man will ever face.)

Having noted that physical entities, plants and animals are non-self-aware, we come to the humans who are partly non-self-aware and partly self-aware. (with further evolution, they will become fully self-aware). We have noted more than once that the human has six layers or selves. Of these, the physical (food, air, water level), the physiological (the plant level), the instinctual (the animal level) and the psychological (primitive human level) are non-self-aware. The psychological and its drives consist of the unconscious, preconscious and the thought – spray, which are all non-self-aware. All these levels, though human, have no I-hood and are therefore termed the non-I. As already mentioned earlier, awareness of the non-I is of the nature of non-self-awareness. The ascetic, the theological and the religious look upon these areas of non-self-awareness as lower selves, appetitive self or plain evil. To cognitive meditators, it is a natural and inevitable phase of the cosmic evolution. If at all there is any evil, it is not in non-self-awareness but in disinclination to overcome it, which is possible for most human beings through self-knowledge for which the best route is cognitive meditation.

Non-self-awareness is at its densest and self-awareness at its most potential at the birth of the universe. As the universe unfolds, so does non-self-awareness, and the process of its attenuation sets in. This attenuation increases progressively through the plant, animal and human body. The last outpost of non-self-awareness in the human (and therefore in the universe too) is at the fag end of the psychological, the thought- spray, where non-self-awareness is at its thinnest and its grip on the 'imprisoned' (potential) self-awareness the weakest.

It is at the level of the attenuated thought-spray that the 'imprisoned' self-awareness escapes and becomes manifest for the first time in the universe. It ceases to be a potentiality and becomes a living, throbbing entity. Now it makes its entry into the universe as a concrete manifestation. It has a glimmer of I-hood and a glimmer of self-awareness and is none else than the much-abused ego. As cognitive meditation does not pass any judgement on non-self-awareness, it extends this non-judgmental attitude to the ego as well. The ego is just the beginning of self-awareness, which is in a very incipient form. It is surrounded by the 'amniotic medium' of the psychological, contaminated with all its impulses, desires, cravings, passions.... The ego unwittingly has earned an odious reputation. The beginning of self-awareness Is a bit murky as its birth has taken place in a dubious uninviting location.

The Ego

The Ego is just the beginning, however humble and unpromising, of a most glorious future. As we saw earlier, the I evolves in three stages, the ego, the current I, the free I, which is the higher self or spirit (not necessarily equivalent to the 'spirit' or 'atma' of other philosophies).

At the current level of evolution, we are endowed with both the ego and the current I. The current I is also contaminated with the psychological but much less so than the ego. Also, its self-awareness is much higher than that of the ego. Someday, through the route of meditation, the current I will consciously evolve into the pure I – the spirit.

The ego and the current I constitute the psycho-spiritual self, which is a transition stage, a bridge, between the psychological and the spiritual.

If non-self-awareness has an age of fifteen to eighteen billion years according to John Eccles (1979), self-awareness is supposed to have made its appearance with the Neanderthal man, (one of the stages of homo sapiens), who appeared a hundred thousand years ago. (this is a sobering thought. Those who undertake any kind of meditation where non-self-awareness is to be replaced by self-awareness, should keep in mind that to start with, as compared to non-self-awareness, self-awareness is extremely incipient and frail. Apparently, it is no match for non-self-awareness. Still one has to work with whatever self-awareness is available. This could lead to initial disappointments. Another name for meditation, particularly cognitive meditation, is patience.)

Evolving Nature of Non-self-awareness and Self-awareness

Thus, non-self-awareness and self-awareness are both subject to evolutionary development. The I and its self-awareness evolve in three stages. The ego, the current I, and the pure I (of the future). The objective of cognitive meditation is to move from the current I to the pure I.

We remarked that non-self-awareness, which was densest at the physical level, thins out as cosmic evolution proceeds and is at its most dilute at the level of the psychological in its thought-spray phase. Concurrently, self-awareness, which was at its most potential at the physical level, becomes less and less potential and is least potential at the level of the thought – spray.

From the level of the thought-spray onwards, self-awareness becomes more and more manifest and non-self-awareness starts becoming potential. At the level of true I, self-awareness is at its maximum and non-self-awareness diminished.

The Birth of Self-awareness (Emergence from the potential state)

I am sure by now you must be wondering as to how, in the first instance, the ego sprouted from the thought-spray, how the I arose from the non-I, and how self-awareness sprang from non-self-awareness.

The emergence of self-awareness is a revolutionary event – the third of its kind. The first revolutionary event was the big bang and its associated non-self-awareness. The second one, the emergence of life along with its non-self-awareness. Third, the arising of self-awareness. And, to anticipate the fourth, the mergence of self-awareness into THAT, thus completing the existential cycle, from THAT to non-self-awareness, from non-self-awareness to self-awareness and from self-awareness to THAT.

We now concern ourselves with the third revolutionary event.

The response to the problem of the birth of self-awareness has to be divided into two parts.

1. Self-awareness gifted by nature.
2. Self-awareness cultivated by man (through meditation).

Initial Self-awareness gifted by Nature

Self-awareness gifted by nature is an involuntary process and practically a one-time occurrence. It could have arisen from non-self-awareness in three ways.

a. We have already noted that non-self-awareness and self-awareness are evolutionary processes.

From the moment of the big bang, non-self-awareness progressively decreases, till it is at its most diluted, at the level of the thought-spray. With the thrust of evolutionary movement, the

150

state of the thought-spray may just leap into the state of the ego, as non-life jumped into life.

b. Self-awareness could be a mutation with obviously fantastically favourable possibilities for survival and advancement.

c. The birth of self-awareness through frustration and pain; an example would be the trauma of birth. The foetus in the mother's womb is in a state of perfect, sleepy bliss. It feeds and excretes and carries out all physiological functions without the least disturbance and of course in a non-self-aware way. The turmoil starts with the trauma of birth, when the feotal paradise is suddenly snatched away. Henceforth, as a neonate, it will have to 'face life'. Discomforts and deprivations would set in. The blissful automaticity while in the womb would be no more. The deprivations associated with feeding, excreting, sleeping, etc. make the neonate cry. And crying means frustration and pain; which lead to awakening from non-self-awareness.

Pain has the property of restructuring non-self-awareness into self-awareness, through a dialectical leap. The pain could be physiological or psychological – the so-called lessons of life. Non-self-awareness 'turns upon itself', gets reversed and becomes self-awareness.

Self-awareness cultivated by man

The 'seed capital' of self-awareness, gifted by nature through mutation or pain is a one-time affair. It is involuntary. Further growth could be sporadic, unplanned, uneven. It could be squandered. But if the 'seed capital' of self-awareness is used to generate more self-awareness, extraordinary developments can take place. This is a route involving choice and conscious decision. It leads to the building of the higher self, the pure I or the spirit. Each man has to make this choice and undertake this responsibility. Even God cannot help in this undertaking.

As we shall see later, one of the most important dynamics of self-awareness is voluntariness and therefore, even by definition, its development is an activity by choice only.

This process of development of greater and greater self-awareness and its extraordinary dynamics, through its existing 'seed capital', is the process of cognitive meditation.

If one refuses to grow through self-awareness, which is already existing, having been gifted by nature, one will have to grow through self-awareness, which is generated by pain. The former is called meditation and the latter, 'lessons of life'.

An acute reader will have noticed by now that the process of the birth of self-awareness is a repetition of the story of the birth of the I. This is bound to be so. The I and self-awareness go together and the non-I and non-self-awareness go together, being two sides of the same Reality. The I is the vehicle of self-awareness, as non-I, that of non-self-awareness.

When we talk of the concept of self, we talk of the non-I and the I. And when we talk of the concept of awareness, we talk of non-self-awareness and self-awareness.

The Ages of Non-self-awareness and Self-awareness

The big bang is assigned various ages — ten, fifteen, eighteen billion years or whatever is the latest thinking. Since non-self-awareness begins with the big bang and continues till today, both in the universe at large and in the human being, it would also be ten, fifteen, eighteen billion years old.

A neuroscientists who paid attention to the phenomenon of self-awareness was Eccles. According to him, self-awareness had already made its appearance at the time of the Neanderthal man (one of the stages of homo sapiens), who emerged about hundred thousand years ago. These rough approximations would mean that the 18 billion-years-old non-self-awareness is 180,000 times older than self-awareness. Rather, something equivalent.

This is most sobering thought. No wonder, at the current level of evolution, non-self-awareness completely overshadows, outstrips and storms ahead of self-awareness. All those expecting a very high standard of behaviour from man have not carried out this simple calculation.

Freud's statement that the conscious (self-aware) mind is only the tip of the iceberg, is a very, very gross underestimate. Even then, Freud has been indicted for his pessimism. But nobody, who has looked so closely into non-self-awareness, i.e. the unconscious, can but succumb to a brooding pessimism. Most of the prophets, particularly the Buddha, have been pessimists, either belittling man or teaching turning away from life. They project a dismal future for man, only to be redeemed by the grace of

God or the Buddha. A startling exception is Zarathrustra, who perhaps knew evil better than anybody. But he apparently also knew how to overcome — transmute it. He threw in his lot on the side of Vohuman (the awakened mind), Asha (purity) and order) and Vohu-Kshathra (the spiritual will). He called upon mankind to become soldiers of Ahura-Mazda — the supreme wisdom. No renunciation and no whining for him. No downgrading of man and woman. Though today his formal followers are reduced to an insignificant number, those who came to hear his clarion call through the millennia, to fight darkness and its evil to eventual victory, can understand his faith in man and his optimistic future.

The question naturally arises, if self-awareness is so frail as compared to non-self-awareness, why should we cultivate it and how is it going to help us either materially or spiritually.

The truth is, non-self-awareness, however strong and mighty, is the force of yesterday. Self-awareness, however fragile is the force of today and tomorrow. The future is with self-awareness. Non-self-awareness can but get exhausted and wane. Self-awareness can but grow. Besides, non-self-awareness has already lost its overwhelming domination. Man can already see through its chinks and stir out of the non-self-aware swoon. He now realizes that his material and spiritual salvation lies in cultivating self-awareness. And the way to self-awareness is cognitive meditation.

Currently, there are only intimations of self-awareness. The kingdom of self-awareness will arrive when the pure I, the full-fledged vehicle of self-awareness, or the higher self or the spiritual self is actually established.

CHAPTER VI

COGNITIVE ASPECTS OF NON-SELF-AWARENESS AND SELF-AWARENESS

The cognitive aspects of non-self-awareness and self-awareness is a vast subject – as vast as the universe. In fact, it is another name for existence. It is doubtful whether any human can master it in its entirety. I am concerned here with only a few aspects related to cognitive meditation.

The Terms

Awareness (or self-awareness, loosely used, interchangeably) is just another buzz word of the second half of the 20th century. When one is not talking of tension, stress or relaxation, one jumps on the awareness bandwagon. Everybody seems to be talking about it, but nobody seems to define what awareness actually is, what it stands for, what it means, from where it is derived, what it can do, where it is leading us and so on.

Let us refer to a couple of dictionaries for the meaning of the terms 'Self-awareness' and 'Non-self-awareness' (it will be an enlightening experience to refer to other general and psychological dictionaries).

Penguin Dictionary of Psychology (Reber, 1952) defines awareness as "Mere experience of an object, an idea, sometimes equivalent to consciousness". The term 'self-awareness' does not occur in this edition. One has to wait till the next edition, where the term does appear and is defined as 'Generally, the condition of being aware of or conscious of oneself .." (Reber, 1995).

Both the terms 'awareness' and 'self-awareness' do not occur in The International Dictionary of Psychology, second Edition 1996 by Stuart Sutherland. However, while attempting to define the term 'consciousness' (unsuccessfully), the word 'awareness' is used. So, 'consciousness' is 'awareness' and 'awareness' could be consciousness, while both of these terms remain undefined.

The great Oxford English Dictionary, 1989, defines 'aware' as 'watchful', 'vigilant', 'cognisant'. 'To be aware of: to take cognizance of, to know', etc. 'Awareness' is defined as "the quality or state of being aware, "consciousness".

However, I will never be able to fully recover from my shock, when I found that the term 'self-awareness' does not occur in this 16-volume dictionary.

After these experiences, it is obvious that there is no question of encountering the term 'non-self-awareness' in any dictionary, though it is as fundamental as 'self-awareness'.

Similar Concepts in Ancient and Modern Thinking

Western thinkers, psychologists, philosophers are under the impression that 'awareness or self-awareness' are recent concepts. However, similar concepts are five thousand years old, at least in India. They are synonymous with spiritual praxis. Eventually these practices were crystallised in certain technical terms in Buddhism and Vedanta. In Buddhism the terms are 'Vipassana' or 'Pragna'. They are generally translated as 'awareness' or 'insight'. Similarly, in Vedanta, it is 'gnana' roughly translated as 'knowledge' but practically meaning 'awareness', 'self-awareness' 'insight' or 'realisation'. In Zoroastrian thinking, Zarathrustra's concept of 'Vohuman' has been mechanically translated by academically robust but spiritually sterile philologists, as the 'good mind'. It could mean anything and therefore nothing in particular. But those involved in meditation will understand it as the 'awakened mind'. This realisation is further strengthened, when the meditator dwells on associated terms like 'Asha', 'Vohuxathra', etc. the 'awakened mind' means 'the self-aware mind'.

To some extent, psychoanalytic cure is based on making the unconscious, conscious. This is obviously an exercise in self-awareness.

In our daily life too, phenomena like 'awakening', 'meaning', 'understanding', 'comprehension', 'insight', 'realisation', 'self-transformation', 'change of heart' or 'transmutation' as called here, do occur.

Both in Buddhism and Vedanta, there are specific technical terms, which are the opposite of 'self-awareness'. In both the systems, they are 'agnana' or 'ignorance'. In Vedanta, there are additional terms like 'avidya' or 'vismruti', (loss of recollection). These terms can be compared to 'non-self-awareness' or 'absence of insight'.

For me, both 'non-self-awareness' and 'self-awareness' are technical terms with specific meaning and action. They are the most pregnant terms, as far as cognitive meditation is concerned.

I would like to point out that the term 'awareness' is likely to be restricted for most of us to only cognition or observation. Really, it is a much wider and deeper concept; an umbrella term covering emotional and volitional activities too.

What is Awareness, non-self-awareness and Self-awareness?

If we try to understand 'awareness' as we have seen earlier, it comes to cognition, sensing, perceiving, introspecting, recognising, experiencing, observing. Such an understanding or a definition is obviously a circular exercise, in fact tautology.

Awareness is an ultimate category, not dependent on any precursory categories. One cannot go behind awareness.

What is more confounding, there is nothing like 'awareness' as such. In this universe, it always occurs as non-self-awareness or self-awareness. Whenever we talk of 'awareness', we are talking of either 'non-self-awareness' or 'self-awareness'.

For instance, everyone knows that the sunflower is 'aware' of the movement of the sun. Similarly, everyone knows that man is also "aware" of the movement of the sun. But there is a fundamental difference between the two kinds of 'awareness'. The sunflower has no 'I' and man has an 'I'. The sunflower becomes aware through the non-I, while man becomes aware through the I. If we use the term 'self' for the I, we can say the sunflower is aware, in a non-self-aware way. Similarly, man is aware in a self-aware way. (incidentally, as we shall see later, man in addition to self-awareness is also capable of non-self-awareness).

By now, it must have become quite clear, that non-self-awareness is not non-awareness. It is full-fledged awareness but by the non-I or of the non-self variety.

Evolutionary levels of Awareness

Having clarified the two terms, non-self-awareness and self-awareness, we can consider them a little more systematically. Earlier, we talked of the three levels of the universe, which are also incorporated in man, who in turn has developed three additional selves or levels. All these are stated below.

In the Universe	In Man
1. The Physical level. Physical Objects	Physical Self, air, food, water in the Body (but still unabsorbed)
2. The Physiological level. Plant	Physiological Self-The vegetative activities.
3. The Instinctual level. Animal	Instinctual/ Appetitive self.
4. The Psychological level. Primitive Man	Psychological self-Impulses wishes, desires, cravings, passions (Excludes the I)
5. The Psycho-spiritual level. 'Current Man'.	The Psycho-spiritual self. Part psychological, part spiritual or self-aware. (refer to the current I)
6. The spiritual level. The higher Man.	The spiritual self. The purified, fully self-aware I

The first three levels, which belong to the universe at large, have no 'I'. Similarly, the fourth or psychological level, which is a component of man (who of course is also a part of the universe), has also no I.

All these four levels, even though they have no I, are capable of 'awareness', an example of which was the sunflower.

The fifth level also takes cognizance of, in a way which is routine with us. As far as the sixth or the spiritual or the purified I level is concerned, most of us have no experience of the same. It may only be said at this stage that it is the highest self-aware level.

The Nature of Awareness at each Evolutionary Level

To me, the entire universe from the physical to the spiritual is aware, though the quality of awareness varies. It became aware, at the moment of its birth, i.e. the big bang, and continues to be aware and will remain so till the end, if there is any.

There are many paradoxes about awareness. One of them is that it cannot be defined with reference to a more fundamental entity. Awareness is awareness.

Another paradox is that awareness does not occur as awareness. It either occurs as non-self-awareness or as self-awareness. In this formulation, the term 'self' means the 'I'. Thus, the term 'non-self-awareness' means awareness or cognition by the non-I. Thus, "non-self-awareness" does not mean non-awareness, but awareness by the non-I. 'Knowing' takes place both in non-self-awareness and self-awareness. But in non-self-awareness one knows, without knowing, that one knows. In self-awareness, one knows that one knows. This happens because, in the former, there is no 'I' to register the knowing, whereas in the latter, such registering is done by the 'I'. Non-self-awareness means awareness or cognition by the non I. And self-awareness means awareness or cognition by the I.

Generally, the physical level is considered to be non-sentient and therefore devoid of awareness. But it is obvious that the physical level is capable of recognizing phenomena, which can be considered awareness of a special kind. For example, the atom is governed by positive and negative electrical charges. The subatomic particles are capable of recognizing and responding to each other, which obviously involves a kind of awareness. To take another crude example, a magnet can differentiate between iron and non-iron filings. Perhaps the entire behaviour of the physical universe is based on this kind of awareness, which is of a non-self-aware variety, there being no I to the physical objects. It is a case of non-I awareness. The plants, as we saw in the case of the sunflower, display various kinds of tropisms and sensitivities to the environment and the seasons. Some believe they are aware of human presence and respond to them. Yes, plants are very aware, though in a non-self-aware way, there being no I. That the animals are capable of awareness or rather non-self-awareness, requires no discussion. There are serious discussions amongst psychologists/ theologians whether animals have consciousness. As we shall see later, the use of the term consciousness itself is confusing, leading to endless debate. But even the animal has non-self-awareness, which is constantly exhibited by its behaviour. The non-self-aware cognition by migratory birds continues to be an all-time wonder.

When it comes to man, the situation is much more complicated. As we saw earlier, man harbours within himself, through recapitulation, the physical objects level (food, air, water, etc.), the physiological level, (the 'plant'), and the instinctual level (the 'animal'). As the physical object, the plant and the animal are capable of non-self-awareness, so also these levels incorporated in man. Some may call it unconscious or non-conscious cognition. I would call it non-self-awareness or non-self-aware cognition, since these levels have no I. They are the non-I components of the human being. Man has one more non-I component – the psychological. It is the 'mental equivalent' (a phrase used by Freud -1933) of the instinctual level. The instincts are 'psychologised' and re-christened 'drives'. Instincts belong to the physiological level, drives to the psychological level. As the 'animal' original as well as residual in man is non-self-aware, the psychological component in man is also non-self-aware. This mean, impulses, desires, longings, cravings, passions are non-self-aware. In fact, they are called 'blind'.

But man has two more levels, the psycho-spiritual and the spiritual. For most human beings, the spiritual level is only a theoretical possibility with the potential of becoming a reality, which is the objective of cognitive meditation. The psycho-spiritual is a hybrid level – one component being the psychological – which is capable of only non-self-awareness. The spiritual component consists of the ego and the current I (which in the course of development will become the purified I). The awareness by the I component in man is self-awareness.

Thus, man is capable of both non-self-awareness and self-awareness. Psychologists and philosophers, who endlessly and inconclusively go on discussing 'consciousness' in man, will never resolve their problem. It is only when they realise that by 'consciousness' they imply self-awareness, which is quite distinct from non-self-awareness, that the tangle will show signs of resolution. Till I-cognition and non-I-cognition are realised and accepted, the confusion will continue. When some of these thinkers are trying to establish the non-existence of the I, what they are actually doing is unknowingly falling back upon non-self-awareness and its workings to explain their concept of 'consciousness'. What they are talking of is not 'consciousness' but 'non-self-consciousness', i.e. consciousness in which the I is not involved. But such considerations are not going to negate the existence of the 'I', which strongly exists, in addition to 'non-self-consciousness' or 'non-self-awareness'.

Examples of Non-self-awareness and Self-awareness Cognition by Man

We have noted that, unlike physical objects, plants and animals, which are capable of only non-self-aware cognition, man is capable of both non-self-aware and self-aware cognition. A few stray examples would illustrate this.

If one is driving a car in India, statistically there are good chances of somebody suddenly darting across in front of the car. If you are lucky, before you know what is happening, you will have applied the brakes. This is known as reflex action. It took place before the I could grasp what was happening. The 'I' does realise what occurred, but only when everything is over. Here, the cognition took place at the non-I level, a case of non-self-aware cognition.

Take the case of a mosquito bite when one is deeply asleep. The mosquito may be swatted and even killed without the sleeping man ever knowing anything about the incident. This is non-self-aware cognition and action.

When the human system is invaded by pathogenic organisms, it immediately takes cognisance of the invaders and goes into action.

Homeostasis is another example of non-self-aware cognition, helping in maintaining the balance of the physiological states.

Utilizing psychoanalytic concepts, one can say that, though both the id and the superego belong to the unconscious area, they can perceive each other's activities, producing neurotic symptoms. The I does not play any part in these cognitions and activities. A typical case of non-self-awareness.

Perhaps the most interesting and controversial instance of non-self-aware cognition is extra-sensory perception. The phenomenon is not only non-self-aware but also sporadic. At the current level of evolution, it is not possible to produce ESP consciously and to order, i.e. in a self-aware and voluntary way. Therefore, certain scientists conclude that it does not exist!

Now a few examples of self-aware cognition.

Searching for a face in a crowd is a self-aware activity in which the I is involved.

Peering through the microscope or the telescope is carrying out self-aware cognition.

Making observations in a scientific experiment is self-aware cognition.

Studying a site of crime is a self-aware observation.

But the most significant and pregnant act of self-awareness is cognitive meditation. All these discussions on non-self-awareness and self-awareness ultimately zero in on the central theme of cognitive meditation. This also is the story of spiritual alchemy.

Non-self-awareness And Self-awareness Summarised

These discussions help to create a few formal statements.

Non-self-awareness

1. Non-self-awareness is awareness, cognition, recognition, observation, experiencing, perception by the non-I.

   Thus, cognition by entities which have no I, like physical objects, plants, animals and the psychological component of man, is non-self-aware cognition.
2. Non-self-awareness is definitely not non-awareness. It is as much positive awareness as self-awareness except for the fact that it is by the non-I.
3. It is an emotion-bound, interest-driven/involuntary cognition. Non-self-awareness cannot help cognition and has no choice about the objects of cognition.
4. Non-self-awareness, being awareness, knows but, due to not having the I, does not know that it knows. Therefore, its knowing is called 'blind' or unconscious.
5. Most important, as we shall see later, non-self-awareness projects beyond mere awareness and generates emotion and drive which mean tension and bondage. This is the human condition.
6. We shall also see later that if non-self-awareness is capable of generating emotion and drive, it is also capable of producing behaviour modification, and what can produce modification is designated as energies or energy. We shall learn that non-self-awareness is a conglomerate of energies. It is a bundle of disparate energies.

Self-awareness

1. Self-awareness is awareness, cognition, observation, perception, recognition, introspection, experiencing, comprehension, understanding, meaning, realisation by the I. These belong at the

psycho-spiritual level. The transmutation, produced by realisation, belongs at the spiritual level. Here also, the self means the I. In this presentation, self-awareness is not awareness of the self, as understood by some thinkers, but awareness by the I. Self-aware cognition can be carried out by the I- structures- the ego, the current I and the purified I. At this state of evolution, it is carried out by the ego and the current I only. The purified I is yet to develop (through cognitive meditation) and its mention here is only for theoretical comprehensiveness.

2. Self-awareness is disinterested, emotion-free voluntary cognition. It may or may not cause cognition as per its choice.

3. Self-awareness can perceive non-self-awareness to a certain extent. By technique and practice, this penetration of the non-self- aware self can be extended. This technique happens to be cognitive meditation.

4. Self-awareness, being awareness, knows and due to having the I, knows that it knows. Therefore, its activity is self-illuminating.

5. Momentously, self-awareness projects beyond mere cognition and generates equipoise and freedom, for which every human being knowingly or unknowingly is struggling. This is the significance of self-awareness and, in turn, of cognitive meditation, which leads to self-awareness.

6. If self-awareness can generate equipoise and freedom, it means self-awareness is capable of generating modification. And what can modify turns out to be energy. Self-awareness turns out to be a unitary energy. It is a single homogenous energy.

7. The 'products' of self-awareness are diametrically opposite to those of non-self-awareness. These are the worldly and spiritual felicities. How one transmutes the multiple non-self-aware energies into unitary self-awareness is the theme of spiritual alchemy. Its technique and process is cognitive meditation.

The Freudian Unconscious and Non-self-awareness

The Freudian term 'unconscious' is frequently criticised, not without justification. It can confuse. For Freud, the id and the superego belong to the unconscious, while the ego (Freud's technical term for the 'I') is conscious (also to some extent unconscious).

One possible explanation is that the ego is not fully conscious of the id and the superego, which is a fact. But in that case, it is the ego, which is not fully conscious, that should be labeled as 'unconscious'. This certainly is not the intention. It is implied that the id and the super-ego are unconscious or belong to an unconscious environment. Actually, the id is conscious of the super-ego and vice-versa. So, in a sense, even the id and the super-ego are not unconscious. As a matter of fact, not only are they not comatose, but are alive, kicking and 'seething' to use Freud's own term.

Freud probably meant that the area of which the ego is not conscious constitutes the 'unconscious'. Though the phenomenon described is most valid, the terminological exercise is not up to the mark. A great opportunity for hair-splitters and pin-prickers. For the intellectually-dishonest, the fuzziness of the term becomes an excuse for creating doubts about the phenomenon itself, and prove Freud wrong!

In any case, the term 'unconscious' was first used by Brener and not by Freud (1974), though it could be under the influence of Freud. Before finally settling on the term 'unconscious'. Freud used the term 'sub-conscious' as well. He may have eventually been influenced by the German philosopher, Hartmann's, great work, 'The Philosophy of the Unconscious' 1869. (the term superego is also equally infelicitous as we note elsewhere).

My submission is the term non-self-aware is much more appropriate for areas covered by the psychoanalytical term 'the unconscious'. Once again, referring to the id and the superego, they can become 'aware' of each other and are therefore not unconscious but are unaware of their own selves, they not having the structure 'I'. Such entities are best described as non-self-aware. However, the term 'unconscious' is by now so highly entrenched, apart from being one of the greatest concepts of Freud, that it is no more possible to displace it. I have myself continued to use this term in a particular context, where I have described the anatomical sub-divisions of the psychological self. Otherwise, I have of course struck to the term 'non-self-awareness'.

Pestonji K Sholapurwala

Self-Awareness and 'Consciousness'

The term 'unconscious' is more of a terminological tangle than any conceptual confusion. Surprisingly, the term 'consciousness' is not only another fuzzy cobweb, but also suffers from a lack of any conceptual uniformity or clarity. The terms 'consciousness', 'self-consciousness', 'mind', even 'soul' are merrily interchangeable with psychologists, philosophers, cognitive psychologists, neuroscientists and even poets. They, some Nobel laureates, have all convinced themselves that they are talking science. But unlike in science, there are no common principles, statements, laws derived. Most of them contradict each other. They even run each other down. The variety of concepts is simply awe-inspiring. They range from 'there is nothing like consciousness' to 'there is nothing besides consciousness'. 'Consciousness' has become a hot subject with a fast and expanding literature. However, we are not concerned here with these intellectual jigsaw puzzles.

I am concerned here with those who believe in consciousness and are using this term. My submission is the term 'consciousness' pre-empts the acceptance of two kinds of 'consciousness' – one through I and the other through the non-I. From usage, it seems that what is meant by 'consciousness' is 'self-consciousness' – i.e. consciousness through the I. Then there should be another term 'non-self-consciousness' to accommodate consciousness by the non-I. No such term occurs in literature and, at times, it seems the term 'consciousness' doubles for both kinds. This is bound to cause immense confusion, apart from leading to false conclusions. The term 'self-consciousness' is a bit jarring as it has another connotation, 'a mental state of embarrassment'.

Neuroscientists, like Nobel laureate Eccles, generally use the term 'self-consciousness'; but on one occasion he has accepted the term 'self-awareness' also (page 115, 1984). There are titles like 'Aspects of consciousness', Vol. 3, 'Awareness' and 'self-awareness' (Ed. G. Underwood, 1982), which seem to recognise the term 'self-awareness'. Another title I came across was 'Awareness' (Nunn, 1996), which from its context seemed to mean 'self-awareness'.

I suggest that all concerned should make up their mind about the terms to be used. If a standard term is accepted, a fruitful dialogue can take place. My submission is the term that will eventually make it to the winning post is 'self-awareness' and the term 'consciousness' will straggle far behind. As compared to 'consciousness', the term 'self-awareness' is much more elegant, evocative, communicative and productive.

Meanwhile, for the time being, the terms 'consciousness' and 'self-consciousness' as used by cognitive psychologists (i.e. those who believe in it) can be said to be more or less the same as self-awareness.

If the term 'consciousness' is the favourite of cognitive psychologists, 'self-awareness' is the favourite of those dealing with meditation. All spiritual enterprises (excluding the pseudo-spiritual) are based on self-awareness. And therefore, the importance of cognitive meditation, which generates self-awareness.

CHAPTER VII

THE COGNITIVE RANGE OF NON-SELF-AWARENESS AND SELF-AWARENESS

The cognitive range of non-self-awareness and self-awareness is a very fast subject. We however are only concerned with those aspects related to cognitive meditation.

We are all familiar with self-aware cognition, i.e. cognition by the I. As a matter of fact, what passes off as cognition in psychology, unless otherwise stated, means self-aware cognition only. This is paradoxical as most of our cognition is non-self-aware cognition. The refusal to distinguish between the two can lead to unexpected confusions. Before we proceed further, let us once and for all grasp that non-self-aware cognition is as much positive cognition as self-aware cognition.

We have already noticed that physical objects, plants, animals, are all capable of cognition, though of a non-self-aware type. Here, we are concerned with the range of such cognitions and in this connection, shall restrict ourselves to man alone.

Non-self-awareness or Non-I Cognition in Man

As man is composed of physical, plant, animal, psychological, psycho-spiritual and spiritual components, he is capable of both kinds of cognition. Let us start with the range of non-self-aware cognition in man which is resorted to by the first four selves.

The Cognitive abilities of Non-self-awareness

1. Cognition of the external world. Most of the cognition of the external world is of a non-self-aware type.

2. Man, like plants and animals, is also capable of paranormal cognition. What is normal for plants and animals is 'paranormal' for man. As a matter of fact, this is also cognition of the external world, but with more subtle levels by more subtle senses.

3. Perhaps, maximum non-self-aware cognition takes place at the physiological level. But for such cognition, it would be impossible for the various systems and organs to maintain the viability of the body. Myriads of reactions and processes are going on in the body, which are interdependent, which would be impossible without mutual cognition by the system and the organs. Any process from a text book of physiology would illustrate this point.

4. At the psychological level, the same situation prevails, though in a more dramatic way. Not that the unconscious was unknown to man; but it required the genius of Freud to scientifically establish unconscious psychological processes which, like physiological processes, depend upon mutual non-self-aware cognition. The best example is the inter-relationship between the super-ego and the id, to use psycho-analytical terminology. There is a vast number of major and subsidiary entities, as we shall see later, in the psychological self composed of the unconscious, preconscious and the thought-spray. All these are interacting all the time, perceiving each other in a non-self-aware way.

Limitations of cognition of non-self-awareness

1. Non-self-aware entities, on the physical, physiological and psychological levels, cannot take cognisance of themselves. They are 'blind' and inertia-driven and do not know what they are doing. They are not even aware of their own existence. The superego can 'see' the workings of the id, but not itself. This extraordinary state of affairs is due to the fact that these entities do not have any I. If the 'id' were capable of becoming aware of its own existence, it would no more remain the 'id'.

   This 'blindness' of psychological entities which is a cognitive state, is responsible for their 'inertial' action (in the sense of the first law of Newton). Thus, the cognitive state projects beyond itself into a dynamic state. It is because of this that non-self-awareness results in 'blind', 'inertial, 'reactionary', 'bound', 'involuntary' behaviour, which has its own further complications.

2. The non-self-awareness of man can discern all the levels from the physical to the physiological, the instinctual to the psychological, and may even be in contact with the rest of the universe, being a part of it, but not the self-aware levels of the psycho-spiritual, much less the spiritual. The utmost it can do is to mechanically surround, suffocate, strangulate, contaminate, downgrade, pull down and then overpower self-awareness. And all this blindly. If ever somebody wants to equate Satan with non-self-awareness, he will have to be denuded of all conscious purpose, cunning, not to talk of intelligence, intrigue and scheming.

Self-awareness or the I Cognition in Man

Being much younger than non-self-awareness, the range of self-awareness at the current level of evolution is much more restricted. Hence, it is more convenient to start with the limitations of self-awareness.

What self-awareness cannot perceive

1. The cognition of the external world is less than that of non-self-awareness. For example, it is not capable of that kind of cognition which results in reflex action. Or in subliminal perception.
2. It is also not capable of paranormal cognition. It requires to evolve much more for this purpose. This is why the phenomenon of ESP cannot be produced at will. I wonder how long scientists will take to recognize this elementary limitation and its consequences.
3. On the physiological level also, the cognitive ability of self-awareness is quite poor. The 'I' is aware of the limbs, the skin, the sense organs, etc. It is totally unaware of 90 percent of the physiology. It has hardly any experiential contact with the internal organs or with that processes. In fact, at any given moment, myriads of processes are going on within the body of which the I, and its self-awareness, are blissfully and completely ignorant. The greatest joke is that the brain is supposed to be the seat of awareness of both kinds. But the I has no cognition, no direct knowledge of even the existence of its own brain!! These days we are exhorted to use the left brain and the right brain! The fact is, of the billions of neurons in the brain, the I cannot cognise a

single neuron, forget the left and right brains. All you have to do is procure a physiology textbook with an intimate description of our body and its workings. All this knowledge had to be established in a laboratory from the bodies of others because the I is incapable of direct cognition of its own body.

4. The story of the psychological level is no different. As we have noted earlier, the psychological consists of (a) the unconscious and its drives, (b) the pre-conscious containing the flows from the unconscious and the backflows from the thought-spray and (c) the thought-spray, otherwise known as the 'stream of consciousness'. (Factually, it has no consciousness of its own, except that beamed upon it by the I, because of its contiguity to the thought-spray).

    Of these three, the I has no capacity to discern the unconscious. Though it sounds so common place today, it required the genius of Freud to scientifically establish the existence of the unconscious, its ways and the indirect methods of making it accessible to the I.

As far as the pre-conscious is concerned, the I has partial cognition. It has the capacity to recall the back-flows from the thought-spray. Also, to some extent, the flows from the unconscious. After all, the preconscious lives next door to the thought spray.

As far as the thought-spray is concerned, self-awareness or the I is in direct contact with it, as we shall soon learn.

What Self-awareness or the I can perceive

1. As we constantly experience, the I has cognition of the external world as long as it is awake. (Non-self-aware cognition goes on in both the states of waking and sleeping).
2. It discerns superficial physiology and anatomy as also disturbed physiology.
3. Its area includes the thought-spray of the psychological level. We must recollect three points – (1) The thought-spray and the I are distinct entities (2) both are neighbours (3) In view of the proximity, the I takes cognisance of the thought spray and not vise versa, since the I is a higher entity. At the most, the thought spray can contaminate the I.
4. The I can take cognisance of itself. This is the very foundation of self-awareness. As I have stated earlier, the I knows that it knows.

Pestonji K Sholapurwala

The Significance of Self-awareness

I narrated rather blandly the strengths and weaknesses of the cognitive ranges of non-self-awareness and self-awareness. We saw that non-self-awareness, which is billions of years old, has been calling the shots. Self-awareness was found to be a fledgeling struggling to stand up. If this is the state of affairs, is it advisable to devote time and energy to the pursuit of self-awareness?

There is no doubt about the answer. Non-self-awareness belongs to the past, though to a great extent its reign continues even today. But it is only a matter of time. As surely as the sun will rise in the morning, self-awareness will take over in time to come.

However, we have not to wait until the near or distant future. Though non-self-awareness may be billions of years strong and self-awareness just a sprout, what this incipient self-awareness can do can never be even dreamt of by non-self-awareness. Self-awareness can discern non-self-awareness, at least the thought spray and some portions of the preconscious. Non-self-awareness cannot recognise even itself, much less self-awareness. It is this power of cognition, observation and insight that enables even the fledgeling self-awareness to modify and transmute non-self-awareness. Such cognition of non-self-awareness by self-awareness is the foundation of our psychological and spiritual health. It is also the basis of cognitive meditation, which is a systematic application of such cognition. Anyone following this meditation is already on the path of self-awareness and its rewards. However weak, current fragile self-awareness is quite capable of changing our life if the correct strategy is utilised.

CHAPTER VIII

BUILDING OF THE HIGHER SELF (PRELIMINARY)

Until now, I have been dealing with the theories concerning the precursors of the higher self. The higher self is the final objective of cosmic evolution and meditation. The building of the higher self has theoretical and practical aspects. The theoretical themes have been taken up in the following chapters:

1. 'Acquaintance with the Higher Self' – This Is already dealt with in the chapter on the three 'I's.
2. 'Building of the Higher Self' (Preliminary) – this is being dealt with in this chapter.
3. 'Energies' – This deals with the energy of the higher self and is discussed in a later chapter.
4. 'The Dynamics of Non-self-awareness and Self-awareness' or the 'Ways of the higher self' – This is also dealt with in a later chapter.

To recapitulate, all the selves, leading to the psycho-spiritual self, have been involuntarily built by nature. The last one, the higher self, has to be built consciously and by choice by the current I. I in other words, the higher self is a potentiality, which has to be actualised by the current I. Here, building and actualising mean the same thing.

I would like to reiterate that the higher self cannot be built by suppression or repression. It can be built by transmutation only – transmutation of the lower selves into the higher self. Transmutation involves an encounter between the non-self-aware and the self-aware, between the non-I and the I, between the lower and the higher. The non-self-aware, the non-I and the lower are represented by the psychological self and its impulses, desires, cravings. The self-aware, the I and the higher are represented by the spiritual component of the psycho-spiritual self, which has been gifted by nature. The process of generating encounters and the consequent transmutations is cognitive meditation.

With this background, I would like to reconstruct an experience, which broadly illustrates the building of the higher self.

Incidentally, the theories expounded in the 'Building of the Higher Self' have not been culled out of thin air but are derived from the actual experience of the building of the higher self through cognitive meditation. These theories will also help you understand better the rationale behind the techniques prescribed in the chapter for practice.

Anger

Anger is an excellent example to illustrate the building of the higher self. According to usual experience, there is either an outburst or a smothering of anger. The former is an 'expression' of the drive belonging to the psychological self, which is anger, and the latter, its 'suppression'.

Observation and Transmutation

There is also a third way — the angry man counts to ten, presuming that the quantum of his anger permits him to do so. When the counting is in progress, the person may happen to observe his anger. Here, the observer is the I, the current I, and the observed is the anger, the non-I. the current I sights the anger. Or, since the anger is within, the current I develops an 'Insight'. In other words, the current I develops self-awareness of the anger.

Thus, there is an encounter between the anger and the current I. Between the non-I and the current I, or non-self-awareness and self-awareness. If, during such an encounter, the current I and the anger come face to face as two separate entities and the anger does not overwhelm the current I, a miracle happens. The anger vanishes and is replaced by composure. There is a leap. Anger has leapt out; in its place composure has leapt in. This does not happen gradually but is a sudden and instant process: therefore, a leap.

There is no reason to believe that the law of conservation of energy, which is applicable throughout the universe is not applicable to psychological and spiritual areas. If this is so, where did the anger of our example, which is also a form of energy, go? Since it was neither expressed nor suppressed, what happened to it? It could not have vanished into nothing, for this would upset the law of conservation of energy. Similarly, from where did composure, which is also energy, materialise? Such an emergence of energy from nowhere would also upset the law of conservation. When one undergoes many such experiences, one will realise that the energy of anger has been restructured into the energy of composure. Anger has been 'transmuted' into composure.

How can anger become composure? Sounds incredible? Not so incredible when we recall other similar phenomena. Ice, which is solid and cold, when subjected to the influence of heat, becomes steam, which is invisible and scalding. Ice has become its opposite, i.e. steam. Similarly, when anger is subjected to the fire of self-awareness (of the current I), it becomes composure.

This restructuring into the opposite is called transmutation, which we have already dealt with earlier. To repeat, transmutation is not sublimation, which is only a refinement of the crude drive. For example, aggression becomes sport. But sport is still aggression, though being sublimated and refined, it becomes socially acceptable.

Transmutation is a restructuring into the opposite, either into the higher or the lower. When manure is restructured into a fragrant rose, it is a positive transmutation into the higher. When the flower is restructured into manure, it is a negative transmutation into the lower. Transmutation is a dialectical leap into the opposite; it may be higher or lower. Certain schools are involved in physical alchemy in which 'base metal' is restructured into 'nobel metal'. There are other schools that are involved in spiritual alchemy in which the lower is transmuted into the higher. For example, anger into composure. This phenomenon of transmutation, which is dependent on the observation of anger (or any other drive) by the current I, is what I have called 'The Observation Effect'.

The Prism

What applies to anger applies to the other drives as well, like fear, sex, greed, revenge and so on. Affection, sympathy and compassion are also drives belonging to the psychological self and they are also subject to transmutation. This is where we encounter another miracle. Though anger, sex, fear, greed, sympathy and compassion are disparate, distinct and specific energies, they all 'melt' into the one energy when transmuted. To a certain extent, the example of the transmutation of anger into composure is misleading. The actual transmutation is into a unique, single, non-specific energy of which composure is one facet among others.

When the spectrum of various colours from red to violet is passed through a prism, it becomes a single, non-coloured, white light. Similarly, when different drives or psychological energies are passed through the prism of self-awareness, they become a single, 'colourless', non-specific energy. I have called this 'The Prism Effect'.

The Quantity

Under 'Observation and transmutation', I mentioned: '…presuming that the quantum of his anger permits him to do so (to observe)'. If the anger was explosive, instead of the I observing the anger, the anger would drown the I. Here, the quantity factor is in operation. If the quantity of the I, or its self-awareness, is greater, positive transmutation into composure will take place. If the quantity of anger is more, the individual will be beside himself with rage and his 'I' will not know what it is doing. A case of negative transmutation. It is only when all anger is exhausted that the I is in a position to find out what has happened.

Obviously, this quantity factor applies to all the drives and not merely to anger. Thus positive or negative transmutation depends on which side is more powerful- the self-aware or the non-self-aware. Mere self-awareness, as many mistakenly think, is not enough. It should be quantitatively more than the opposing non-self-awareness of the drive, desire, craving or particular emotion. Non-recognition of this would result in disenchantment with the concept and practice of self-awareness. I have called this 'The Quantitative Effect'.

The Critical Mass

If observation and positive transmutation are regularly carried out, which is what meditation essentially is, the balance of power will change in course of time. Anger will diminish and composure will increase. Earlier, the balance of power was in favour of anger; now it will be in favour of composure. The same change in the balance of power will also take place in case of the other drives.

Composure is just a facet of self-awareness or its vehicle, the higher self. All drives, such as anger, are non-self-aware energies of disparate and specific kinds. When positively transmuted, thanks to the prism effect, they become the homogenous self-aware energy. NON-SELF-AWARE ENREGIES ARE MANY, BUT THERE IS ONLY ONE SELF-AWARE ENERGY.

With repeated positive transmutations, which are the building blocks, the mass of self-aware energy goes on increasing and one day when a critical mass is reached, the birth of the higher self will take place. I have called this 'The Critical Mass Effect'.

The Lesson

In caseyou have not already drawn the lesson, let me state it for you. The suppression of anger or any other drive is toxic and leads to pathology. Giving way to or expressing a drive is considered normal and healthy. But it may not be possible in many cases. For example, you may not be able to slap your boss. Thus, one is forced to suppress or lump the drive and face the pathological consequences. This has been a human dilemma over ages.

EVEN IF THE EXPRESSION OF THE DRIVE (INCLUDING SUBLIMATION) IS DILEMMA-FREE AND PERMISSIBLE, IT ONLY ACTS AS A PLEASURE ACTIVITY, RELEASING TENSION. IT COULD BE WASTEFUL OR IMPOVERISHING. IT CAN NEVER LEAD TO GROWTH.

The third way, besides suppression and expression, is that of transmutation. It leads from the darkness of non-self-awareness to the light of self-awareness. It leads to growth – to the development of the higher self. This self, whose dynamics are 'purity', 'wholeness', 'equipoise', 'transcendence', etc, which are different facets of the homogenous energy of self-awareness, is wonderful and useful not only in daily life but also in the spiritual life to come.

The concepts of observation and other effects are the nuts and bolts for the building of the higher self and it is time to consider them in greater detail.

The Observation Effect

Earlier, we came across the observation effect. Its treatment was obviously an over-simplification.

Dynamic Process

The observation effect is not a descriptive situation but a dynamic process, being associated with change. Meditation begins with the observation of the internal world.

It seems that the observation effect has spread into quantum physics as well. However, some maintain that even physicists do not understand quantum physics. Niels Bohr is reported to have said: 'If you think you understand it, that only shows that you don't know the first thing about it.' (John Horgan, 1997). But I can't resist the temptation to observe that the concepts of quantum physics are so bizarre that, in comparison, the concepts of ESP seem sheer sobriety. Yet scientists would rather believe in quantum physics and its associated near-crazy speculations than in the occasional verifiable episodes of ESP.

Capacity to Observe

The capacity to observe the inner world is uneven, as all capacities are. Different people have varying capacities. The same person may have varying capacities at different times. Progress in meditation will enhance the capacity to observe both the external and inner worlds.

In the inner world what the I can observe is what is generally called the thought stream, what I call the thought-spray. The psychological self is divided into three broad porous divisions: the unconscious, the preconscious and the thought- spray. Geographically, the thought spray is most contiguous to the current I. Hence, the light of self-awareness falls on the thought-spray as well, so that it appears to be self-aware on borrowed light despite belonging to the psychological self and the non-self-aware. The current I has limited access to the preconscious and none at all to the unconscious.

The Meditative Zigzag

When we talk of the encounter, it is between the current I and the thought spray, which is the last outpost of the psychological self. The intensity of the thought spray varies from day to day due to internal and external stimulations. The psychological self is a stratified terrain wherein weak and powerful strata alternate. When one is passing through the phase of observing the weak stratum, observation and meditation make rapid progress. When one confronts the powerful stratum, i.e. when the internal landscape is stormy, there is a sudden drop in observation and meditation. This can cause considerable discouragement, even depression. Feelings of frustration and failure may supervene. In advanced spiritual stages, it could be 'the dark night of the soul'. If you realise that you are just passing through difficult terrain, with patience and continued practice of meditation you can get over this difficult period. It must be remembered that progress in meditation can never be linear. It is always zigzag.

The Two Birds

Two birds, companions (who are) always united, cling to the same tree. Of these two, one eats the sweet fruit and the other looks on without eating. (Mundaka Upanishad 111.1 Radhakrishnan, 1996)

It takes two to carry out the act of observation – the observed and the observer. The former belongs to the psychological self, the non-self-aware, and the latter to the psycho-spiritual or the spiritual self-the self aware.

When a person says 'I am angry' or 'I am afraid', there is part fusion and part separation between anger or fear and the I. There being part fusion, it is difficult for the current I to observe. With sustained observation, the current I, on the one hand, and fear/anger, on the other, can be segregated. Then both the observed and the observer come face to face and an encounter takes place. Whichever the stronger, absorbs the other. It is only when the two are properly segregated and come face to face that a transmutation takes place.

The sequence of events in the case of fear (or any other drive) goes something like this:

1. Arousal of fear from the unconscious area of the psychological self, where it generally dwells.
2. Its ascent through the preconscious as thought spray and infiltration of the current I.
3. The current I says 'I am afraid'.
4. Observation by the current I of the partially fused fear and its segregation.
5. Encounter by the current I of the fear, which is now face to face, and its observation.

6. Transmutation of the fear (presuming that the current I is stronger) by the observation effect. The fear observed by the current I is restructured, absorbed and homogenised with the current I.

If transmutations (even on a lower scale) take place a number of times, they all add up and constitute a new self- the higher self or the pure I. The current I, a component of the psycho-spiritual self, feeds on the psychological component, which becomes smaller and smaller even as the current I becomes bigger. With the diminishing of the psychological component, the admixture of the current I also reduces and it becomes purer and purer. It ceases to be the current I and becomes the pure I.

All the above steps, which take place rapidly, are hardly registered by the non-meditator. But they become visible to the cognitive meditator.

Analysis is Synthesis

The observation effect is a deeper phenomenon than made out. Observation or cognition is of two types:

1. Surface Cognition.
2. Deep Cognition.

Behind every drive of anger (and this applies to all the other drives), there is a deeper drive or series of drives. I have called this deeper drive 'the propellant' that fuels the anger. This propellant is the triggering cause.

Cognitive meditation demands not only the perception of anger but also the propellant behind it. No amount of merely perceiving the anger will help. It is only when the propellant behind it is perceived that transmutation takes place. Anger collapses, is resolved, rearranged and restructured into its opposite and higher — composure. The non-self-aware, non-I nature of anger takes a dialectical leap into composure, the self-aware, the pure I.

Identifying the propellant is to realise the meaning of anger. Unraveling the meaning of anger is analysis. The transmutation of anger into composure or the pure I is synthesis. Analysis leads to synthesis. Since the process is instantaneous analysis is synthesis.

The Self-awareness Prism

I had referred to prism effect, which is a derivation of the observation effect. The multi-coloured spectrum, while passing through the prism, becomes a colourless white light. Similarly, the many 'coloured' various energies of the psychological self — love, hate, greed, fear and so on — while passing through the prism of self-awareness, lose all their 'colour' and are transmuted into a single colourless energy — the pure consciousness of the pure I or the higher self.

The self-awareness prism, which is associated with the observation effect, operates much beyond the 'colour' or mere transmutation of the various psychological energies. It not only transmutes the impure (coloured) into the pure (colourless) but also transmutes chaos into order, tension into equipoise, bondage into freedom, conventional morality into higher morality, becoming into being, and stagnancy into transcendence. All this will be treated in some detail in 'The Dynamics of Non-self-awareness and Self-awareness'.

Such is the power of the observation effect of self-awareness that it turns around your entire life. It makes you a new man, a higher man.

The Quantitative Effect

The detail example of the transmutation of anger into composure is incomplete. It is not every time that a person is able to count to ten when anger is aroused. And it is not every time that anger is transmuted into composure. Far from it.

Instead of the I overcoming the anger, anger could also overcome the I. which is the more frequent case. Anger (or any other drive) could 'flood' the I and overrun it so that the I would be drowned for that period of time. It is a state in which one does not know what one is doing, in which one is lost and in which one forgets oneself.

Whether the I will overcome anger and transmute it or whether anger will overcome the I and regressively transmute it depends purely on the quantitative factor. If, in any given case, the I is quantitatively more powerful, anger will be resolved. If anger is quantitatively more powerful, the I will be dissolved. If this were not so, all the drives that rose to the surface and became objects of the self-awareness of the I would be transmuted in all cases. Within no time, man would be free from the forces of the lower selves. It is through our daily experience that we become self-aware of our anger, sex, hunger or envy, but no change is brought about in them. In spite of the self-awareness of the I, all these drives persist. Those who think that making the unconscious conscious is the solution to all the problems are mistaken. Something more than just 'making conscious' is necessary and that is the higher quantitative power of the I. All these encounters are ultimately between the non-I and the I or non-self-awareness and self-awareness. Whichever one is quantitatively more will win. The problem is not only to become self-aware but also to become self-aware in such quantities as to be able to quantitatively overcome the non-self-aware forces. One must not forget that the non-self-aware forces are much more powerful than they appear on the surface because they are deeply embedded.

Positive and Negative Transmutations

Now we see that there are two types of transmutations – anger into composure and composure into anger. The dialectical leap, which is always into the opposite, can be both forward and backward. The transmutation can be both progressive and positive or regressive and negative. COGNITIVE MEDITATION IS THE ART AND SCIENCE OF BRINGING ABOUT POSITIVE TRANSMUTATIONS.

The Law of Reverse Effort

The quantitative factor is also related to the phenomenon of the 'law of reverse effort', most probably first enunciated by Charles Baudelaire. Suppose you want to read when the TV is blaring. The more you try to ignore the disturbance, the more obnoxious it gets, the less you can read. This is because the power of the decision of the I to read is much weaker than the inclination of the non-I to listen to the TV. If, on the other hand, the reading material is of great interest to the non-I, no amount of blaring of the TV will be able to interfere. Mind you, in both the cases, whether you are able or unable to read, it is the triumph of the quantitatively stronger non-I. But the law of reverse effort is not a permanent feature. If the I is made powerful, which is what happens in cognitive meditation, it will be able to overcome non-co-operation and sabotage by the non-I. Those who have practiced cognitive meditation will be able to read without distraction (or very little distraction) even in a noisy environment.

Of course, the area of the law of reverse effort is much wider than merely reading before a TV. For example, you may want to concentrate on a particular issue but there is constant distraction and derailing by the disturbing thoughts within. The more you try to concentrate, the more you are disturbed. For a person who has undergone cognitive meditation, concentration is effortless. The inner disturbances are either dissolved or much attenuated to offer resistance to the meditatively developed I.

The Middle Path

This finally brings us to the theme of the middle path, usually attributed to the Buddha. Actually, it is both pre- and post- Buddhist. It is the same as the Greek rule of the 'golden mean' or a life of moderation. The non-mediating I has limited powers of taming the drives — both hedonistic and ascetic. In the life of moderation, neither hedonism nor asceticism predominates. If there were too much hedonism, the ignored drives of asceticism would create trouble and vice versa. In either case the I would be subject to destabilisation. And since the I is the principal agent in the act of meditation, a destabilised I will not succeed in its meditative enterprise. Till such time that the I is strengthened, the practice of meditation has the best chance when there is a balance between hedonism and asceticism.

Having said this, please bear in mind that there is no general uniform formula for the middle path. Each individual will have to assess his own hedonistic and ascetic drives and work out his own individualised middle path. Hence, the middle path will vary from individual to individual. One individual may require six hours of sleep; another may need eight.

The Cognitive Meditation Strategy

Everyone wants to change, i.e. for the better. Three ways immediately come to mind:

1. Deep moving experience
2. Deep psychotherapeutic analysis
3. Moment-to-moment analysis, as in cognitive meditation.

All these are based on insight and self-awareness. There are other non-insight-based, non-self-aware techniques founded on fear, punishment, reward or incentive, Skinnerian pigeons (or mice) or Pavlovian dogs may not only show other pigeons and dogs how to change but also humans beings, who can be conditioned and manipulated by punishments and rewards. After all, as we have already seen, man has a thick layer of the animal within him. Hence, what works on animals will also work on man. But one has to decide whether he wants to invest in the 'animal' (conditioning) or in the higher self (liberating), whether he wants to become more of a machine or more of a human being. The end product of conditioning may be change, but it's one of pressured behaviour, a change that can disappear as soon as the conditioning pressure is released. Change produced by insight is effortless and enduring. We are concerned here with change towards the higher self through self-awareness and its insight.

The quantitative factor has great relevance for change through meditation. ACCORDING TO ME, MEDITATION IS THE BUILDING OF THE HIGHER SELF BY THE TRANSMUTATION OF RAW MATERIAL PROVIDED BY THE LOWER SELVES. The pre-meditative I, I.e. the current I, has its own limitations. It can only deal with the highly attenuated versions of the non-I (the non-self-aware or the lower self). These are the day-to-day routine contents of the thought streams and thought sprays — impulses, thoughts, feelings, likes and dislikes, the flotsam and the jetsam. Strength and quantity-wise, they are tiny weak and manageable. This is the initial raw material with which a beginning is made for the building of the higher self. These are encounters in which the current I can win most of the times. Any grandiose attempt to take on the elemental and raw forces of sleep, hunger, sex, anger, the temptations, would not only be bad strategy but also prove counter-productive.

Much of conventional meditation is associated with ascetic practices, fortified by vows and guilt complexes. As we shall see later, asceticism, like hedonism, is a cluster of blind non-self-aware drives. Both cause bondage and both are anti-spiritual. They are just neurotic. The spiritual is a state of blissful freedom from both.

The I can free itself from the stranglehold of the primordial forces of hedonism and asceticism only by gradually building itself, starting from the humble, ordinary, day-to-day thought spray that constantly rises and falls before the inner eyes of the current I. In meditation there is no scope for heroics or for romanticising the temptations. As the I builds itself brick by brick of small and weak impulses and thoughts and their transmutations, it will automatically be able to face bigger and bigger inner challenges in the course of time. Some day, theoretically at least, the

I will have entirely resolved the lower self and will shine incandescently with all the transmuted fuels derived from the lower self.

Thus, the quantitative factor throws up the most important issue of the strategy — how to systematically and gradually transmute the lower self out of which is fashioned the higher. This concerns the technique and practice of cognitive meditation, which will be dealt with later.

Further Comments on the strategy of Cognitive Meditation

There are certain similarities between psychoanalysis and cognitive meditation. Both are involved in progressive change in human beings. The objective of psychoanalysis is to build a sound ego and attenuate the id. This is chiefly done by analysing one's childhood and its residual complexes and emotional charges. Cognitive meditation is also involved in building an I-structure that is of a much higher type than the sound ego of psychoanalysis. However, cognitive meditation is not at all preoccupied with childhood complexes and their resolution but is rather involved in analysing the day-to-day disturbances reflected in the thought-spray. The strategy of psychoanalysis is to transmute the raw material of childhood, while that of cognitive meditation is to utilise routine raw material consisting of the day-to-day thought spray. Thus, the differences between the two are:

1. Cognitive meditation does not involve itself in childhood analysis. It believes in dealing with the present, the here and now.
2. The energies released by the resolution of childhood complexes are good enough to build a sound ego, a modest objective. The energies released by cognitive meditation, though of a much less dramatic type than those of childhood, are so enormous in quantity, being daily generated over a long period, that they can contribute to the building of the higher self.

Where Psychoanalysis Ends, Cognitive Meditation Begins.

The resolution of childhood complexes is full of drama. But there is no scope for heroics in cognitive meditation. The day-to-day raw material of the thought spray is dull and drab, with an occasional sparkle or punch. But its transmutation is available on a day-to-day basis, releasing enormous quantities of energy over a period that is required for building the higher self. By the time the deeper and elemental forces of the lower self reach the surface, the I is so strengthened that it can then successfully deal with these explosive, surging forces and in the bargain, become the higher self.

A major portion of Freud's life was devoted to the exploration of the id. By the time he studied the development of ego psychology (1923), he had to undergo his first cancer operation and only a few productive years were left to him. He had no time to explore the ego as he had done the id. Even then, his pronouncement "where id was, there shall ego be" (1933) attains the same peak spiritual status as the Upanishadic 'from darkness lead me to light' (Brhad Aranyaka Upanishad I, 3.28).

Unfortunately, Freud's successors also did not apply themselves to ego psychology, notable exceptions being Hartmann (1981) and a few others like Gertrude and Rubin Blanck (1974, 1979, 1986). The net result is that psychoanalysis continues to be the 'science of the id' while cognitive meditation becomes the 'science of the ego' and its metamorphosis into the higher self.

CHAPTER IX

ENERGIES – ENUMERATION AND CLASSIFICATION

There is a lot of material available about the structure of the human unit. Anatomists, physiologists, biochemists, psychologists, depth psychologists, philosophers and meditators have all made their contributions. But when it comes to energy, there is hardly anything to go by, either factually or even speculatively. I came across McDougall's 'The Energies of Man' (1935). Freud was always interested in dynamical forces acting in the human psyche and wound up with his celebrated and controversial formulation of Eros and Thanatos, energies of life and death.

As a meditator, I have become conscious of the various forces working within me and I have made an attempt to chart them in a formal way. For reasons that I will mention later, this chart will always be imperfect as these life energies can never be pinned down and schematised.

However, in a very broad way, the working of these energies can be understood. Unless we do this, we shall never understand the moving forces behind meditation.

I have already talked of the six selves or sheaths or levels of the human unit. Each self has its own energy. Thus, we have physical, physiological, instinctual, psychological, and psycho-spiritual energies and finally, the spiritual energy (of the higher self).

Instincts and Drives

I am now concerned only with the psychological and spiritual energies, with a passing reference to instincts or instinctual energies, which are a highly specialised brand of physiological energies. Plants, animals and human beings, all have physiological energies related to birth, growth, decay and death. But plants do not have instincts which manifest themselves as a special class of physiological energies and require to be given distinct recognition. However, even though they are physiological, instincts have been segregated as a distinct class of energies.

Now, in our scheme, instincts and psychological energies are most intimately related. Before we proceed further, we shall christen the psychological energies as 'drives' because all these energies literally drive a human being.

We may identify a psychological entity which moves on its own and forces the organism in a specific direction towards a particular goal, as a drive. It could be an appetite, a desire, craving, wanting, not wanting, wish, need, longing, motivation, yearning, tendency, hankering, aspiration, striving impulse, unfinished work, interest, preoccupation, inclination, sentiment, passion, and so on.

No matter how significant it may be, every thought is also a drive because it moves on its own and pushes the organism in a particular direction. Every thought is a distant derivative of a well-identifiable drive. It is, in fact, a very mini drive. Another characteristic of a drive is that it constantly seeks expression. If such an expression is blocked, there is unease, discomfort, tension and stress. Any entity whose stalling causes stress is a drive. Compulsiveness is one of the fundamental characteristics that identifies a drive. Each drive is somnambulistic and lives in its own world.

Having clarified our concept of the drive, we shall try to understand its relationship to instinct. To put it succinctly, both instinct and drive are the same forces in two different and independent modes. One is physiological and the other 'psychological'. Thus, there is an instinct of sex, which is physiological and a drive for sex, which is psychological, A drive is a 'psychologised' instinct. The structure of one is physiological; that of the other, psychological. One of the functions of the higher brain is to move the physiological energy of an instinct into the physiological energy of the drive. The higher brain is a transducer.

I am extremely conscious that certain current academic thinking refuses to give an independent status to the psychological because it is tantamount to splitting man in body and 'mind'. For the 'currently scientific', the mind is the brain, which in turn is a part of the body. They sincerely believe that 'mental', 'psychological', not to mention 'spiritual', are only misnomers. There is no level higher than the body and its brain. There are undoubtedly discordant notes like those of Popper (1977) and Eccles (1984), but they are in a minority. As far as the meditator is concerned, he has a clear experience of the physiological and the psychological being distinct. Para-psychological phenomena also postulate the distinction of the psychological from the physiological. This must be one of the main reasons why believers in 'body only' so hotly contest para-psychological phenomena. (The Russians have solved this difficulty by explaining telepathy as some kind of a brain wave. This dispenses with the need for accepting a psychological level).

Drives are a set of energies which propel a human being. There is one more kind of energy of which practically nothing is heard even from psychologists, not to mention physicists. This is the self-aware energy of the I and the higher I or the higher self. Even the spiritual make only hazy references to it. This is one of the main themes of cognitive meditation, where this self-aware energy is so definitely identified and described.

Enumeration, Classification and Levels of Energies

We have just noted what cannot be more than mere tautology, that drives are entities that drive. Issues that immediately arise are the classification of these energies, their levels and derivations constituting hierarchies, their individual identification and so on.

The fundamental classification is that of non-self-aware energies and self-aware energy. The energies of the four selves — the physical, the physiological, the instinctual, and the psychological — are non-self-aware. The psycho-spiritual self being a dual structure has both kinds of energies — non-self-aware and self-aware. The energies of the psychological component, which harbours the drives, are non-self-aware. The energy of the self-aware or spiritual component is self-aware. The energy of the higher I or the spiritual self is fully self-aware.

Physical energies are studied by physicists and chemists, physiological energies by biochemists. Instinctive energies are the field of ethologists, and psychological energies of dynamic psychologists. As already stated earlier, we are concerned here only with the psychological energies or drives and the self-aware or spiritual energy.

Perhaps the profoundest observation on drives can be credited to Freud (1959, 1927). His hypothesis of life and death energies, Eros and Thanatos, as he modestly calls it, offers one of the deepest insights that one can attain. Because of the fact that most of his time and energy were devoted to the explorations of the id, he did not have enough opportunity to explore the development of ego psychology. If this opportunity were granted to him, he could have gone beyond Eros and Thanatos and arrived at a still deeper duality of the non-self-aware energies and self-aware energy. He had already formulated the concept of desexualised, this displaceable energy. The next step would surely have been self-aware energy to mesh in with the self-aware structure of the ego (psychoanalytical) or the I. For Freud, the ego partly belonged to the 'conscious' system. Keeping in mind the context, Freud's 'conscious' is what we call 'self-aware' here. In other words, Freud came right up to the highest sublimation of the libido, but did not take the final dialectical leap from sublimation to transmutation. This could have brought him face to face with the self-aware energy, which is beyond the pleasure principle and has several other extraordinary dynamic properties.

The experience of the segregation of non-self-aware energies and self-aware energy comes quite naturally to the cognitive meditator. If morality deals with sublimation, it still leaves the concerned energy non-self-aware. Meditation deals with transmutation, the original non-self-awareness being changed into self-awareness. The dynamics of sublimated energies and transmuted energy are contrary, one being non-self-aware and the other, self-aware. For example, the highest sublimated energy still remains a drive that is subject to the pleasure principle, while the transmuted self-aware energy is no more a drive but an equipoised self-aware pool of energy. Of course, self-awareness has several other extraordinary dynamics.

Thus, the primary classification of energies is that of non-self-aware energies and self-aware energy. The former belong to the first four selves, though we are only concerned here with the energies (drives) of the fourth, i.e. the psychological self. The self-aware energy belongs to the higher I or the higher self. A mixture of the two prevails in the psycho-spiritual self or the current I.

All life energies have infinite shades, which cannot be reduced to 'one' final classification. There could be several versions, all arbitrary but linked to the expediency of instant communication. As far as non-self-aware energies are concerned, I divided them into four levels, deriving one from the other. As far as self-aware energy is concerned, it stands alone. It has no derivations and therefore no levels.

Primary Level

This represents the drive energies and the non-drive energy. The drive energies are non-self-aware while the non-drive energy is self-aware. Non-self-aware energies are many or even innumerable, but there is only one self-aware energy.

Secondary Level

This is derived from the primary level. The drives or non-self-aware energies involves us into existence, i.e. into the processes of birth and death (and rebirth). The non-drive or self-aware energy is neither involving nor is it non-involving. (Had it been merely non-involving, it would also have become a drive, which it is not).

Tertiary Level

This is derived from the secondary level. At this level, existence-oriented energies are further classified into life and death energies. These roughly correspond to the Freudian life and death instincts. We have to bear in mind that existence is a spectrum of which one end is birth and the other, death. In other words, death is as much a part of existence as birth. Without birth, there is no death, and without death, there is no birth. Existence constantly oscillates between these two points. Any leap beyond the non-self-aware and into the self-aware is a leap beyond birth and death. The tertiary level actually makes an attempt to enumerate the individual drives. However, this is a futile exercise and its only usefulness lies in its ability to be illustrative. A reference to the chart where these drives are enumerated will show any number of drives missing or those stated may probably be wrongly included or seem capable of being alternatively named. Take the following quotation from Chuang Tzu:

"There are eight faults that men may possess.
To do what is not your business to do, is called officiousness.
To rush forward when no one has nodded in your direction, is called obsequiousness.
To echo a man's opinions and try to draw him out in speech, is called sycophancy.
To speak without regard for what is right and wrong, is called flattery.
To delight in talking about other men's failings, is called calumny.
To break up friendships and set kinfolk at odds, is called maliciousness.
To praise falsely and hypocritically so as to cause injury and evil to others, is called wickedness.
Without thought for right and wrong, to try to face in two directions at once so as to steal a glimpse of the other party's wishes, is called treachery.

These eight faults inflict chaos on others and injury on the possessor. A gentleman will not befriend the man who possesses them, an enlightened ruler will not have him for a minister."

Each of these faults is a drive but not one finds place in our chart. This will give you a idea of the impossibility of making such charts perfect. I have been foolhardy enough to make a chart of these energies (drives). Before I proceed further, I must warn the reader that I am not the first, nor would I be the last, to make such charts. Such projects are attempted all the time by psychologists, depth psychologists, psychoanalysts, psychiatrists, biologists, ethologists and philosophers. Compared to these efforts, my scheme is going to appear amateurish, confused, unscientific, even bizarre. I could easily have made myself acceptable, but only at the cost of what I have experienced.

I have finally come to the conclusion that it is not possible to prepare neat and slick tables of life's energies without producing ugly bumps and dents. The energies of man, in spite of all the efforts to fathom them, will continue to remain inscrutable and inexplicable. There are scores, hundreds, thousands or innumerable threads and filaments of various lengths and widths, colours and textures, forms and shapes, timbers and pitches, all inextricably woven into webs and networks, incessantly glowing and darkening, one shading into the next and at times into the opposite: from time to time the visible becoming invisible and the latent becoming manifest, constantly arising and extinguishing. It would be rash or arrogant to impose design or any order on this throbbing, palpitating, totally indefinable mass.

Of what I am certain is this. Man has a set of energies, which are non-self-aware, and an energy, which is self-aware. The former force us into involvement in life, whereas the latter cares neither for involvement nor for non-involvement, which alone is true detachment. A hatred of life is not detachment. It is an attachment from another end.

By the time we come to the third level, life breaks out in a wild, mad luxuriance, a proliferation beyond both mathematics and philosophy. In spite of it all, chart making, however inappropriate, is necessary to illustrate what we are talking about.

Quaternary Level

To many, the concept of a thought as a drive would appear novel. The tyranny of thoughts is well known to everyone who has tried to control them. A thought is an entity moving on its own and anything that moves on its own and exerts pressure is a drive. It is a mini drive. There are end derivatives of major drives like sex, hunger, aggression, compassion and so on. The rising and falling spray of thoughts is one of the most enchanting spectacles that man can behold. Thoughts are the uppermost tips of the deep-seated and invisible drives. The thought-spray and the current I are neighbours, the latter staying in the storey above. It is because of this contiguity that they can interact, one of the most profound of such encounters being meditation. The effortless cessation of thought in cognitive meditation and the occupation of space previously occupied by the thought-spray by the stillness of equipoise is one of the most rewarding and pregnant experiences of man. It is the beginning of a new life, new skills, new ways, new objectives.

The Chart of the Energies of Man

There are all kinds of maps of the mind. I have added one more. I fondly believe that it is the ultimate one. Maybe, at the tertiary level, there is scope, and plenty of it, for redrawing it in a number of different ways, but the overall concept is ultimate. It deals not only with the mind i.e., the psychological self but also with the no-mind, the self-aware self.

The chart is full of oddities. I do confess that there is a certain deliberateness about it. I could have made it more 'academic' or at least refined the terms and made them less objectionable. But I have purposely allowed a certain rusticity to have its way. Mind you, I am talking of the drives and the non-drive, the pushers and the non-pusher. Some items like hunger and sex are instincts, some like love are drives, some like birth and death are events, while some others like the ego and super-ego are entities, some like melody or theory are artistic or scientific concepts and some are mere thoughts. They all make a strange collection. Whatever they may be, they are basically drives. And this chart is about them (and naturally about the non-drive as well).

The chart below deals with certain items. Some of them may appear odd but there is a good justification for them to be there. (The headings and the items on the chart are cross-referenced by alphabetical letters).

The Energies of Man (A)

The difference between the formulation here and the 'scientific' ones can easily be discerned by referring to the formulation of William McDougall, (1935). He gives a tentative list of eighteen propensities (drives).

1. Food seeking propensity
2. Disgust propensity
3. Sex propensity
4. Fear propensity
5. Curiosity propensity
6. Protective or parental propensity
7. Gregarious propensity
8. Self-assertive propensity
9. Submissive propensity
10. Anger propensity
11. Appeal propensity
12. Constructive propensity
13. Acquisitive propensity
14. Laughter propensity
15. Comfort propensity
16. Sleep propensity
17. Migratory propensity
18. Coughing, sneezing, breathing, evacuation propensities.

One can add to this list. McDougall claims no finality about it. Nobody can. Since then, others must also have prepared such lists. If my list is complex, peculiar, even odd, it is not my fault. I am trying to reflect life itself, though as succinctly as possible. If life is made of innumerable contraries, each contrary is made of innumerable shades. All of which can never be classified. Each one of us can make an attempt and leave it at that.

Involvement in Existence and Non-involvement in Existence (B, C) Life Drives, Death Drives (D, E)

Normally, whenever we talk of drives, they are existence-oriented, be it hunger, sex, sleep, etc. Only Freud has spoken of a drive for death. Eros is from inorganic to organic and Thanatos is from organic back to inorganic. Since death is very much a part of life, indirectly it also implies involvement in existence. Birth and death go together and existence is something that comprises both. Non-involvement in existence is something altogether different from death. In non-involvement both life and death are excluded. It is a state entirely unknown to psychologists and even depth psychologists. Freud occasionally speaks of the nirvana principle but he has completely misunderstood the Buddha, who enunciated the state of nirvana. The Buddhist concept of nirvana goes beyond life and death.

For life and death to be produced, drives are required. Drives can subsist only in non-self-aware states. The moment self-awareness replaces non-self-awareness all the drives are dissolved. When this happens, birth and death, which are drive-dependent, are also dissolved. Those who are comfortable with the concept of rebirth will also find it drive-dependent. Hence, rebirth will also disappear when the drives are dissolved.

All of us have self-awareness, but to an insignificant extent. Therefore, we continue to be under the sway of life and death. It is only very advanced, self-aware 'I's or selves, who are disengaged from life and death forces, who can experience the state of non-involvement. Mere talk of 'detachment' by those clouded with non-self-awareness is pious humbug. When psychologists become meditators, then alone will they experience non-involvement in existence and make the corresponding changes in their textbooks.

A concluding caveat. Non-involvement is not withdrawal from existence. Withdrawal is the opposite of involvement. Just as there are drives for involvement, there are drives for withdrawal. But the moment the drives come into operation we revert to a state of non-self-awareness. In self-awareness there is no drive and, hence, no compulsiveness to either get involved or to withdraw. Self-awareness is neutral towards both. Those experiencing withdrawal are most probably suffering a variant of the death wish, which is as anti-spiritual as the wish for life. The Jain monk, who considers living itself as undesirable and kills himself by indefinite fasting, hoping to obtain 'relief' from life is succumbing to the death drive rather than building the spiritual. If it were otherwise, all those people who committed suicide would attain instantaneous spiritual enlightenment!

Genetic and Acquired Drives (F, G)

A drive by definition is assumed to be genetic. I may perhaps be the first one to talk of acquired drives. It doesn't seem to me all that great an innovation. I don't have to argue that beliefs, habits and conditioned reflexes are great drives. They fall within my definition of drives. A belief, even one that's wrong, can change not only one's life but also that of one's community or civilisation. Habits and conditioned reflexes also push humans in their own way, not infrequently into disaster. Perhaps, the most driven creature known to man is a drug addict, a horrible example of an acquired drive.

Birth, Death (H, I)

Obviously, these are events. How did they come to be classified as drives? Perhaps I should have called this pair the birth and death processes. But I would have gained nothing more than to mollify the objectors. I have accepted that events, in their pristine majesty, are also harbingers of change; in other words, they are drives.

Awakening (Physical) (J)

Another multi-dimensional term. In fact, there are three type of awakenings: an awakening to the external world, followed by an awakening to the internal psychological world, ultimately followed by an awakening to the spiritual world. What has always intrigued me is that the instinct or propernsity for sleep has been included in the pantheon of instincts, but its opposite, the instinct for physical awakening, finds no mention. Most probably, academics do not acknowledge its existence. I believe that one cannot go to sleep but for an instinct of sleep and correspondingly, one cannot awaken but for an instinct for physical awakening. Maybe, like everything in life, instincts also contribute to dualities. I would not be surprised if this unstated factor led Freud to the concept of the instinct of death as a contrary to the instinct of life.

Ego (K)

If events can constitute drives, so can entities. The ego is a hybrid structure consisting of the fledgling I, which is riddled with all kinds of cravings (drives). Perhaps, the only difference between a simple drive and the ego as a drive is that the latter, at any moment, is a bunch or collective of various drives. Also, drives by definition are non-self-aware or unconscious. But by sheer contiguity, the ego imparts its incipient self-awareness to the drives enmeshing it, enabling them to bask in the ego's self-awareness, however dim. It is no wonder then that the ego is considered to be the fountainhead of all mischief. It pays for the company it keeps, however unavoidable. (It should be obvious that the term ego is used here not in the psychoanalytical sense but as a primitive-I).

Superego(L)

Yet another entity besides the ego, which doubles as a drive or a cluster of drives.

Here I am dealing with one more oddity. You will find this item under both life and death categories. The super ego is a culturally acquired entity. Being multidimensional, on the life instinct side, it contributes to the civilising of the individual, thereby allowing for an orderly life-protecting society. On the other hand, it can act as a savage force of self-punishment, which can at times endanger life.

Enhancement of Existence Drives (L)

To most, it would appear to be quite novel to treat artistic, scientific and philosophical pursuits as drives. But come to think of it, what else are they? Inspiration is too obvious a drive, particularly on the artistic side. There are also forces in the artist, which navigate him towards particular melodies, forms and compositions. If he resists, he will suffer discomfort, tension and stress. There is a compulsiveness about these forces, which characterises them as obvious drives. Similar is the case with scientists. All genuine science is compulsive activity. Even philosophers are drive-ridden. They will be disturbed unless they indulge in building hypotheses, theories, world views and so on. The need to extract order in scientific and philosophical areas is almost like an itch. However rational they may seem, scientists and philosophers are basically drive-driven.

Self-abasement, etc. (M)

Self-abasement, self-denial, puritanism, fasting celibacy, asceticism, hatred of the body, and hatred of life have traditionally been considered to be spiritual traits the world over at all times. I am sorry to strike a discordant note. These tendencies are not only anti-life but also anti-spiritual. They are as anti-spiritual as hedonistic tendencies likes sex and gastronomy. All the above tendencies whether ascetic or hedonistic, are typical drives. They satisfy all the characteristics of drives, some of which are blindness, inertia and compulsiveness. The spiritual is beyond all drives, whether hedonistic or ascetic. As a matter of fact, any excess in hedonism or asceticism is pathological, not just below the spiritual but also below the normal. Contracting life is not becoming spiritual but only encouraging death, which is one of the states of worldly existence.

Thoughts (N)

Everyone has heard of the trouble that thoughts cause. They continuously distract, can never be controlled, and behave like monkeys. Above all, they are the subject matter of the famous second sutra (aphorism) of Book First of the 'Yoga system of Patanjali' – 'Yoga is the restriction of the fluctuations of the mind.' (Woods, 1927). "Fluctuations" can be roughly translated as "thoughts". Thoughts, I submit, are also drives. This may be treated as yet another novel affirmation of the many that I have made in this chapter. They, like the drives, move on their own and pressurise the I. They have their way. If held up, they can cause distress. They have their own kind of compulsiveness. And, contrary to popular assumption, they are non-self-aware. Actually, they are as unconscious as the drives. Thoughts, being geographically contiguous to the I, are lit up by the self-awareness of the I. This reflected consciousness is mistaken for the consciousness or self-awareness of the thoughts.

At the most, they have travelled far enough to become the contents of consciousness even though they themselves are non-self-aware.

The chart shows that 'thoughts' are derived from the first level of non-self-aware energies and occupy the fourth and last level. These derivatives, because of the distance they travel from their sources, become attenuated. They can be called mini drives or drivelets. Of course, thoughts are much maligned because of the disturbance they cause, but they are not the real culprits. The culprit of culprits are the first-level non-self-aware energies, the great-grandfathers of thoughts. Each of the life and death drives generates its own kinds of thoughts. Thoughts can be truly infinite. It is no wonder then that, again and again, the question arises: 'How to still the thoughts?

Why one thought should be succeeded by another, which in turn is succeeded by still another, is a most interesting problem.

The I encounters the non-self-aware drives only at the level of thoughts. As discussed earlier, it is an encounter in which either the I prevails or the thoughts do, mostly the latter. Also, it is this encounter of the I with the thoughts that forms the basis of meditation, particularly cognitive meditation. It is in this encounter, when certain conditions prevail, that the non-self-awareness of thoughts is transmuted into the self-awareness of the I. And it is this enhancement of the I that is a progression in cosmic evolution. Incidentally, it is also the basis of an improved day-to-day family, social and professional life.

Awakening (Spiritual) (O)

The involvement energies are hierarchical. They are an unfolding, resulting in several levels. It is an uncoiling. It is a graduated manifestation of latent layers. It starts with non-self-awareness that unfolds in life's involvements, which in turn unfolds in birth and death, which in turn unfold in subsidiary life and death drives, until the final unraveling into the thought spray.

The self-aware energy, which for most of us would be a tentative and strange energy, has no hierarchies, no levels, no drives, no subsidiary drives and no thoughts. It is frequently referred to as silence. Spiritual awakening (which succeeds physical and psychological awakening) does not lead to self-awareness or the I. Spiritual awakening itself is self-awareness; it is the I. Once spiritual awakening sets in, there is no further evolution. There is no birth or death or rebirth, as of the physical, the physiological or the psychological. It is neither static nor moving, but dynamically equipoised. It can move as it wants, or rest. It is supremely voluntary. It is self-enhancing and self-limiting, self-stilling and self-moving. Non-self-aware energies are innumerable, but there is only one self-aware energy. Non-self-aware energies are 'colourful' and kaleidoscopic, self-aware energy is 'colourless'.

Concluding Remarks

Even a brief acquaintance with the 'chart' should be enough to register that man is dominated by the empire of drives, that he is a creature of drives. For all practical purposes, man is what his drives make him. Bhartuhari, an ancient Indian poet, aesthete, philosopher, maintains:

"We do not enjoy enjoyments
The enjoyments enjoy us
We do not perform austerities
The austerities perform through us."

The hedonist who thinks he enjoys and the ascetic who thinks he is practicing penance are both mistaken. Both are just vehicles for the drives, whether hedonistic or ascetic. If the hedonist tried to renounce pleasure or the ascetic, penance, both of them would become distressed and tense due to the bottling up of their respective drives. Both are bound, compelled by their drives. Both are anti-spiritual. The spiritual is free and non-compulsive.

I am sure Georg Groddeck, 'The Wild Analyst' (1965), had never heard of Bhartuhari. But he came to exactly the same conclusions. We are all 'lived' by our drives. Our form, structure, functioning of organs, thoughts, action, course of life, destiny, ups and downs, our beginning and end are all determined by the drives. Groddeck collectively named all these various drives the It. ('It' became Freud's 'Id', a term borrowed by him from Groddeck but with change in emphasis). For Groddeck, the I is a helpless, passive entity, suffering an onslaught of the drives. For Freud, the ego (or the current I) is a more active entity, trying to manage with limited success the id, the superego and the external world.

For the meditator, the I has three stages"
The ego, the incipient weakling, Groddeck's I
The current I, or what psychoanalysts call the ego
The purified, fully self-aware higher I, which is the meditator's I.

The ego, the current I, and the higher I are an evolving continuum. The task of meditation is to break the hegemony of the drives and transmute the current I into the truly self-aware higher I.

I am dismayed to find that psychologists and depth psychologists have been lavish in their attention to the drives or non-self-aware energies. None of the them, however, have made an unambiguous attempt to concretise and identify the self-aware energy. This should be expected because, not being meditators, they do not come across this energy, which meditation alone can unfold.

THE ENERGIES OF A SAMKALPA

PRIMARY LEVEL

- NON-SELF-AWARENESS ENERGIES (DRIVE ENERGY)
- SELF-AWARENESS ENERGY (NON-DRIVE ENERGY)

SECONDARY LEVEL

- DRIVEN MOVEMENT IN EXISTENCE (IN)
- BIRTH, GROWTH, DECAY & REBIRTH
- NEITHER ENGAGEMENT NOR NON-ENGAGEMENT IN EXISTENCE
- NEITHER BIRTH, NOR DEATH, NOR REBIRTH

TERTIARY LEVEL

- LIFE DRIVES (IT)
- DEATH DRIVES (E)
- NO DRIVES

QUATERNARY LEVEL

LIFE DRIVES (IT)

SUSTAINING DRIVES (P)

SELF PRESERVATION
- BIRTH
- GROWTH
- ANABOLIC PROCESSES
- SLEEP
- AWAKENING (PHYSICAL)
- HUNGER
- SELF AGGRANDIZEMENT
- ACQUISITIVENESS
- FEAR
- COURAGE
- SELF-PRESERVES
- EGOISTIC

→ DERIVED THOUGHTS (N)

SPECIES PRESERVATION
- SEX
- LOVE
- EMPATHY
- COMPASSION
- ALTRUISM
- PITY
- UNSELFISHNESS
- NON-VIOLENCE
- SACRIFICE

→ DERIVED THOUGHTS (N)

ENGAGEMENT(S) OF EXISTENCE

ARTISTIC DRIVES
- INSPIRATION
- FORM
- MELODY
- COMBINATION

→ DERIVED THOUGHTS (N)

SCIENTIFIC/PHILOSOPHIC DRIVES
- CURIOSITY
- INVESTIGATION
- DISCOVERY
- THEORISING
- SEARCH FOR ORDER

→ DERIVED THOUGHTS (N)

ACQUIRED DRIVES (A)
- BELIEFS
- DOGMAS
- CONDITIONING
- REFLEXES
- SUPER EGO

→ DERIVED THOUGHTS (N)

DEATH DRIVES (E)

GENETIC DRIVES (P)

INDIVIDUAL DESTRUCTION
- CATABOLIC PROCESSES
- AGEING
- DISEASE
- DECAY
- DEATH (E)

→ DERIVED THOUGHTS (N)

SPECIES DESTRUCTION
- ANGER
- HATRED
- AGGRESSION
- CRUELTY
- REVENGE
- MURDER
- WAR

→ DERIVED THOUGHTS (N)

CONSTRUCTION OF LIFE
- SELF ABASEMENT (M)
- SELF HATRED
- PURITANISM
- ASCETICISM
- FASTING
- CELIBACY
- HATRED OF ONE'S BODY
- HATRED OF ONE'S LIFE

→ DERIVED THOUGHTS (N)

ACQUIRED DRIVES (G)
- BELIEFS
- HABITS
- CONDITIONING
- REFLEXES
- SUPER EGO

→ DERIVED THOUGHTS (N)

NO DRIVES

- AWAKENING (SPIRITUALISATION)
- I AM HIGHER / HIGHER SELF
- PURITY OF SELF AWARENESS (FREE OF CONTAMINATION OF GOOD AND BAD THOUGHTS)
- WHOLENESS/INTEGRATION
- EQUIPOISE/ANANDA
- FREEDOM FROM TENSION AND RELEASE
- STILLNESS/SILENCE
- ORDER/HARMONY
- POWER/PHENOMENON
- DETERMINATION
- UNINHIBITED BACKGROUND
- UNRELATED STILLNESS
- CHOICE/VOLUNTEERNESS
- HIGHER NEUTRALITY
- BEYOND CONVENTIONAL GOOD AND BAD
- DOING GOOD FOR THE SAKE OF GOOD
- BEING
- TRANSCENDENCE
- FROM MAN TO HIGHER MAN TO A GOD
- FROM MORTALITY TO IMMORTALITY

→ NO DERIVED THOUGHTS AS PURE SELF AWARENESS IS "SILENT"

CHAPTER X

THE DYNAMICS OF NON-SELF-AWARENESS AND SELF-AWARENESS

Introductory Note — Allotropes

This chapter is the heart of cognitive meditation. In Energies, I dealt with the energies of man --- non-self-aware energies and self-aware energy. I also dealt with the classification and levels of non-self-aware energies. Self-aware energy being one such energy, requires no classification.

Non-self-awareness and self-awareness occur not only as such, but also in their respective innumerable manifestations. These innumerable manifestations are basically only non-self-awareness and self-awareness. Therefore, I have called these manifestations allotropes of non-self-awareness and self-awareness. These allotropes are the modes of operation of both kinds of energies.

These innumerable manifestations are the pairs of contraries e.g., the tension of non-self-awareness on the one hand and equipoise of self-awareness on the other, or fragmentation and wholeness. All these are bound to be in pairs for the simple reason that they are all derived from the basic pair - non-self-awareness energies and self-awareness energy.

Fortunately, it is possible to categorise these innumerable pairs under a few manageable groups. The number of these groups could be three, six, seven, nine or more, according to one's taste and predilections. I have settled for six.

1. Non-self-awareness and self-awareness (Basic Dynamics).
2. Impurity and Purity (Principal allotropes)
3. Impotence and Power (Principal allotropes)
4. Conventional morality and Higher morality (Principal allotropes)

5. Becoming and Being (Principal allotropes)
6. Stagnance and Transcendence (Principal allotropes)

The meaning of these terms become clear, when they are commented upon individually.

Impurity and Purity, Impotence and Power, Conventional morality and Higher morality, Becoming and Being, Stagnance and Transcendence are five principal allotropes of Non-self-awareness and Self-awareness. Each of these pairs have several derivatives or sub-allotropes.

The sub-allotropes are of two kinds - primary and secondary. Primary allotropes are rather theoretical or ideal --- like the first law of Newton, based on totally frictionless surfaces, which can only exist ideally. Similarly, as far as primary allotropes go, one may get closer to them, but perhaps never fully experience them.

The secondary allotropes belong to our day-to-day existence and are susceptible to full experience. As a matter of fact, when we talk of meditation, for all practical purposes, we mean the processing of these secondary allotropes of non-self-awareness and self-awareness. We can also say that advanced spiritual states, are intimately related to primary allotropes. The spiritual aspects of day-to-day life are confined to the secondary allotropes of self-awareness.

The unfolding of these allotropes is an evolutionary process. As far as non-self-awareness is concerned, all its allotropes, primary and secondary, have already unfolded and are being experienced by us. As far as allotropes of self -awareness are concerned, they are still in the process of being revealed. For example, at the moment of the big bang, it is non-self-awareness which comes into overt existence while self-awareness remains latent. This self-awareness started manifesting only at the psycho-spiritual level, when non-self-awareness was considerably attenuated. However, for the purposes of tables, comparing the primary and secondary allotropes, both non-self-awareness and self-awareness and their manifestations are shown as contemporaneous This is the only way a non-complicated table can be prepared.

So, even though we may have experienced the entire range of non-self awareness allotropes, we have still to experience allotropes of self-awareness. We may have already experienced a few of them, but a whole lot remains to be realised. The royal way to develop the allotropes of self-awareness is through cognitive meditation.

Unfolding the allotropes of self-awareness is a long drawn evolutionary process and, as far as primary allotropes relevant to advanced spiritual states are concerned, their realisation will definitely require more than a lifetime.

As non-self-awareness and self-awareness constitute a dualistic pair, so also do their respective allotropes. This phenomenon incidentally helps in understanding intellectually certain advanced allotropes of self-awareness without actually experiencing them. A typical example would be 'transcendence'. Even for regular meditators, its actual realisation would be a distant dream. But we can still comprehend it intellectually, as a symmetrical contrary of 'stagnation', which all of us have experienced and continue to experience.

It is quite amusing, to say the least, the way modern godmen pose, as if they have experienced the farthest reaches of spirituality and all the allotropes of self-awareness to their fullest extent.

To fortify their posturing, they indulge in pious drivel, hoping to impress their listeners. It is to be taken for granted that they have already attained the highest spiritual altitudes. Their talks are largely nothing more than empty words, with no meaning, much less actual experience. Some of them, even resort to sleights of hand to enhance their influence - the modern day mini-miracles. Quite a few of them are either humbugs or frauds. It is quite tragic to see throngs of followers even when these frauds and criminals are booked by the police. Their modus operandi is to run ashrams or social service institutions, preferably for girls as a front for their nefarious activities.

Before I conclude this introductory note, I would like to draw attention to two themes concerning allotropes.

1. Various Skills

All allotropes of self-awareness are skills, e.g. skills of concentration, tranquility, decisive action, productive interpersonal relations, family, social and professional, creativity, sensitivity, penetration of the object of study, realistic and effective planning, leadership, administrative capacity, implementation of team spirit, achievement of objectives changing one's life for the better, maintenance of psychosomatic health and so on. There is an avalanche of 'how to' books for each of these and more. It is implied that each of these is an independent skill, requiring a tailor-made, exclusive, separate training programme. My submission in the present climate, is revolutionary. I believe, from experience, that all these apparently varied skills are expressions of one common basic skill. The skill of self-awareness. It is not necessary, in fact, it is not possible to cultivate all these skills one after another. If one cultivates self-awareness, all these skills automatically sprout. Self-awareness, the source of all skills, is attained through cognitive meditation Therefore, meditation is the fountainhead of all these skills; not disparate, miscellaneous training programmes. This theme becomes more obvious when one goes through the allotropes of self-awareness.

2. Transmutation of Energy and mode of operation of Energy

We have seen earlier that non-self-aware energies, when subjected to the fire of self-aware energy, become transmuted into self-awareness Thus anger, which is a non-self-aware energy, is transmuted into self-aware or I energy. So also another non- self-aware energy like greed is also transmuted into self-aware or I energy and so on. Non-self-aware energies which are many and various are resolved or transmuted into a single homogenous self-aware energy. It is like the energies of many colours becoming a single white colour, when they pass through the prism.

The entire range of non-self energies have some common states like tension, fragmentation, involuntariness etc. Similarly, the energy of self-awareness has different states like equipoise, wholeness voluntariness etc. As the same entity assumes different states, I have called them allotropes.

There can be transmutation of energies only, not of their states. Thus, the non-self-aware energy of anger can be transmuted into self-awareness or I energy, but the state of tension caused by anger cannot be directly transmuted into a state of equipoise. This is what most people try-to 'calm' themselves, to 'compose' themselves and fail. What is required is the transmutation of the non-self energy behind the state of tension and not the transmutation of a particular state. The skill of transmutation works in a more complicated and indirect fashion than anticipated.

When a person becomes angry he also develops certain tension. When the process of self-awareness through self-observation and insight is applied, he first registers the tension which is a state (or allotrope). When the process is continued, the anger which is the energy behind the tension is eventually registered and the flash of transmutation takes place, producing the light of self-awareness

When self-awareness takes place, the entire dynamics change. Instead of the dynamics of tension, it is now the dynamics of equipoise. But equipoise is only a characteristic of self-awareness or I – energy. Similarly, wholeness, voluntariness etc are characteristics of I-energy. Wherever there is I-energy or self-awareness, all these characteristics or allotropes of self-awareness are present. One shouldn't make futile attempts to reach equipoise, to integrate oneself but only to become self-aware and still more self-aware. From the basic skill of self-awareness, all the various skills are obtained. One has not to collect, but to recollect. Recollection is the process of meditation, leading to self-awareness.

The allotropes of both non-self-aware energies and self-aware energy encompass the entire non-spiritual and spiritual existence of man. The primary allotropes of self-awareness deal with advanced spiritual states. The secondary allotropes deal with the skills required for our day-to-day as well as professional life. Most of us are interested in acquiring skills related to secondary allotropes. These would be the first fruits of practicing cognitive meditation.

The dynamics of the non-self-aware energies and the self-aware energy are presented in tabular form with the allotropes of these energies. The primary allotropes are commented upon separately. As far as secondary allotropes are concerned, except in some cases, no comments are offered since they are more or less self-explanatory. The entries against the allotropes, particularly the secondary ones, should be treated as illustrative rather than exhaustive.

I realise I have put the cart before the horse by giving this introductory note before presenting the tables of the dynamics of non-self-awareness and self awareness in the paradoxical hope of quicker communication. But I earnestly suggest that, after going through the tables, and the comments within, this introductory note is given a once-over again.

A Note on the Tables

Instead of dealing with the allotropes in descriptive manner, I have chosen to present them in tabular form. This makes for concise presentation. Wherever elaboration is necessary, it has been offered in the next chapter on 'Comments', by a system of cross-references.

The allotropes form a hierarchical arrangement.

At the top of this hierarchy is the basic dynamic of non-self-awareness and self-awareness. This gives rise to the five principal allotropes, also in a sub-hierarchy. The principal allotropes are further divided into primary and secondary allotropes (The last two principal allotropes have only primary allotropes).

Now let us deal with these allotropes in a reverse order.

The secondary allotropes, particularly of non-self-awareness, are the ones we are familiar with. This is because they are a part of our daily life. They are innumerable. The list can only be illustrative and not exhaustive.

The primary allotropes are at a deeper level. However, some of them may also be involved in our day-to-day life.

The principal allotropes are at a much deeper level. We may not have their direct experience. They appear almost like abstract concepts. In reality, they are factual dynamic entities that we shall encounter in deeper states of meditation.

The basic dynamic of non-self-awareness and self-awareness is the most fundamental fact of our entire existence, from the beginning to the end. Their actuality is realised in the deepest states of meditation.

The play of the basic dynamic and its five principal allotropes does not cease even for a moment. But we become aware of their activities in our day-to-day life, indirectly through their derivatives.

The hierarchy is a process of unfolding. The basic dynamic of non-self-awareness and self-awareness leads to the principal allotropes and they, in turn, lead to the primary and secondary allotropes. The principal allotropes are also hierarchical amongst themselves. On the self-awareness side, they start with purity and end in transcendence.

The Tables

Table I is concerned with the basic dynamic and its five principal allotropes. Some of the terminology is likely to be unfamiliar to you and even quaint. It has not been easy christening them. But I hope their significance becomes clear in the next chapter on 'Comments'.

Table II deals with the primary and secondary allotropes of the basic dynamic.

Table III deals with the .primary and secondary allotropes of the principal allotrope of 'Impurity and Purity'

Table IV relates to the primary and secondary allotropes of the principal allotrope, 'Impotence and Power'.

Table V is concerned with the primary and secondary allotropes of the principal allotrope, 'Conventional Morality and Higher Morality'.

Table VI is concerned with the primary allotropes only of the principal allotrope 'Becoming and Being'.

Table VII is connected with the primary allotropes only of the principal allotrope, 'Stagnance and Transcendence'.

TABLE 1 BASIC DYNAMIC		
1	Non-Self-awareness	Self-awareness
PRINCIPAL ALLOTROPES		
2	Impurity	Purity (of self-awareness or 'consciousness')
3	Impotence	Power
4	Conventional morality	Higher morality
5	Becoming	Being
6	Stagnance	Transcendence

TABLE II BASIC DYNAMIC		
7	Non-self-awareness (Non-I-hood)	Self-awareness (I-hood)
PRIMARY ALLOTROPES **Of Non-Self-awareness and Self-awareness**		
8	Blindness (spiritual)	Insight
9	Mindlessness / suppression Repression / expression / sublimation	Mindfulness, Transmutation
10	Ignorance / Agnana / Oblivion / Sleep (spiritual) / Unconsciousness	Knowledge / Gnana / Awakening (spiritual) / Consciousness / Understanding / Meaning / Realisation / Wisdom
11	Subjectivity / Rationalisation	Objectivity / Reality.

SECONDARY ALLOTROPES	
Of Non-self-Awareness and Self-Awareness	
12	Pseudo-spirituality/called trance, so- called meditations	Genuine spirituality/ Genuine meditations
13	Incapacity to takes cognizance of the internal world.	Capacity to comprehend internal World – deeper and deeper.
14	Contraction of Consciousness	Expansion of consciousness.
15	Obtuseness / Dullness / Denseness / Indiscrimination	Intelligence / Sharpness / Discrimination / Hindsight/Insight.
16	Confusion	Analysis.
17	Insensitivity	Sensitivity / Appreciation
18	Irrationality	Rationality
19	Immaturity	Maturity
20	Shallowness / Superficiality / Thoughtlessness / Immaturity	Reflectiveness / Depth / Thoughtfulness / Maturity
21	Incomprehension	Comprehension
22	Partiality / Injustice	Impartiality / Justice
23	Poor judgement of people And situations.	Good reading of People and situations.
24	Inability to Learn from experience	Capacity to learn from experience
25	Closed mind / Rejection of Good arguments and accomplishments of opponents.	Open mind / Appreciation of good Arguments and Appreciation of opponents

TABLE III		
PRINCIPAL ALLOTROPE		
26	Impurity and Purity	
PRIMARY ALLOTROPES		
27	Contamination of awareness by bad as well as good drives, impulses, thoughts, desires, inclinations.	Purification of awareness of all bad as well as good drives, impulses, thoughts, desires, inclinations.

28	Consciousness stained with bad and good thoughts, leaving no space for I-hood, i.e. leading to non-I-hood and Non-Self-awareness.	Pure consciousness only. Purified consciousness of all bad, and good thoughts, leaving behind only I-hood, i.e. selfawareness. Only 'I am'.
29	Fragmentation / Conflict/ Disintegration	Wholeness / Harmony / Integration
30	Chaos	Order
31	Tension and Discharge, Pain and Pleasure / Stress and Psychosomatic desease	Equipoise / Bliss / Ananda Psychosomatic health.
SECONDARY ALLOTROPS		
32	**Impurity and purity**	
33	Presence of bad and good thoughts, impulses, desires, craving, ideas, feelings in the mind, i.e. contents of Non-Self-awareness.	Absence of bad and good, thoughts, ideas, etc. just pure consciousness.
34	Turbulence	Stillness
35	Fragmentation	Wholeness
36	Multiplicity of dualistic, conflicting, specific, individualized drives, leading to friction, clash, collision, conflict/inner discord/ Disintegration/ To be or not to be / paralysis (Psychological) / Distraction / Wandering of the mind / cacophony/ Tower of Babel	No drive /No specificity / Entire pool of non-specific homogenous energy / Inner accord / Integration / Decisiveness / Productiveness Quick mind / Silence
37	Friction / conflict / waste of Energy / Exhaustion.	Build up of energy / Freshness
38	Chaos	Order
39	Randomness / Disorder / Irregularity / Confusion	Law / Regularity
40	No system	System

41	Chance	Cause
42	Disarray / Untidiness / Disorganisation	Neatness / Organisation
43	Disharmony	Harmony
44	Bedlam / Anarchy	Law / Order
45	Aperiodicity	Periodicity
46	Disequilibrium	Equilibrium
47	Uncertainty	Certainty
48	Asymmetry / Ugliness	Symmetry / Beauty
49	Mismanagement of time / Energy	Management of time /Energy
	Tension – Discharge	**Equipoise**
50	Generation of specific energies of specific drives	No generation of specific energies from specific drives
51	Build up of pressure and tension by suppression / repression of drives seeking expression.	No build up or pressure or tension, there being no drive.
52	Expression of energies of drives leading to the discharge of the same.	No drives and no expression / discharge of their energies.
53	Tension leads to pain. Discharge to pleasure, relief and relaxation	No pain or pleasure but a state of equipoise which is bliss or 'ananda'
54	Blank and passive trance.	Equipoise
55	Tension and stress lead to Psychosomatic disease.	Tension and stress lead to physiological, psychological health after being transmuted.
56	Expression and consumption of energy in the trivial ways of Day-to-day life – Perpetuation of Non-Self-awareness.	Transmutation of energies, generally wasted otherwise. Building of Self-awareness.

TABLE IV		
PRINCIPAL ALLOTROPE		
57	Impotence and power	
PRIMARY ALLOTROPES		
58	Drivenness	Self-navigation
59	Involuntariness	Voluntariness
60	Determinism / Bondage	Free will / Freedom
61	Stimulus and response	Beyond stimulus and response.
62	Reaction	Action
63	Inertia, Inertial movement Inertial stillness	II- generated movement I – generated stillness
64	Effort	Effortlessness
SECONDARY ALLOTROPES		
65	Involuntariness of cognition, of feeling, of action	Voluntariness of cognition, of feeling, of action.
66	Habits / Compulsiveness	Capacity to dissolve habits.
67	Incapacity for choice	Capacity for choice
68	Inspired creation, Inspiration	Conscious creation, Perspiration.
69	Automatism / somnambulism	Self-aware action
70	Grooved thinking	Creativity
71	Movement due to pressure of the drives	Movement due to decision of the I.
72	'Imported' peace	Self / I-generated peace.
73	Floating on the floods of non-self-aware drives	Swimming / Navigation by the I.
74	Destiny	Mastery of circumstances.

TABLE V	
PRINCIPAL ALLOTROPES	
75	Conventional Morality and Higher Morality
PRIMARY ALLOTROPES	
76	Immoral and moral conduct produced by genetic non-self-aware drives. Another source of conventional morality is acquired non-self-aware drives of the superego.	Higher conduct arising from equipoise without pressure of any kind of drive --- good or bad.
77	Moral conduct imposed by scriptures and social conventions.	Higher conduct arising from the self-aware still mind, irrespective of scriptures and social conventions.
78	Experience of guilt on failure to observe conventional morality	Renewal of effort towards more self-awareness, in case higher conduct is not attained. No guilt.
SECONDARY ALLOTROPES	
79	Conventional morality mostly consists of non-self-aware drives of puritanism and ascetism.	Higher morality is free of and beyond all hedonistic and ascetic drives.
80	Conventional morality is full of numerous dos and don'ts / Oughts and Ought nots / Rigid responses to situations.	Higher conduct which is totally unpredictable and spontaneous, arising from a drive-free still mind.
81	Conventional morality --- a hidden agenda in the hope of acquiring wealth, prosperity, advancement in social life, respectability, insurance against ill-health, misfortune, merit, higher position in next life.	Higher morality has no Expectations. Doing good for the sake of goodness.

	TABLE VI	
	PRINCIPAL OF ALLOTROPE	
82	**Becoming and being**	
	PRIMARY ALLOTROPE	
83	Cosmic evolutionary movements from the physical to the physiological, to the instinctual, to the psychological, to the psycho-spiritual to the spiritual.	Culmination of the evolutionary movement in the spiritual.
84	Incessant movement and flux / Incessant yearning to be on the move	Cessation of movement. A perception of having arrived
85	Movement involves succession of events, and succession of events involves time	No movement, no succession of events. No time / timelessness
86	Divine discontent / in spite of achievement after achievement, persistence of a mysterious discontent.	Peace that passeth all understanding.
87	Suffering due to non-attainment of the ultimate goal, which cannot be identified.	Happiness of identifying the ultimate goal and reaching nearer to it
88	Incompleteness / Imperfection of the 'unfinished products' / Becoming.	Completeness / Perfection of the 'finished product' 'higher self' / Being
89	Non-Self-awareness. The non-I.	Self-awareness / The pure I.
	NO SECONDARY ALLOTROPES	

TABLE VII	
PRINCIPAL ALLOTROPE	
90	Stagnance and Transcendence
PRIMARY ALLOTROPES	
91	From Non-Self-awareness to Non-Self-awareness	From Non-Self-awareness to Self-awareness.
92	Compulsion to be repetitive	Ever fresh and free
93	From meaningless to meaninglessness.	From meaninglessness to ultimate meaning
94	From existence to existence	From existence to mergence into **THAT**
95	From blindness to blindness	From blindness to insight.
96	From awakening (physical) to eating, to working, to sleep, to awakening.......	From awakening, etc. to breaking through the routine of life.
97	From impurity to impurity	From Impurity to purity
98	From fragmentation to fragmentation	From fragmentation to wholeness
99	From chaos to chaos	From Chaos to order.
100	From Tension and discharge to tension and discharge.	From tension and discharge to equipoise.
101	From pain and pleasure to pain and pleasure.	From pain and pleasure to bliss (ananda)
102	From drivenness to drivenness.	From drivenness to freedom.
103	From the merry-go-round of life to the merry-go-round of life	From the merry-go-round of life to the examined life.
104	From Bondage to bondage.	From bondage to liberation
105	From becoming to becoming.	From becoming to being.
106	From man to man.	From man to higher self
107	From birth, growth, decay, death, survival, to birth, growth, decay, death, survival, to birth. Chain of births.	From birth, growth, decay, death to beyond birth and death / beyond survival and rebirth.
108	From mortality to mortality	From mortality to immortality
NO SECONDARY ALLOTROPES	

CHAPTER XI

COMMENTS ON THE VARIOUS ALLOTROPES

Chapter X deals with the dynamics of non-self-awareness and self-awareness. It also deals with their principal, primary and secondary allotropes, which are serially numbered; some significant allotropes are commented upon below. (Numbers in the brackets have cross-references with the previous chapter).

Basic Dynamic

We have already dealt with non-self-awareness and self-awareness in several Chapters. It may be added that these two contribute to the basic dynamics. From these arise the various principal, primary and secondary allotropes.

(8) Blindness / 'Insight'

At one time 'insight' was the buzz word. It turns out to be an aspect or allotrope of self-awareness.

(9) Suppression - Repression/Transmutation

Non-self-aware energies exist either in suppressed (conscious inhibition), repressed (unconscious inhibition) or expressed states. Sublimation is a refined expression. In self-awareness, none of these states exist. On being subjected to self-awareness, they are all transmuted into self-awareness. In fact, all self-awareness, is transmuted non-self-awareness of various varieties.

(10) Ignorance/Knowledge

The terms 'ignorance' and 'knowledge' do not refer to academic areas. By ignorance is meant non-self-awareness and by knowledge, self-awareness.

(11) Subjectivity/Objectivity

Not only in the case of ordinary humans but also in the case of scientists and philosophers, thinking and conclusions are tainted by desires, prejudices and partialities. Otherwise, given the facts, there should have been no difference of opinion between Einstein and Niels Bohr.

Even in the case of someone gifted by constitutional objectivity, the main source is self-awareness which by definition is free of prejudice and partiality. The best route to objectivity, a highly valued and rare state, is cognitive meditation and the self-awareness generated by it. A typical modern example of the 'blind spot' is the denial of ESP by a class of scientists and philosophers, who are keen to establish their 'scientific' credentials. It is only when desires subside through meditation that one can take cognisance of the reality and become objective.

(12) Pseudo-spirituality/Genuine Spirituality

There are few terms which are as mutilated as the 'spiritual'. Religion is most frequently mistaken for the spiritual. The study of religious texts, performance of religious ceremonies, practice of puritanism, fasting, bathing, visiting sacred places, performance of austerities pass off as spiritual activities. Even Marxists talk of the spiritual, when they are actually referring to the cultural. Practically, all these activities are propelled by non-self-aware drives and wherever there is a drive, there is non-spirituality or pseudo-spirituality. Genuine spirituality arises when the drives subside. Even good drives like unselfishness, co-operation, compassion are still drives and exclude genuine spirituality. This of course does not mean that 'good' drives are on the same level as 'bad' drives. From an evolutionary angle, 'good' drives are at a higher level than 'bad' drives and much more precious. But at the most, they are a higher variety of the non-spiritual.

Sankara, one of the greatest Indian spiritual geniuses and teachers, says neither the study of spiritual texts, nor performance of rituals, nor worship of gods, nor performance of acts, nor practice of yoga can lead to liberation. (Vivek Chudamani 6, 56).

More pernicious than the conventional pseudo-spirituality is the new fangled pseudo-spirituality induced by chemicals. Dangerous are the determined efforts made by the high priests of LSD, mescaline or plain narcotics. We are persuaded to believe that the chemically induced allied states of the mind are the same as those produced by meditation. To be established in meditation may take a long time; the chemical high is superior, being instantaneous. If ever there was nonsense, this is it. There is absolutely no basis for any such equivalence. There is no comparison between the two. What we do know is that substances lead to addiction, which is bondage, which is most anti-spiritual. Further, it causes physiological and psychological damage which is the very opposite of what meditation does. Meditation is a great source of psychosomatic health. Psychedelics can only lead to ruim, whatever wonderful 'highs', they may offer initially.

(13) Incapacity and the capacity to take cognisance of the internal world

All meditations, including cognitive meditation are based on the voluntary capacity to observe the inner world of impulses, desires, thoughts, etc.. For the densely non-self-aware, this is not possible. This capacity should not be confused with that of introversion, which is no capacity but an involuntary compulsive state. It cannot lead to any transmutation.

(16) Confusion/Analysis

Self-awareness is capable of analysis, which is also the basis of cognitive meditation. Analysis means the capacity to identify the 'propellant' behind each impulse, thought, etc. Mere observation of a particular thought does not produce any transmutation. But the moment the drive behind a thought is identified, instantaneous transmutation takes place.

(17) Insensitivity/Sensitivity --- Appreciation

Practice of cognitive meditation makes one sensitive to all aspects of life, be it art, events, interpersonal relations, needs of others, above all one's own deeper requirements.

(18) Irrationality/Rationality

It is too well-known that where drives, desires abound, cravings, passions, irrationality flourish. The treatment for irrationality is not reason but self-awareness, of which reason is an allotrope.

(19) Immaturity/ Maturity

Maturity is a ripened complex of various self-aware skills. Experience also makes one mature. As a matter of fact, next to meditation, experience is the other factor that generates self-awareness. Only it is slow, sporadic and above all unsystematic. Experience is self-awareness by hindsight, whereas meditation is self-awareness by insight.

(22) Injustice/Justice

No management, administration, governance is possible without justice. And no justice is possible without self-awareness. Managers and administrators under the thrall of desires, partialities, prejudices, which are some of the commonest expressions of non-self-awareness, can never be just. Meditation, generating self-awareness, is a sovereign remedy for acquiring justice. No amount of sermons can inculcate justice.

(24) Incapacity/Capacity to learn from experience

Both the phenomena are well-known. The capacity to learn from experience is an unfailing sign of self-awareness. An accumulation of such experience leads to maturity. Those who do not want to meditate may become self-aware by acquiring maturity, a long -drawn, haphazard process with uncertain results.

(26) Impurity/Purity

I am not talking of conventional moral cleanliness or purity. The main difference between non-self-awareness and self-awareness is that the former is cluttered with feelings and thoughts, both 'good' and 'bad', whereas the latter is free from all feelings and thoughts, except that of 'I am' or I-hood. It is pure awareness or consciousness. For modern psychologists, it is a very difficult state to comprehend. But it is basically an empirical fact, one of the ultimate results of meditation. Some call it stillness and still others, silence. So, 'pure' thoughts are still thoughts which contaminate awareness and cause impurity. By purity is meant pure consciousness, which is neither moral nor immoral nor amoral and is effortlessly free of all thoughts, feelings, desires, intentions, etc.

(29) Fragmentation/Wholeness

Wholeness or completeness is another buzz word, which everyone uses but mostly no one understands. We saw that man not only has innumerable drives, but that they are all conflicting with their contraries. The endless 'To be or not to be';These innumerable conflicting drives tear man apart - fragment him. But if these drives subside, which is bound to happen as self-awareness advances through meditation, transmuting all drives into further self-awareness, man becomes a seamless whole. In practical terms, it means that conflicts are reduced, fragmentation is minimal, and integration enhanced. Man may not become completely conflict-free, but certainly conflict-reduced. The paralysis caused by internal contradictions wanes and clarity and productivity is enhanced.

(30) Chaos/Order

These states are corollaries of fragmentation and wholeness. As self-awareness is the restructuring by transmutation of an earlier state of non-self-awareness, so wholeness is a transmutation of fragmentation. So also is order a transmutation of chaos.

(31) Tension-Discharge/Equipoise

This is perhaps one of the most famous dyads in healing psychologies. As long as the drives are allowed to flow, express and consume themselves, nothing special happens. But it is not possible, for obvious reasons, to give vent to all the drives. Either the situation does not permit it or it may just be repression. One cannot slap his boss. One is compelled to stifle much anger. If the drives, particularly of anger, aggression, sex, fear, are not allowed free expression, they get bottled up. These compressed energies, trapped and seeking to burst, create pressure, either in the unconscious or in the thought-spray. This is the state of pressure popularly known as tension. The tension is felt directly, if the blockage has taken place in the thought-spray (suppression) or indirectly, if it takes place at the unconscious level (repression). Such tension causes unease, discomfort, pain and pathology. If the blocked drive gets released, there is a .discharge of the drive, which is accompanied by relief, pleasure and relaxation.

Blockage of drives, leading to tension, can eventually lead to stress, neurosis, and psychosomatic disorders. It also leads to blighting of interpersonal relations, relating to family, social life and profession. Modern life, with all its deadlines, speed, competition, conflicts and consumerism, arouses more and more drives, having no prospect of expression or release and satisfaction. Tension and stress surge by leaps and bounds, developing an exclusive pathology of the times. This pathology generates yearnings for getting away from it all, for relaxation, for peace, for tranquility or just plain diversion. The response to this pathology is billion-dollar industries --- entertainment, tourism, psychotherapies.

Self-improvement literature, 'how to' books, yoga, tantra, chakra books, pop religion, T.V. evangelism, soporifics, tranquilisers, energisers, narcotics, psychedelics, hippy movements, rock music, smoking, alcoholism, godmen cults, mind-benders ... are all a response to tension and stress. Faith in God, faith in guru are excellent preventives for panic which seizes modern man from time to time. Religion is the most popular bulwark against anxiety neurosis. But these resources have their own shortcomings.

There are deeper strategies to cope with tension and stress, besides progressive relaxation exercises. Sitting alone on a solitary river bank during sunset can immediately calm one down. To be in a church or an old isolated temple, where there is minimum or no traffic, brings peace. (This has nothing to do with religion. Perhaps, the architecture contributes to the effect). The physical presence of a realised spiritual master or even a good, composed man can instantly tranquilise. Soft 'meditative' music is yet another method well-known to soothe the nerves.

There is one common denominator in all the above strategies — such tranquility is generated by external factors. Such tranquility has to be imported. It is not self-generated.

The last observation brings us to equipoise. When tension and discharge, or rather the forces behind them, are subjected to self-awareness, they are transmuted into self-awareness, which in this case manifests as equipoise.

In the case of tension, the energies behind it are coiled and in the case of discharge, they are uncoiled. It is altogether different in the case of equipoise. Equipoise is a pool of energy, which is never coiled and therefore never uncoils. It is energy, in a state of stillness, equipotential at all points, from the centre to the periphery.

The technique of producing these equipoises is called meditation. This technique is not dependent on any external factor and thus is self-generated and autonomous.

Modern situation has made man so distraught and bewildered, that he can think of nothing else but composure, peace and tranquility. This is the beginning of the cult of relaxation. More the tension and stress, more the indulgence in relaxation. An altogether new guru, the relaxation guru, makes his appearance and rapidly multiplies.

Most of these gurus mistake relaxation for equipoise. It is a serious mistake. Relaxation and equipoise are altogether different phenomena, with different consequences.

We are all familiar with the concept of suppression (as also repression) of drives at the psychological level. There is also an equally common similar phenomenon, at the muscular level, but conceptually not recognised.

When a man becomes angry, the anger is displayed at two levels. Partly at the psychological level and partly at the muscular level. During anger the muscles of the hand are primed to administer a slap. They become tense. However, for more than one reason, as usual, the slap is not effected, the muscular anger is suppressed and the muscles of the hand continue to remain tense. If such tension becomes chronic, it can cause pathological consequences. With the passage of time, or by conscious practice of relaxation, the energies of muscular anger will be pushed deep down, leaving the muscles relaxed. It becomes a case of surface placidity and deeper turbulence. The same thing happens in case of psychological suppression - surface placidity, deeper turbulence. As is now well-known, the suppressed energies are neither neutralised nor destroyed but continue to fester. In the case of psychological suppression, there is a chance of sublimation or transmutation by cognitive meditation. No such possibility exists in the case of muscular suppression. Such muscular level suppressed energies are frozen and blocked. The constant practice of relaxation keeps the excitement down.

To return to the comparison between relaxation and equipoise. Equipoise is a still, non-specific dynamic pool of energy, available to the I, for all minor and major undertakings. In relaxation, energy is frozen and inaccessible. Relaxation can only be inaction. Equipoise being free, non-specific, non-coiled, non-driven energy can act or 'not act' at the voluntary decision of the self-aware I. The serenity of equipoise is at all levels, not deceptive as in the case of relaxation – superficially quiet, deep down simmering. Equipoise is produced through cognitive mediation, by transmutation of non-self-aware energies by self-awareness. Relaxation is produced by the suppression of tension in the muscle. Relaxation is the intensification of non-self-awareness, equipoise is the blossoming of self-awareness. Those who practice equipoise do not have to practice relaxation.

(53) Tension – Discharge/Ananda – Bliss

Earlier we came across pain caused by tension, i.e. by the blockage of the drives and pleasure by their discharge or release. Tension and discharge are typical non-self-aware phenomena. In the case of equipoise, we come across an altogether new state of 'ananda' or bliss, which is neither pain nor pleasure. One who experiences ananda will no more care for pleasure. Ananda is one of the hallmarks of the spiritual. Running after pleasure is running away from the spiritual.

Equipoise of the thought-spray and to some extent of the preconscious is possible in one lifetime only. But the equipoise of the unconscious, wherein the seeds of all the drives are harboring, would take several lifetimes. But then, it is final liberation.

(54) Blank and Passive Trance/Equipoise

If relaxation is not equipoise, much less is a blank or passive trance. We have to be careful about these two pseudo-equipoises.

Everyone is aware of the incessant movement of thoughts – the thought-spray, rising and falling incessantly, even in sleep. But the moment one begins to mediate, i.e. the I starts observing the thought-spray, rising and falling incessantly, even in sleep. But the moment one beings to meditate, i.e. the I starts observing the thought-spray, the movements of the thoughts suddenly cease. The thoughts just won't flow. A blank develops. This happens to everyone in the beginning and thereafter occasionally. This blank is not to be mistaken for equipoise and its stillness. In the case of the blank, the thoughts are very much there, but they just won't rise. Shy? Perverse? The psychological system is not at all accustomed to being observed, and the sudden change of gears momentarily paralyses and the blank ensues.

In the case of equipoise, there are no thoughts which can rise to the surface. On the surface, both the blank and the equipoise are still. But in the case of the blank, there is a vague pressure at a deeper level. In the case of equipoise there is none, either at the surface or deep down. The state of the blank is discomforting, equipoise is exhilaration, 'ananda' or bliss as we noted earlier.

The passive trance could be more insidious. It is a state in which one is neither awake nor asleep. There is no I either, it having been lost in the trance. This state is more like a cultivated absent-mindedness. The ignorant, both the meditators and their followers, mistake this state for spiritual accomplishment. It is nothing of the sort. When the I and its self-awareness and alertness are lost, there cannot be, even by definition, any spiritual state. The trance, being a non-self-aware phenomenon, could be highly addictive. It is a case of natural pleasure, being substituted by perverted pleasure. It is spiritual perversion.

(57) Impotence and Power

In a way, non-self-awareness has bewildering power. A mad man has the strength of five. But at the same time, non-self-awareness is drivenness and that is its impotence. Self-awareness is self-navigation and therefore power. The weakness of non-self-awareness is its reactiveness; the strength of self-awareness, its proactiveness.

The impotence of non-self-awareness lies in its involuntariness, bondage and stagnance, while the power of self-awareness lies in its voluntariness, freedom and transcendence.

The issue of impotence and power has been discussed for centuries under various names – free will and determination, freedom and bondage, voluntariness and involuntariness, destiny and mastery of fate and so on.

This subject is as popular and perennial as the mind-body problem. Though psychologists have started jumping into this field, it is mostly the preserve of philosophers.

For reasons not quite clear, philosophers on the whole are either exclusively for free will or exclusively for determinism. Never partly for free will and partly for determinisms.

The case of Freud is interesting. His discovery of unconscious motivation led him to opt for determinism. But it was also Freud who proved that analysis and insight can set a man free of his unconscious compulsions. Still, for reasons unknown, in spite of his demonstration of man's capacity for freedom, Freud stuck to his vision of man determined and bound by his unconscious forces.

It seems modern'cognitive' psychologist and neuroscientists just refuse to believe in free will and even refuse to discuss the issue.

For example, Francis Crick, a Nobel laureate, discoverer of the molecular structure of DNA, along with James D. Watson, has now shifted from molecular biology to the psychology of consciousness. In 'The Astonishing Hypothesis' (1995) he has relegated the subject of free will to an appendix and states that psychologists and neuroscientists are no more interested in the subject. The term 'free-will' just does not occur in 'The International Dictionary of Psychology' by Stuart Sutherland (1996). However, this does not prevent him from using the term to explain another term 'voluntary admission'. More interesting, even if a term like 'free will' is excluded, a term like 'Vitamin' does get included in this dictionary. The psychology of such exclusion and inclusion is difficult to understand. According to Kuhn's 'The Structure of Scientific Revolutions' (1970), which should be obligatory reading for all, particularly scientists, the extant scientific theories and paradigms have built in large components of the current scientific fashion. And these fashions change from cycle to cycle. Scientific fashion is more powerful than science itself. If today's fashion is not to believe in free will, a time will certainly come when it will be scientifically fashionable to do so.

The truth, as is frequently the case, is somewhere in between. Man is partly (mostly) bound and partly (to some extent) free. This can be verified on both the physiological and psychological levels. While most of physiology is bound, some of it is free. The former is called involuntary function and the latter, voluntary. The beating of the heart is involuntary, the movement of the hand, voluntary.

Some physiological system like breathing is both involuntary and voluntary. This phenomenon is the basis of Patanjali and Vipassana systems of meditation. Paradoxically, the same phenomenon is used in opposite ways. In Patanjali Yoga, it is suppression (disciplining) of breath, in Vipassana, it is expression (letting go) of breath.

On the psychological level too, most activity is involuntary or determined. Freud is mainly responsible for this kind of thinking. But there is a small area where psychological activity is voluntary or free. This was also demonstrated by Freud in the action of insight. But those who are most familiar with voluntariness and freedom at the psychological level are the mediators. The capacity to perform cognitive meditation, i.e. the observation of the non-I by the I, is a typical voluntary or free activity.

Involuntariness or bondage is the consequence of non-self-awareness and voluntariness or freedom that of self-awareness. And as man, at the present stage of evolution, is part non-self-aware and part self-aware, so also he is part bound and part free.

The acute reader is likely to face a difficulty. Throughout, I have maintained, that the physiological and psychological selves are non-self aware and therefore involuntary.

Then how is it that there are areas of voluntariness and therefore of self-awareness at both these levels? The reply is, from the moment of the big bang, self-awareness is a constantly unfolding and increasingly manifesting force. It makes its first appearance at the physiological level, enhancing its presence at the psychological. At the psychological level, which is our current level, it is already a well-established force. At the spiritual level, it is of course all self-awareness.

(59) Involuntariness/Voluntariness

These are of three kinds.

a) Involuntary / voluntary cognition
b) Involuntary / voluntary feeling
c) Involuntary / voluntary action.

Most of our cognition, through eyes, ears and other senses, is involuntary or compulsive. We cannot help seeing, hearing, etc. But what is worse, the more we try not to see or hear something, the more we see or hear it.

Our feelings are also involuntary. We are creatures of our sentiments, emotions, impulses, moods, transports. It is very difficult to voluntarily create feelings. Great actors do have this talent.

Most of our actions including physiological functions are also involuntary. But limbs like hands and legs are voluntary.

Most interesting is the breathing function. Normally, it is involuntary, but it can also be made voluntary. No wonder, the breathing function occupies the center stage for several meditation systems.

Cognition of the internal world -- the thought-spray is also an involuntary activity. But it can be made considerably voluntary, and this is the foundation of cognitive meditation.

Practice of cognitive meditation decreases the area of involuntariness and augments voluntariness. A meditator can or may not see or hear at will. He can at will generate special kinds of psychological states of stillness or movement. Normally, meditators do not get involved at the physiological level. But if they do so they can voluntarise the body more and more.

Biofeedback is an unrecognized form of meditation.

(60) Determinism - Bondage — Free will - Freedom.

Both sets of terms mean the same thing. One of them is used by philosophers and the other one by the spiritual. The terms 'involuntariness' and 'voluntariness', generally used by physiologists and psychologists, also mean the same. This shows that the same phenomenon occurs on physiological, psychological and spiritual levels. Few seem to realise this. But what most do not realise is that the basic phenomenon is non-self-awareness and self-awareness.

Stimulus and response and freedom from this mechanism also belongs to this category.

(63) Inertia/Generated movement

There is still one more pair belonging to the above category. If a thought chain starts, it will keep moving indefinitely, unless stopped by another thought chain. If a thought chain comes to a halt, it will continue to remain so till prodded to move by another thought chain. All this is the non-self aware, involuntary working of the non-I. In self-awareness, thoughts are moved or stilled by the I. Only the genetically gifted and the meditators experience this phenomenon.

(64) Effort/Effortlessness

Effort, in the sense of overcoming resistance, belongs to the world of non self-awareness. Under the rubric fragmentation and wholeness, we found that in non-self-awareness, a number of drives, some of them conflicting, are having a field day. If you want to concentrate on a book but are really more interested in the TV, a typical effort situation is precipitated. One has to make considerable effort to concentrate on the book. In a state of self-awareness and its equipoise, there is no such effort. In equipoise, there are no drives and no conflicts and no effort. In non-self-awareness also, there is a particular kind of effortlessness. This is when the subject studied is of great interest. This 'interest' is itself a very powerful drive, which easily rides roughshod over other drives. It is a case of one segment of non-self-awareness overpowering other segments of non-self-awareness. The term 'concentration' is frequently used for such a phenomenon. To maintain clarity of concepts, non-self-aware "concentration" should be termed 'interest' and the term concentration be retained for self-aware application.

(72) 'Imported' Peace/Self I-generated Peace

Man is supposed to want money the most. But after making money, what he wants most is peace and tranquility. Thus, the final pursuit of both, those who have no money and those who have made money, is peace and tranquility.

The demand for peace and tranquility is met in various ways. One is through chemical substance. Sedatives followed by tranquilisers. Sedatives provide peace and tranquility by putting one to sleep. Tranquilisers claim that they achieve the same result without simultaneously causing drowsiness. Whatever the claims of the pharmaceutical industry, tranquilisers do not tranquilise. They merely cause a temporary benumbing. One of the editions of Goodman andGilman's 'The Pharmacological Basis of Therapeutics', started the chapter on tranquilisers with the remark that they would not use the term 'tranquiliser'. Whatever the nomenclature, the fact is the tranquiliser market runs into billions of dollars.

Alcohol is another route to its own kind of peace and tranquility. Some claim that they soothe their excitement by smoking. That certain kinds of music can tranquilise is universal experience. Apart from conventional music, all kinds of nature sound tapes have appeared on the market. .

Sound's of waterfalls, sea waves, winds, exotic bells, gongs and unheard-of instruments contribute their mite.

Churches, temples, and other places of worship have their own peaceful atmosphere, particularly when there is no traffic. A solitary place on a river bank during sunset can induce extraordinary peace and tranquility. But perhaps the greatest source of peace and tranquility is the company of a genuinely spiritually advanced being. His mere proximity can tranquilise. However, there is one disturbing fact about these kinds of peace. Such peace is 'imported', being dependent upon absorbing some external factor. There is another kind of peace and tranquility — one generated by one's self. The most effective route to I/self-generated peace is meditation. Philosophers are fond of talking about maintaining tranquility in times of adversity. But, besides sermonizing, they have no contribution to make; only those who meditate, wherein the non-self-aware drives of fear and anxiety are attenuated by transmutation into self-awareness, genuinely and voluntarily acquire peace and tranquility. Self-awareness itself is self-generated and so the accompanying peace and tranquility.

(74) Destiny/Mastery of Circumstances

This is an extension of belief either in determinism or free will. For those believing in determinism, life obviously is completely subject to destiny. For those on the side of free will, life is something to be mastered. Much philosophy and poetry is devoted to both the themes.

As we have seen, we are partly determined and partly free, so also we are partly destined and partly masters of circumstances. This is obvious and commonsensical. What is essential to note is this: For those who meditate, not only does non-self-awareness wane and self-awareness wax, but simultaneously destiny, which is nothing else but the drive of non-self-awareness, diminishes and mastery of fate enhances. No amount of inspirational talk and positive thinking can really conquer fate. The self-aware, whose drives are attenuated or extinguished, are by definition free of fate. To conquer fate, one must conquer non-self-awareness, the source of all fate.

(75) Conventional Morality/Higher Morality

Have meditation and self-awareness anything to do with morality? Reading some modern treatises on meditation, one may conclude that there is a relation between the two.

The two great systems of meditation, Patanjali Yoga and Buddhist Vipassana, are intimately based on morality. The first two steps of the former are 'Yama' and 'Niyama' (abstentions and observances) and the first step in Vipassana is Shila (moral purity). I may anticipate here that any scheme in which morality precedes spiritual training may not be the right approach. I go one step further. Practice of morality at any stage, in the beginning or later, is an obstruction in the way of spiritual enterprise.

This attitude may disconcert some. But the fact is, all morality is based on suppression or repression. Neither of these are good for mental health.

And mental health is a condition precedent for undertaking the spiritual adventure. In some quarters, a strange view does prevail that only the odd, freakish, abnormal qualify for the spiritual. Nothing can be further from the truth. The eccentric are fit only for pseudo-spirituality

However, the fact stands that there is an intimate relationship between meditation, self-awareness, and the spiritual on the one hand, and morality on the other.

If it were really possible to practice the moralities laid down by Yoga and Vipassana, the latter would be redundant. The truth is, the moral cannot give birth to the spiritual, but it is the spiritual which is the source of the moral.

And morality which is generated by the spiritual is the higher morality, which is altogether different from conventional morality.

In the chapter dealing with drives, we came across what are conventionally called 'bad' and 'good' drives. Some examples of 'bad' drives are anger, hatred, aggression, exploitation, revenge and so on. Examples of 'good drives are love, sympathy, compassion, co-operation and so on.

It is these drives which make the conventional immorality or morality. These drives are genetic forces. Thus, man is born with certain bad and good moralities.

We have already seen that the cosmic evolution is an unfolding process. The 'bad' drives precede the 'good' drives and have already unfolded. The good drives are just unfolding. Thus, at the present stage, man appears to be predominantly 'evil' and minimally 'good'. The good drives which are just unfolding, much of them being still potential, are still to blossom. They are not in a position to meet the current requirements of smooth social organization. Hence; a need arises for producing 'acquired' 'good' drives in the growing individual. These are implanted in the child by the parents and constitute the Freudian superego. Incidentally, for Freud, natural or genetic man can only be bad, a view remarkably close to some Chastain thinkers. He does not believe in the natural, genetic or constitutional goodness of man. The only good that man knows is the superego morality implanted in the child by the parents and teachers. This is acquired goodness. The position held here is that as far as evil is concerned, it is wholly natural or genetic. But as far as good is concerned, particularly conventional good, man is a mixture of predominantly acquired goodness plus a modicum of natural goodness, still unfolding.

Further, acquired morality is relative. In one culture, marrying four wives would be in order while in another, it would be a sin.

The ethical philosopher being a philosopher will go on arguing about these issues till the end of time. It is not so for the meditator with his expanding self-awareness. For him, the situation changes dramatically. As we saw, conventional immorality and morality are drives or energies of non-self-awareness. As the meditator progresses the non-self awareness and its drives representing conventional immorality and morality become progressively attenuated. They are transmuted into self-awareness. And self-awareness being pure - consciousness is uncontaminated by drives and their respective moralities. To many, the meditator may appear amoral. But this is the birth of a new and higher morality. The higher morality is certainly not in conformity with the conventional one. The sources of both are different and opposite: that of conventional morality, the non-self-aware blind drive of the superego, and that of higher morality the self-aware, still pool of pure consciousness. This higher morality has no scripture, no rules, no format. It has no predictability and no respectability. It is a creative morality. It has no sense of guilt and self-punishment. If there is a perception of a failure, there is no self-denigration. Instead, there is an enhanced effort to raise self-awareness, which in turn generates the higher morality. Such morality has tolerance not only for others, but also for oneself. Compassion begins at home. If ever a formula can be forced upon higher morality, whatever is advancing self-awareness is moral. Self-awareness is the highest morality. Beyond self-awareness lies **THAT**, which is beyond immorality and morality, beyond lower and higher, a state not of immediate concern to us.

There is nothing relative about higher morality. It is a single-minded, unvarying pursuit of self-awareness, which is an absolute pursuit. If at all the higher morality is to be elaborated, it is wholeness, equipoise, power, freedom, transcendence, all synonymous with self-awareness.

Behind all that pious talk, much of conventional morality is a hidden agenda for petty worldly pursuits - acquiring respectability, social status, wealth. Without "correct" behaviour no status may be acquired in this world. More insidious is the concept of scriptural morality as an insurance against ill-health, misfortune, failure. Conventional morality is fear morality.

Discussion about conventional morality is not so academic as it might appear. Any person who has entered the world of meditation becomes more and more sensitive to these issues, which turn out to be of everyday occurrence.

However, a concrete, conscious application of an unconventional higher morality, rank immorality, in the eyes of the world does take place in the practice of Tantra. As already noted, the two great Aryan systems of meditation, Patanjali Yoga and Buddhist Vipassana, make conventional morality a precondition for the meditational practice. The solution of Tantra is unabashed and realistic. It divides the spiritual undertaking into three stages.

1) Pashvachar - the way of the pashu or the animal. Tantriks have a certain disdain for the conventional and the respectable. By 'pashu' or animal, they mean the 'square' in modern slang.
2) Virachar - the way of the hero. 'Vira' means hero - a spiritual athlete.
3) Divyachar - the illuminated, divine or spiritual way.

In the first stage, the tantra aspirant has to stabilise himself, in the conventional, social way With all its moral constraints. Obviously, tantra believes that moral constraint are required for the 'pashu' or the animal, or the square.

In the second stage, which is characteristic of tantra, there are various deviations from conventional morality. Members of orthodox society, who are vegetarians and teetotalers, have to partake of meat and alcohol in the prescribed way as part of the ritual. Sex also becomes a part of the ritual and depending upon the sub-cult, it is either with one's own wife or there is group sex, again as a part of the ritual. Tantra makes no distinction between higher and lower castes, all castes can become followers of tantra and are treated as equals in the ritual circle.

In the third stage, there is a resolution of the various animal and human tendencies, which are deliberately aroused, encountered and transmuted. This leads to self-realization and merger with the ultimate reality — the cosmic Mother.

What appears like free sex in Virachar — the second stage of the tantra system - is the cause of both notoriety and popularity of tantra in certain sections of Western society.

Tantra does allow, within closed and secret circles, practices which are conventionally immoral and appear like orgies. However, it is a highly ritually-controlled activity to deliberately quicken, loosen and raise to self-awareness, frozen, repressed lower tendencies. The usual encounter between the lower tendencies or drives takes place, with consequent transmutation into further self-awareness. This is the much misunderstood technique of tantra — "to make the very obstacle a stepping stone to spiritual success". (Mahanirvana Tantra 1953). For example, the obstacle of sex is overcome not by running away from it but by facing it and resolving it into the higher. It is like deliberately inviting temptation in order to overcome it. In a much diluted way this is happening all the time, in everyday life. Hence, the superiority of the householder's way, with its opportunities for challenges, over that of the monastic. Of course, there are black sheep everywhere and so in tantra. They indulge for the sake of indulgence. The Tibetan proverb sums up the situation in one sentence. "Some drink in order to perform the ceremony and some perform the ceremony in order to drink." Tantra consigns the latter to hell.

What appears to be promiscuous to the conventional is pre-spiritual to the tantric. The heroic way is not meant for the faint-hearted, squeamish or those subject to giddiness. It is a fast but dangerous way to reach the top of the hill, not by going in circles but by climbing vertically.

(82) Becoming / Being

This is a very important theme with philosophers. I am not concerned with their treatment of the subject. But as a meditator, I also come across the same theme.

Becoming is basically related to the cosmic evolutionary movement. This evolution starts with the physical (mineral) through the physiological (the 'plant'), the instinctual (the 'animal'), the psychological (the "primitive man"), the psycho-spiritual (the 'current man') to the spiritual, (the higher or "self-aware man").

From the physical to the psycho-spiritual (excluding the spiritual component), it is becoming. From the spiritual component of the psycho spiritual to the spiritual, it is Being. Loosely, one may call it 'spirit' or atman', though I would prefer to call it the 'higher self. Both 'spirit' and 'atman' have their own backgrounds and their own varying connotations.

(85) Time Timelessness

This evolutionary' process is a kind of 'uncoiling' or 'unwinding', from the physical onwards, the physical being the 'tightest' coil. This uncoiling produces an incessant movement, of one kind or another. Some have called it 'change' or 'flux'. As long as the evolutionary coil is not fully unwound, the incessant change or flux will continue. This change necessarily means succession of one event after another. This, succession of events gives rise to the experience of time.

When the stage of the spiritual is reached, the unwinding is exhausted and there is no more change for the particular individual. This is the experience of having arrived, of having reached the final 'Home'. There being no uncoiling, there is no more succession of events, no more passage or experience of time. The fully self-aware lives in the timeless. .

(86) Divine discontent / Peace that passeth understanding

Till the spiritual is reached one has to experience the unwinding of the energies of non-self-awareness. When they are discharged or expended, there is pleasure and when they are choked, there is pain.

But there is also a deeper, vague, unidentified pain. There is a constant sense of something wanting or something missing. But what is lacking cannot be identified. This is 'divine discontent'.

It is only when the uncoiling is exhausted, either by itself (over aeons) or in an accelerated way by meditation, that this pain gives way. Instead, one is left with the happiness of the 'peace which passeth all understanding'.

(88) Imperfection/Perfection

The 'products' of the cosmic evolutionary change are themselves constantly changing. They suffer from a built-in imperfection. This 'product' is being constantly 'improved' but never perfected. Something is always missing and something is always incomplete. It is only when the spiritual is reached, the 'product' becomes perfected. It is perfection in which no further improvement is required or even possible. Nothing is missing and nothing is wanting. Being is completeness and perfection.

(90) Stagnance / Transcendence

Like Becoming and Being, philosophers, particularly the existentialists, are fond of 'transcendence'. For the meditator, it is not something to be discussed but to be experienced.

Come to think of it, Being is itself a transcendence. Both the themes, Becoming / Being and Stagnance/Transcendence are the same. All the allotropes of non-self-awareness mean the same and so also all the allotropes of self-awareness. In fact, they are synonyms of non-self-awareness and self-awareness. Only time, geography and culture, create varying presentations. And each presentation develops its own language: The more one uses such languages, the more one converges on the basic understanding. The different allotropes are only different languages, the root language having only two words - non-self-awareness and self-awareness. Stagnance is ever getting off and never arriving. Endless progressing, regressing progressing..... . Moving, moving and remaining rooted to the same spot.

The frenetic, universal, merry-go-round, from which one cannot jump off. It is waking -- eating --working -- eating -- sleeping — waking ... It is being born -- growing --dying -- being born again..... . It is the cosmic repetition-compulsion of which the Freudian repetition-compulsion is a tiny holographic fragment.

Transcendence is a complete break. A new being, a new way, a new life.

It is the diametric opposite of stagnance.

Transcendence is going beyond the physical, the physiological, the instinctual, the psychological, and arriving at the spiritual. Transcendence is the other bank of the river of manifestation. On the one bank are non-self-awareness and its blindness, impurity, impotence, fragmentation, chaos, tension and discharge, pain and pleasure, stress and psychosomatic disease, drivenness, bondage and so on. On the other bank are self-awareness and its insight, purity, power, wholeness, equipoise, psychosomatic health, freedom, understanding, meaning, realization and so on.

In this river, waters flow from one bank to another. What is non-self-awareness on the Bank is dissolved in the waters only to re-crystallise on the other bank as self-awareness. The same stagnance reappears as transcendence. Something dies, and out of it, something is born. The dung into the rose. The spiritual alchemy. The cosmic transmutation. Transcendence is the ultimate creative art.

Transcendence is immortality, which is utterly different from mere survival after death. Death is only a variation on life. Death is a renewal of life by other means. Life and death are just two alternating phases of mortality. Everyone automatically survives, everyone does not automatically become immortal. Immortality is going beyond birth, life, death, rebirth...

Both the non-I and the I, stagnance and transcendence dissolve into **THAT**, from where they first sprang. The journey and its consequence, the return journey are completed. Noise and silence, both subside into **THAT** - single, dual, multiple, zero, nothing, everything. Only a meditator can undertake this ultimate experiment -- stagnance into transcendence and beyond both.

CHAPTER XII

COGNITIVE MEDITATION

We have come to the end of theoretical considerations. I have dealt with Cognitive Meditation in various chapters. A second look is called for.

Meditation, as such, seems to have been born in what is now geographically Pakistan (Mohenjodaro), earlier a part of undivided India. This activity is at least 5000 years old. It could be older. What is certain is it grew and flourished in practically the whole of India. The activity reached a peak in the Upanishadic times 8th to 7th Century B.C. There was another wave of meditation generated by Buddhism in 5thCentury B.C. In the course of time, this activity declined. By the end of the 19thCentury, it was more of history than live widespread practice.

If meditation was born in India, it experienced a revival in America beginning in the last decade of the 19th century and spreading over the 20th century. The moving figure was of course Vivekananda the great Indian spiritual teacher. The meditation movement seems to have meshed in with the human growth movement, another typical American activity. It became the subject of academic psychological research. It also became a tool of psychotherapy. Ultimately, in true American style, it became, in some cases, a part of the personal developmental programme of the business executive. It even acquired brand names.

Most meditation systems start abruptly and plunge immediately into their narrow religious or philosophical pursuits. There is no attempt to create a theoretical infrastructure.

Knowing full well that modem science is materialistic, if not fully mechanistic, and that meditation goes beyond crass materialism, I have tried to retain the scientific flavour to the extent possible. My outlook has been evolutionary, even fully accepting Darwinian evolutionary mechanisms as a phase of a larger cosmic evolution. I have accepted the universe, the world, yourself and myself as real. For me, the Universe starts as matter, which in course of time will evolve into spirit. Matter and spirit are not in conflict with each other. Rather, they are differing expressions of a common underlying Reality.

The progress from matter to spirit is not continuous but punctuated with sudden leaps. As this leap is into an opposite and higher state, I have called it a dialectical leap. Because of the nature of dialectic leaps, the starting point (matter) and end point (spirit) are of contrary structures and dynamics. Meditation is a method of producing conscious and planned dialectical leaps.

The tendency to change and 'improve' was ingrained in the very first blob of matter. It has continued till today through billions of years, reincarnating as an urge to move towards something higher. This urge has spawned innumerable cults, religions, philosophies and practices. Meditation is one such practice. It has to compete with many other practices and ideologies. Today, it may be difficult for some to choose between them. But in the next fifty to hundred years, there would be enough data to decide upon the most suitable route to 'self-improvement'. Knowing the other systems, I have no doubt that meditation will score the highest. Not only that, it will also throw bright light on the issue of what is 'self-improvement' and where it will lead.

As for Cognitive Meditation, I have already mentioned earlier that meditations are of three types --- suppressive, expressive and cognitive. The last one is based on the I interacting with the non-I, i.e. thoughts, impulses, desires, cravings, etc. It is a specific interaction based on observation (by the I of the non-I), cognition, comprehension, insight, realisation, leading to transmutation by a dialectical leap into the opposite and higher stage.

I believe cognitive meditation is the only genuine meditation, If other meditations do produce results, it is due to the unavoidable admixture of the cognitive factor, along with suppression or expression.

When I talk of meditation, I mean only cognitive meditation, unless specifically meant otherwise.

I am extremely intrigued by the role observation is supposed to play in quantum physics. I get an impression that the mere act of observation modifies reality at the subatomic level. The full implications of this are not clear to me. But I do know, from the daily experience of cognitive meditation, that observation by the I of the non-I, that is the thought-spray, not only modifies the latter but transmutes it into the opposite and the higher. This means that the I transmutes the non-I into the I.

I keep wondering whether there is any relationship between the observation phenomena of meditation and quantum worlds. Some day I, hope to hear from a quantum physicist, preferably one who is practicing cognitive meditation.

Meditation is a way of life, demanding devotion and time. The current culture is not exactly friendly to meditation. I am looking forward to a more meditation-friendly ambience with liberalised working and leisure hours. To devote the morning hours, the best hours of the day, to livelihood rather than to a higher life is, to say the least, uncivilised.

I have called meditation the ultimate experiment. In all other experiments, the experimenter and the experimented are different entities. It is only in cognitive meditation that the experimenter and the experimented belong to the same human unit --- its I and the non-I.

Barring the spirit, the thought-spray is the ultimate manifestation of the universe. And any experiment concerning it is obviously ultimate.

But cognitive meditation is also, an adventure — an ultimate adventure. Having explored the moon, the urge to explore the within will turn up one day. And if one can completely explore the within, nothing will remain to explore further. This is because the within is the end product of the entire universe.

All meditations seem to be associated with some religious symbol or the other. God, saints, godmen….. This can surely put off the liberated and the serious, amongst the moderns. But their plight could be tragic. It is one thing to abandon religion and another to fill the vacuum so created. They can take to the arts, sciences and other intellectual pursuits. But they really cannot fill the void caused by the disappearance of religion. I would like to bring to the attention of those so deprived, that this void can best be filled by another element called the spiritual. Religion is frequently confused with the spiritual. The truth is, it is something altogether different. The spiritual is the pursuit of the higher self and its way of life, which is described as the dynamics of self-awareness. The development of the spiritual is the function of cognitive meditation. This meditation is secular, non-religious, non-cultic, non-sectarian, humanistic. It is concerned with human categories like the body, mind and the I and the underlying Reality from which they spring.

Every human carries within him the Spiritual and the non-Spiritual. The I and the non-I — the world of thoughts, impulses and desires. The 'experience of the spiritual can be brought about in two ways. The heightening of self-awareness or diminishing of non-self-awareness, i.e.

by the calming of thoughts and desires. The latter is frequently attempted by extraneous means like soothing music, silent spots, river banks in the evening, temples and churches, or in the company of the spiritually realised, in ceremonies and so on. It is obvious that tranquilities so attained are 'imported'. The moment the extraneous aid is absent, turbulence returns. This is not the strategy of cognitive meditation. Its aim is self-generated tranquility, altogether independent of any extraneous aid. It is not the temporary benumbing of the non-self-aware by outside agencies but its transmutation into the self-aware, whose very nature is tranquility in good times and bad. Only cognitive meditation can self-generate the spiritual and its allotropes like tranquility, etc.

I have not touched on the issue of diet. I am a vegetarian, not because of the health benefits (now well-established) but on grounds of consideration for the animal kingdom. The Buddha is called the compassionate. But facts seem to indicate otherwise. He refused to promote a vegetarian diet. Twice the proposal was made in this connection and twice it was rejected by him. The teaching of Buddha's contemporary Mahaveer, the promulgator of Jainism, was altogether different. The concept of non-violence was extended beyond man to the animal kingdom also and that too without any sophistry whatsoever. If anyone is to be called the compassionate, it is Mahaveer.

I want to touch upon a different issue - allergy. Cognitive meditation requires a highly alert and penetrating I, to observe and cognise non-I, i.e. the thought-spray. Different individuals are affected by different foods. Some of them can cause dulling of the mind and can slow down the process of cognitive meditation. In a specialised area of ESP, I have developed a technique, which I call 'feldonics' ('feld' being an archaic term for 'field'), which is a sophisticated version of dowsing with a pendulum. This technique helps in identifying allergy causing foods and substances. Such identification has helped me in sharpening the process of meditation, apart from other benefits.

Classical meditations are associated with partial or complete withdrawal from an active life. The case with cognitive meditation is reverse. It invites an active life. Such a life may also lead to exposure to various kinds of temptations. Such exposure is also welcome to cognitive meditation. The idea is an active life generates a rich, thick, challenging thought-spray. Developing a capacity to cope with and transmute such a lively thought-spray quickens the creation of higher self. The only precaution is not to cross the limits and provoke a thought-spray whose turbulence could be unmanageable.

In this presentation, an attempt has been made to develop a theoretical structure which explains the various phenomena connected with cognitive meditation. Such theoretical structures are generally missing in other systems of meditation. If you find the theoretical structure unconventional, no less would be the practical technique which is related to it. This situation is the response of timeless insight to the specific requirements of today. If some body feels that I have modernised the technique, he is right.

I make a claim that may appear extraordinary that cognitive meditation can enhance intelligence. As usual, intelligence could be partly genetic and partly cultural. It could also be a unitary factor or a conglomerate of several factors. Whatever it is, one of its characteristics is indisputable: that intelligence can be clouded by emotional forces. The various drives, partialities and prejudices, likes and dislikes, wanting and not wanting, can cloud intelligence and play havoc with it. What cognitive meditation can do is to dissolve the emotional clouding and thus liberate intelligence.

Before I wind up the theoretical discussion, let us have a last look at the objectives of meditation.

Two legitimate candidates present themselves immediately — worldly success and spiritual success.

Even though the concept of meditation is making waves these days, it has practically no relevance today for worldly success. In fact, for the worldly successful, any talk of meditation could just be an incongruity.

Worldly success appears to be congenital and does not seem to have any use for meditation. That is, till the consequences of worldly success come to the surface. No one can escape the heavy price that worldly success exacts. The physiological disorders associated with stress are too well known to need recapitulation.

But the psychological disorganisation that stress can cause, even though subtle, is much more damaging. Man can lose direction, balance and more importantly values. Superficiality gradually takes over. Family life can be torn apart. Bizzare goals can take over. Cravings can multiply manifold. Addictions find a ready soil. In trying to develop business, one gets undermined. Business sucks up the businessman. The abnormal becomes the normal. The joy of success is short-lived and is displaced by a mysterious and chronic discontent. Something was always missing and is still missing.

I would prescribe medication to all those suffering from worldly success.

The deep and the sensitive amongst the successful will ultimately turn to the spiritual. Paradoxically, the route to worldly success and spiritual success is the same — self-awareness. In the latter case, it is more advanced.

On the path of self-awareness there are three equipoises or silences. In the case of a business undertaking cultivation of the first equipoise --- that of the thought-spray is enough. In the case of a spiritual enterprise, cultivation of the second equipoise, that of the preconscious is essential. (And there is the third equipoise --- that of the unconscious where the seeds of the drives, hibernate, which would call for several lifetimes and which would grant final liberation). However, if somebody concludes that worldly or spiritual success is the be all and end all of meditation, he is likely to be mistaken.

Meditation eventually leads one to transcendence and beyond that anything can happen One can only speculate or fantasise. Some are stuck in the lower selves and some, after great effort, find themselves perching in the higher self. The one in the lower self is reluctant to rise, and the one perching in the higher, disdains the lower. But the one who has transcended is beyond the lower and the higher. He is at ease at both the levels and can commute between them effortlessly. He is stuck nowhere and can be anywhere. The depth, the width and the height are his. He can roam through all existence. He becomes a god. And when he finds even this inadequate, he leaps into **THAT**, where our story begins and ends.

PRACTICE

'If I do not practice for one day (Piano), I notice it.
If I do not practice for two days, my wife notices it.
If I do not practice for three days, the public notices it.'
- I. Paderewski

'A theorist without practice is a tree without fruit'
(Gulistan by Sheikh Sa'di)

'Practice is nine tenths of perfection'
(Emerson)

'Practice makes perfect'
(Latin Proverb)

'Pick battles big enough to matter, small enough to win'
(J. Kozal)

CHAPTER XIII

INTRODUCTORY REMARKS

The final objective of theory is to lead to practice. The following are the themes of this chapter.

- Two Meditations.
- Two Divisions of the Main Meditations.
  a. Peripherals
  b. Main Meditation
- Obstacles
- Rationale
- Some differences between Cognitive Meditation and other Meditations
- Second Meditation.

The process of meditation can only start at the level of the psycho-spiritual self. And that, too, only by its self-aware components, i.e. the current I. Henceforth, in this chapter, I shall refer to the current I simply as I, to sound less pedantic.

When I look at the human unit, I am deeply grateful to nature. A major portion of the cosmic evolution, from the physical to the psycho –spiritual has already taken place through natural, non-self-aware forces. The job of building just one more self, the spiritual Self, is left to us. The blind, non-self-aware, bound forces cannot help us anymore. Only the partially self-aware I has to choose and decide on the spiritual enterprise.

I would conclude the above remarks by observing that those who denigrate the I and are constantly looking for outside intervention, generally 'divine', are making a great mistake. Even those who believe in God should know that God helps those who help themselves.

Two Meditations

After having developed the main meditation theory, which has been dealt with above, I have also developed another meditation, which I call the second meditation.

The second meditation being of recent origin, it has not been possible to develop a theory about it. Therefore, it is being included directly in this chapter on practice.

The main meditation works on the psychological level, while the second one works on the physiological level. The first is based on the cognition of the psychological — comprising the thought-spray, the preconscious, and the unconscious. The second meditation is based on the cognition of the flow of breath. In this meditation, first the frontal lobes of the brain are equipoised and then the entire body (to the extent possible). This meditation, because it is based on the cognition of the breathing, is deceptively similar to the Buddhist Vipassana (related to breathing technique) and likely to be mistaken for one. But the overall process and the objectives are quite different.

Two Divisions of the Main Meditation

Now, we come to the practice of the main meditation. It is divided into two divisions -- Peripherals and the Main Meditation.

Peripherals

Peripherals consist of Place, Time, Posture, Duration, Regularity, and Lifestyle. These are described below.

Place

An independent room .undisturbed by others. It should be neither bright nor dark, but pleasantly dim. It should be neither noisy nor silent. Similarly, neither hot nor cold.

Time

A very important peripheral. Obviously, morning time, with a fresh mind, is the best time. Nothing is to be eaten before the morning meditation. A cup of tea may do. I am not sure about coffee, excepting for those who routinely take it.

As far as possible, every day, it should be the same time to the extent possible.

To come back to the 'fresh mind'.. A person who has forced himself to get up, by an alarm, by definition cannot have a fresh mind. Such a mind would be able to attend to routine chores like office, technical or professional work but it does not mean it is fresh enough for meditation. In principle, when one gets up naturally, without any outside aid, there is a good possibility of having a really fresh mind, good enough for meditation. Any heaviness in the head will seriously obstruct the meditative process. If one's circumstances do not permit time in the morning, then the only possibility is evening. In such a case, there should be no solid intake for one hour before meditation time. Also, evening meditation must be preceded by at least a twenty minute rest in bed in a dim room followed by a bath.

It is a paradox that good, healthy, natural sleep is essential to awaken spiritually. Those who preach forced reduction of sleep do not know what they are talking. A society which does not provide for and accommodate the highest activity man is capable of— meditation, is not civilised, whatever its trappings.

There is another dimension to the theme of time. It is widely believed that meditation is to be carried out at a particular time of the day. This may be so in the beginning. But there, will be a state when meditation will project beyond the set time. After all, cognitive meditation means an encounter of the I with the thought-spray and the consequent transmutation. This activity can go on even beyond the set meditation period. In fact, throughout the day. Thus, there will be a set period for producing advanced stages, and the rest of the day for routine transmutations.

Meditation, itself the liberator, cannot be time-bound.

Posture

A lot of misunderstanding prevails about posture. It is not possible for everyone to adopt the Buddha posture (padmasana). Nor is it necessary.

One can sit on a chair, with a pillow, below and behind, to ensure a straight back and a comfortable pose. In case you don't know, there are meditative postures, in which one lies down or stands upright. Even Patanjali recommends a posture, which is stable, easy and comfortable (Woods, 1927).

Posture should be such that it can be sustained for an hour or more, and which enables one to forget the body while meditation is in progress.

For the western aspirant, sitting on a chair, with pillows below and behind, is the most sensible posture. It is particularly suitable for those suffering from muscular stiffness or painful joints. One should sit with a straight back like a Pharoah, but with the right palm over the left palm (unlike the Pharoah, who keeps his palms on the knees).

The eyes deserve some attention. Should they be kept open or closed? Each position has its own advantages and disadvantages. This issue will be discussed under the section on Rationale.

Duration

A person can start meditating for a duration of 20 to 30 minutes. But once he picks up the basic skills of encountering thoughts, transmuting them and reaching equipoise, he can extend the duration.

As we shall see later, meditation has a daily goal apart from the long- term goals. The daily goal is to reach a state of equipoise during the particular meditative session. Equipoise means effortless stillness. But reaching equipoise will depend upon the turmoil index on the particular day. If the mind is too agitated or stimulated, it will naturally take longer to reach the equipoise, if at all. Eventually, with daily practice and with correct technique, it should be possible in about 15 minutes.

Regularity

As far as possible, meditation should be a daily exercise without any breaks. I said 'as far as possible' because modern industrial society has no respect for the individual's private time requirements.

In fact, one must be regular in all respects. Same place, same time, same posture, same duration (with provision for extension). Such regularity will accelerate progress.

The steps recommended above relating to regularity will have a conditioning effect. I don't mind accepting this, even though conditioning is a non-self-aware process. This means taking help of non-self-awareness to advance self-awareness. I leave it to you, whether to call it a strategy or a compromise. One step backwards, to advance two steps forward. Needless to say, as one gets more and more stabilised, the need for such conditioning measures will lessen.

Lifestyle

There is a general belief that taking to meditation means taking to a new kind of life. A life full of restraint and regulations, some kind of a suppressive programme.

I would like to emphasise that no drastic change has to be made in one's lifestyle when one starts meditation. The only changes you need to make are to ensure a fresh mind in the morning and providing some time for meditation. This does not apply to life or mind-threatening situations. If someone is suffering from addictions, he must immediately undergo counseling/therapy even if they are of a suppressive nature. Such remedial action is more important than even meditation. To reach the super-normal, one has to start from the normal. One cannot start from the subnormal. In the case of the subnormal, it is only after reaching the normal by therapy that one can start meditation.

This does not apply to light or harmless addictions. They may not be tampered with. They will drop away by themselves when one advances in meditation.

The idea should be to deal with all kinds of abuse through self-awareness only and not through suppression. For those who practice cognitive meditation, the principle is 'To give up nothing. Everything falls away by itself'.

Having finished with the themes of peripherals, we now come to the main meditation.

The Main Meditation

The technique of the main meditation is perhaps the most important section of the book. Whenever possible, I shall try to cross-link a particular aspect of the technique with the theory chapters. Also, my endeavour is to make the reader as autonomous and as independent of me as possible.

In the interest of smooth communication, I shall describe the process, point-wise.

These directions may sound complicated, but in actual practice are easy to follow.

1. The most important input one can bring to the main meditation session is a fresh mind, free from all heaviness and fatigue in the head.

2. As far as possible, the main meditation session should be in the morning, on an empty stomach (except for tea / coffee if unavoidable). The room should be exclusive without disturbance. However, low disturbance is not only permissible but also desirable. Garments should be loose and minimal.

3. The next step is to take the posture and decide whether the eyes are to be kept open or closed. From practice, it is seen that it is better to close the eyes.

4. Now turn the attention inwards and allow the thoughts to run, without any restraint whatsoever. One must, to the extent possible, let go all possible control over the running of the thoughts.

    One has to learn to be non-judgmental towards one's thoughts. No shrinking from a thought, however unpleasant, painful, immoral, dirty, 'sinful' or unacceptable. All the mud and the sludge should be allowed to rise to the surface. This is painful but the only route to self-knowledge, self-awareness and transmutation.

    It must be kept in mind that not only is 'bad' thought to be transmuted but 'good' ones also. The spiritual is certainly not a refinement of the 'good'. Good thoughts are as much non-spiritual as the bad ones. The non-spiritual aspect is not 'bad' or 'good' but thought itself, of any kind.

    The spiritualised consciousness is freed of all thoughts, both bad and good. What is left is only the awareness of I-hood or self-awareness.

5. Once the thoughts come up, the I should attempt to observe/cognise them.

    Since the thoughts belong to the psychological self, they have no I-hood. So, it means that the I is observing/perceiving the non-I.

    This can be framed in a different language. The I equals the spiritual or the self-aware, and the non-I (the thought) equals the psychological (non-spiritual) or non-self-aware. Therefore, the encounter between the I and the non-I is the same as an encounter between the spiritual and the non-spiritual or between the self-aware and the non-self-aware.

In terms of significance, the encounter is as important as the big bang. The big bang meant the birth of the universe, and the encounter that of the higher self.

When such an encounter between the I and the non-I takes place, two results can follow. If the I is stronger, the non-I will be transmuted. If the non-I is stronger, the I will be drowned.

Most of the thoughts running during the meditation session are unimportant, insignificant, inconsequential trifling. They being weaker, the I should be able to transmute them. Transmutation means the thought (the non-I) would take a dialectical leap and get absorbed into the I. (Chapter VIII).

Every time this happens, the non-I decreases and the I increases. Or the spiritual and self-aware increase and the non-spiritual (psychological) and the non-self-aware decrease. This is the main objective of cognitive meditation. Basically, it is achieved by working on thoughts weaker than the I.

Of course, every time it is not going to be a story of positive transmutation. When the thought is not inconsequential, or in case the emotion is stronger than the I, there will be a negative transmutation. The I will get drowned / lost (for the time being) by being flooded by the non-I, i.e. by thoughts, emotions, desires. But since the occasion for positive transmutations are greater, the I will become stronger and in time will be able to take care of stronger emotions. After suitable practice, the I will be able to transmute strong emotions too. If one puts in regular meditation, he will consciously experience these changes.

Before proceeding further, I would like to draw your attention to a special property of the encounter between the I and the non-I.

By thought and similar structures, I do not mean something vague, airy, insubstantial, notional. It is a psychological entity which is 'solid' and palpable, with real existence of its own. When the I encounters a thought, it is as concrete as Mr. A encountering Mr. B.

When the I turns its attention inwards, it finds that the inner space is populated by other independent entities, popularly called thoughts, impulses, drives, desires, cravings.

In order that cognition takes place, it is essential that there is a separation between the I and the non-I. Better the separation, better the cognition. And better the cognition, better the transmutation.

If you do not find thoughts as concrete, live, throbbing entities, it means the cognition by the I is inadequate. But it can be improved by constant daily practice, leading to better and better transmutation.

It is time to draw your attention to a special precaution. During the meditation session, there are bound to be disturbances. And you cannot close your ears as you can close your eyes. Hence, there will be a natural reaction to ward off the disturbance. This would be fatal. The more you try to ward it off, the more you are attending to it. The law of reverse effort (Chapter VIII). The only way you can get rid of a disturbance is to ignore it or suffer it passively. All you have to do is to continue to observe the thoughts, may be less efficiently, because of the disturbance. If you happen to remain busy observing your thoughts, the disturbance will cease disturbing you. Similarly, if you feel like scratching, you should do so and forget it.

6. Perceiving the thought-spray continuously is not going to be easy. As there are external disturbances, which I dealt with above, there are internal ones also. These are (1) wandering of the mind and (2) sleep. Both are derivatives of non-self-awareness.

After much trial and error, I have developed the technique of 'rounds'. It not only deals with mind-wandering and sleep, but also accelerates the process of transmutation and the consequent early development of the higher self.

7. The 'round' consists of questions to ask yourself.

Keeping the attention about eighteen inches in front of the eyes, you ask yourself "What is coming up now?" Repeat the question keeping attention about eighteen inches from the right ear (or the left ear, if it is more comfortable that way), then again for the third time about eighteen inches from the back of the head at the level of the eye. It is once again repeated by shifting attention about eighteen inches from the left ear. Thus, the same question is asked four times in a clockwise fashion (or anti-clockwise, if it so suits you). Then a fifth and final new question is asked in the region of the head 'What has come up now?'

As a result of your consistent questioning, symbolically from all the four directions, and in answer to the fifth question, a response will arise from the depths of the preconscious, in the form of a thought, impulse, desire, emotion, etc. More likely, such a response will come just when you are going through the drill of asking the four questions without waiting for the fifth one. It is such thought, impulse, desire and emotion, which is to be subjected to observation or cognition by the I. Transmutation brought about in the following way is called 'analysis'.

We saw that cognition of the non-I has improved by experiencing its independent live existence. But a still more powerful technique of improving cognition is by verbalising. When a thought surfaces, either while doing the rounds or after finishing the four rounds and asking the fifth question, the I should repeat the thought by verbalising it. This sets the stage for the final step of 'analysis'.

8. Mere cognition of a thought, even after verbalising, is not enough to properly transmute it. It has also to be 'analysed'.

When a thought rises from the preconscious to the surface, it does so because of a propellant. If a thought, remembering a person, rises to the surface, it is because you either love or hate that person. Such love or hate is the propellant. So, when the thought of the remembrance of a person comes up, you should identify the propellant. This is called analysis. The moment cognition of a thought is followed by the identification of the propellant, the thought ceases, on being transmuted by a dialectical leap into the I (i.e. the Spiritual or the Self-aware). The objective should be that every round is followed by a transmutation. And once a transmutation happens, another round is carried out. Thus the process of meditation consists of carrying out round after rounds till equipoise is reached.

In the world of meditation, the involuntary darting movements of thoughts and feelings across inner space are rightly considered to be disturbances. All schools of meditation have as their objective the stilling of this disturbance (to what extent they are really successful is another matter).

In cognitive meditation too, stilling of the disturbance is the immediate objective. (The final objective being establishment of the higher self). I have used the term equipoise for such effortless, dynamic stillness.

Between the starting point of meditation and equipoise at the end, there is a very interesting disturbance pattern. This period can be divided into three parts. The first part is rather dull. There could even be a blank (see below the section on 'obstacles'). The second part gradually warms up and becomes lively, brisk and turbulent. Then, as meditation proceeds and transmutations occur, the inner space starts cooling down and the third period sets in. A great calm starts supervening, finally ending in the equipoise. If the intensities of disturbance could be plotted, it would make a nice bell curve.

The moral is one should not be unduly euphoric during the first period, nor discouraged in the second period, if one patiently persists, some day the new meditator will arrive at the equipoise.

9. What is this equipoise? If you watch carefully, you will find that when a particular thought is transmuted, the event is followed by an effortless stillness or 'void' in which one is fully awake, with nothing else but a sense of I-hood. In one word, by a state of self-awareness uncontaminated by any thought. This state of self-aware, effortless stillness, void or equilibrium, is termed the equipoise. It is a pool of energy in a state of equilibrated, effortless stillness. In spite of the state being full of equilibrated energy, it is also called the void, because it is devoid of all thoughts, impulses, drives, desires, passions, wanting, not wanting. It is pure, colourless consciousness. It is a state of great felicity, peace, tranquility, bliss and above all of voluntary power.

The state of equipoise is an allotrope of self-awareness. When it is reached, several other allotropes are also simultaneously reached, being other facets of self-awareness (Chapter X). But equipoise is a striking and easily identifiable state and therefore, acts as a spiritual marker of having arrived at a particular stage in meditation.

That meditation is successful which ends on the note of equipoise.

10. It is during meditation that one realises the extraordinary difference between the non-I and the I.

The non-I is many and variously 'coloured' and when transmuted into the I, it becomes one and 'colourless'.

The psychological is many since it comprises innumerable and many kinds of impulses, thoughts, drives, desires, passions, etc. it is heterogeneous. On transmutation into the I, these heterogeneous energies of the psychological (or the non-I) become the homogenous energy of the Spiritual (or the I). The many become one.

Similarly, each entity of the non-I is 'coloured'. But the I is 'colourless'. When the I is flooded or suffused with hate, it takes on the 'colour' of hate. And when it is flooded by love, it takes on the 'colour' of love. A glass of water has no colour. When red is added, it becomes red and when blue is added, it becomes blue. Like the colourless water, the I is also basically colourless. However, it can take on any colour, or opposite colours. The same I can become hateful or loving. The I itself is neither hate nor love. As mentioned above, just colourless.

Thus, when hate, love, cruelty, compassion, greed, charity, the good and the evil are transmuted, they all become 'colourless'. The specific energies of the non-I, i.e. the psychological, the non-spiritual, the non-self-aware, become the non-specific energy of the I, i.e. of the Spiritual or the self- aware. The coloured becomes the colourless.

The non-self-aware drive energy is always coiled and compressed, and therefore tense, trying to unwind and uncoil. The self-aware energy of the I is completely unwound and uncoiled and therefore in a state of equipoise, in equilibrium at all points.

Equipoise is an aspect of self-awareness, it is a pool of one, non-differentiated, non-specific, equilibrated, colourless energy.

Just as a prism transmutes many lights of different colours into one and colourless light, self-awareness also transmutes the entire spectrum of many and variously 'coloured' energies of non-self-awareness into one and colourless energy of self-awareness. I have called this the prism effect (Chapter VIII).

The profound experience of the equipoise, which is peace, tranquility, composure, happiness, summarised in one word 'bliss', is the consequence of the equipoise being one, colourless, and equilibrated. No wonder, once the meditator tastes equipoise, it becomes the objective of every meditation session.

11. There are three kinds of equipoise: that attained by the transmutation of a single thought, by the transmutation of several preconscious thoughts, during a particular session, and finally by

the transmutation of the unconscious. The first two are attainable in one life and must be the objective of every meditator.

However, the equipoise of the unconscious, with all its instincts and drives, is a long drawn affair, spread over several lifetimes. For us, it can only be a speculative objective. But when it is achieved, self-awareness will bloom in all its petals — purity, power, higher, morality, being and transcendence. And when transcendence is complete, not only is there full liberation on this earth, but also the readiness any moment to leap back into **THAT**.

12. The reader might have found the above instructions complicated and difficult to follow. Particularly so, if he is a newcomer to meditation. The summary which follows should considerably ease the overall understanding of the technique. The process will become still easier when practiced.

Summary of the Main Meditation Technique

i. Bring a fresh mind to the meditation session.

ii. As far as possible, attempt it in the morning (the other option being evening). Empty stomach. At the most a cup of tea or coffee. Exclusive room without disturbance. (Some background disturbance desirable). Room not too bright, not too dim.

iii. Take a posture, with eyes open or closed. (If in doubt, keep the eyes closed).

iv. Turn attention inwards. Allow the thoughts to run, without any constraint whatsoever.

v. Start observing the thoughts.

vi. In case any external disturbance starts distracting, ignore it. Do not fight it. Continue with the observation practice.

vii. Carry out the observation of the thought-spray, through the technique of 'rounds'. This will minimise mind-wandering and the tendency to slide into sleep.

viii. Whatever thought comes in focus, at the end of each 'round' try to verbalise it.

ix. Achieve the transmutation of the thought which has come into focus after a particular round
   a. by observing and verbalising it.
   b. by indentifying the propellant which moves the thought to the surface.

When these two steps are carried out, transmutation will take place of the single thought and mini-equipoise will develop.

x. During any particular meditation session, a limited number of thoughts are activated in the preconscious for one reason or another. (Other thoughts remain dormant).

At the end of each 'round', a particular thought will be transmuted. In the next round, another thought will be transmuted. In still another 'round', another thought will be transmuted. Someday, in one session, after due patience, all the activated thoughts of the particular session will be transmuted. When this happens, an equipoise of the session will supervene.

After developing a certain proficiency in the technique, attaining equipoise should be the objective of the daily meditation.

xi. When the establishment of the equipoise becomes a frequent, if not a daily affair, someday, self-awareness of which equipoise is made will reach a critical mass and the birth of the higher self will take place.

In the course of time, the higher self will also continue to become more and more stable. (Please be under no illusion that a full-fledged higher self will be developed in one lifetime).

Yet, even in one lifetime, tremendous strides can be taken. The extended, deepened and heightened self-awareness will bring a new life to you and your family, and your professional and social life will enormously improve. Enrichment and empowerment are the rewards.

I will not be surprised if the above technique seems complicated to you. Compared to other systems, it might be so to a certain extent. I am concerned with the efficiency of the technique and the time frame, within which results can be obtained. I am not allowing you to confuse suppression for genuine peace, equanimity and equipoise. I want you to face the inner challenge and come through with a permanent solution. Not of overcoming the lower self but of transmuting it into the higher self and its superior dynamics.

Obstacles

In the previous section, if I have given an impression that meditation is a mechanical process in which certain buttons are to be pressed and the equipoise reached, far from it. It is a dynamic process, highly sensitive to the external and internal forces.

There are two kinds of obstacles. General and Specific. The former are already dealt with in Chapter I. Obstacles specifically related to the meditation process are considered here.

1. Mind-wandering
2. Inability to attend to the inner world.
3. Sleep
4. Blank
5. Aggravation.

These are dealt with below.

Mind-wandering

A notorious obstacle. The main reason is the predominance of non-self-awareness, i.e. the untamed thoughts and feelings accustomed to freely roam in the inner space. Also a tired I. The solution is not 'fixation on a point'. This is never going to succeed, since the root cause — non-self-awareness remains untackled. It is only when some progress is made in transmutation, when self-awareness is enhanced and non-self-awareness decreased, that mind-wandering will be reduced. A fresh mind at the time of meditation would be an added help. The technique of 'rounds' also checks mind-wandering by breaking it and returning the I to observation of the thought-spray.

Inability to attend to the Inner World

This is due to a tired I. It is also due to extroversion. This does not mean that introverts make good mediators. Both extroversion and introversion are non-self-aware, compulsive states, unfavorable to meditation. The inward gaze in meditation is a free and voluntary activity. A trained meditator is neither an extrovert nor an introvert. He can direct his gaze outward or inward as per his choice.

Here too one has to wait until sufficient self-awareness is built up. It will attenuate the extroversion/introversion mechanisms.

Sleep

This is another notorious obstacle to meditation. Apart from a tired I, the very process of inwarding is conducive to sleep. This is one of the reasons for developing the technique of 'rounds' described above.

Blank

This is the opposite extreme of mind-wandering and equally common. In a blank, no thoughts arise and therefore nothing is present to be observed. This defeats the main technique of cognitive meditation --- watching the thought spray. The only thing that can help is to continue with the 'rounds' and at some stage, the thought-spray will suddenly spurt. And then one can resume watching It.

There are two reasons for the blank. In case repressed material is involved, it will not be allowed to surface. But a more common reason is the thought-spray is not accustomed to being watched. As progress in the development of self-awareness takes place, one becomes more and more non-judgmental towards his 'evil' and 'sinful' thoughts, thus enabling them to rise to the surface. Once they rise to the surface, it is both a challenge and an opportunity. Either they may be allowed their physiological or psychological expression or they can be transmuted into self-awareness. This is what life is all about choice. Either indulge or become self-aware. Either salivate or meditate. No amount of moralising, prayer, self-denial, asceticism can help. There is no substitute for waking up to our deeper tendencies and motivations.

This brings us to an important issue of the distinction between a blank and the equipoise. In both the cases, there is no stirring up of thought chains and the blank is likely to be mistaken for the equipoise.

(a) In the case of a blank, no thought might be stirring up to the surface. It does not mean thoughts have been dissolved. It only means that they are repressed and accumulated at the bottom of the preconscious or in the unconscious. In the case of equipoise, during its presence, there are really no thoughts, they being dissolved into self-awareness. (The equipoise ceases when fresh thoughts are generated and activated in the preconscious from dormancy).

(b) In the case of blank, there is a perception of influence, weight, load, heaviness exerted by the repressed thoughts. They cannot come to the surface, but exert their pressure from a distance. They create feelings of discomfort, disequilibrium and anxiety.

In the case of equipoise, there being really no thoughts, there are experiences of lightness, freedom and exhilaration. Feelings of well being, even bliss.

(c) Blank is a state of non-self-awareness and its consequent dynamics (Chapter XI). Energies are either blocked or frittered away. In equipoise, the energy is in its highest state at the voluntary command of the person concerned.

Once the blank is released by 'rounds' and consequent generation of self-awareness, the process of meditation can be resumed -- by watching the restarted thought flow and its transmutation by 'rounds' and cognition.

Aggravation

A novel experience. When a person progresses in meditation, he is looking forward to lessening of anger, aggression, lust, greed, revenge, partiality, injustice, etc. Exactly the reverse happens. As a matter of fact, the early stages of meditation are the best aphrodisiac! A yogi lost to the promptings of the lower self is a well-known phenomenon. He is called 'yogabhrasht', fallen from the grace of yoga. Even one's character can take a turn for the worse.

Come to think of it, there is nothing mysterious about the phenomenon. Meditation means allowing the thoughts to run unabashedly. And since we tightly packed bundles of repressions, on non-inhibition the repressions start spurting and there is a sudden clouding of the mind with various kinds of desires. Those who are systematically practicing cognitive meditation are not at risk. But those following suppressive meditation can get unbalanced by a sudden explosive outburst of desire.

Aggravation is very well-known to the disciplines of naturopathy and homoeopathy. Certain kinds of medication suppress disease, creating an illusion of cure. But the suppressed disease continues to express itself in disturbed ways. With treatment according to the above disciplines, suppression is released and the disease suddenly flares up in a severe way. But thereafter it soon clears away, leaving the person cured. A similar process takes place in the therapy of meditation too. After the aggravation, the desires cool down. This might happen several times. Eventually, the meditator is cleansed and becomes more innocent than a child.

Aggravation is not a setback. It is an inner challenge and an opportunity to grow. According to tantra, the very obstacle is converted into a stepping stone to success. Tantra calls it 'virachar', the way of the hero. He not only deals with the obstacles on the way, but even goes out of his way to invite them ritually.

Rationale

All kinds of ideas prevail about meditation techniques. Since I would like the reader to become autonomous, I feel obliged to convey the rationale of some of the unfamiliar steps recommended in the 'Main Meditation'.

Peripherals

a. Talking of the posture, the Buddha pose is not possible for most people. I have suggested sitting on a chair, which is the best solution for one's lifestyle today. Even the conservative Patanjali recommends 'stable and easy position' (Woods 1927, Book II, 46). The bottom line is the back should remain straight, there should be no pain even if the posture is to be maintained for an hour or more. During meditation, the body should be forgotten. Sitting on a chair meets all these requirements.

b. There could be a debate whether the eyes should be closed or kept open during meditation. My argument is, one cannot 'close' one's ears or nose. One has to meditate with these 'open'. Then why not keep the eyes also the open? When during meditation, attention gets withdrawn from the external world, even with open eyes and ears, one neither sees nor hears. This is the real 'closing'.

However, for some, keeping the eyes open may cause strain. In such a case, it would be best to keep them closed and remain comfortable

c. Meditation requires a fresh mind for better observation and transmutation. A mind fresh enough to carry out daily chores or professional activity may not be fresh enough for meditation. Take common sense steps to maintain high alertness whatever they may be. Otherwise, the entire meditative exercise would be a waste.

d. Whenever a meditation enterprise is undertaken, the gurus and scriptures demand a complete change of lifestyle. One is required to turn towards an ascetic way of life. I consider this unnecessary. One is already considerably suppressed and repressed. Taking an ascetic turn would make the situation worse. I have all along maintained that a suppressive type of meditation is a wrong approach. Ultimately, it is counter-productive. I have also maintained that the only correct meditation is transmutative through self-awareness. Hence, one should leave his life-style as it is and indirectly bring about a change through self-awareness.

The exception is, if one has fallen prey to dangerous habits like drug addiction. In this case, suppressive methods must be adopted. Such cases cannot develop the requisite self-awareness. They require appropriate therapy and not meditation.

Let the thoughts run

To the meditatively naive, this may appear to be odd advice. They believe in concentrating on one fixed point and freezing the mind. Nothing of the sort is possible except creating a voluntary blank. What is to be achieved is equipoise, where the mind is voluntarily and effortlessly still or active. It is not 'concentration' that produces meditation, but meditation that produces concentration.

So what is the rationale of letting the thoughts run?

We have seen earlier that meditation is a spiritual alchemy in which the base is transmuted into the noble. Here the base materials are the thoughts, both good and bad, and the noble element, the higher self. More the transmutations, more the expansion of the higher self. And for more and more transmutations, you require more and more thoughts. Hence, the need to let the thoughts run. More the thoughts, more the 'raw material' available for the growth of the higher self.

The need to become Non-Judgemental

The rationale for this is simple. Conventionally, thoughts are categorised into 'good' and 'sinful'. Transmutation of both is required. However, 'sinful' thoughts are generally repressed and to bring them to the surface is not easy. One of the ways of doing so is to become non-judgemental towards one's thoughts. This is really worthwhile because a non-judgemental attitude will not only facilitate 'sinful' thoughts to rise to the surface, but the transmuted yield of such thoughts would be much richer. Incidentally, those who want to cease judging others will have to first learn to cease judging themselves.

This brings us to the technique of 'free association;' of psychoanalysis. In this procedure, the patient is asked to let the thoughts run without any inhibition. In this procedure, there being as less inhabitation as possible, the repressed thoughts also tumble forth, along with the non-repressed thoughts. The repressed thoughts will be exposed to the insight (self-awareness) of the patient and the disorder rectified (in conjunction with some other psychoanalytic techniques).

The main difference between allowing the thoughts to run by the mediator and the psychoanalytic format is, in the former there is only one human unit and in the latter, two. In the case of meditation, both the observer and the observed belong to one human unit, and in the case of psychoanalysis two, the analyst (the observer) and the analysand (the observed).

The technique of allowing thoughts to run could be 5000 years old. But it is definitely 2500 years old, being one of the components of the Buddhist Vipassana meditation. Freud reinvented it in a modified form.

The Analysis of the Propellant

From the meditative experience it is learnt that mere observation of thought is not enough to bring about transmutation. When we observe a particular thought, a further deeper observation is required to identify the propellant of the thought. For example, if the thought is dislike of Mr. A. its propellant could be jealousy. It is only when one becomes aware of the particular jealousy, not intellectually but as an independent concrete entity in the inner space, that transmutation takes place. This makes one free of jealousy and also adds to the stock of self-awareness, with all its felicitous consequences.

261

The observation of the propellant is the analysis of the thought. And as we saw in Chapter VIII, analysis leads to synthesis (of self-awareness).

Analysis quickens the process of transmutation and the formation of the higher self.

The 'Rounds'

The technique of 'rounds' is an innovation, necessity being the mother of invention. It serves two very important purposes. (1) It prevents the meditator from lapsing into sleep and keeps him alert all the time and (2) it helps in facilitating the rise of thoughts to the surface, where they could be transmuted by the I's self-awareness.

This technique also accelerates transmutation and formation of the higher self.

Equipoise

I have made equipoise the benchmark of progress in meditation out of sheer practical necessity. There must be some marker by which one can measure one's progress in meditation.

Transmutation of a single thought is a mini-equipoise. The collection of several mini-equipoises constitutes the equipoise of a particular meditation session. This represents the transmutation of the various thoughts activated during a particular meditation session in response to current stimulations.

The collection of a number of equipoises over a period becomes a critical mass and the higher self is born, with all its various dynamics. Though there are five principal and several subsidiary dynamics of self-awareness (Chapter X), the easiest to register on a day-to-day basis is the dynamic of equipoise. Hence, whenever a particular meditation succeeds in establishing equipoise, one learns that some progress has been made towards the formation of the higher self.

This explains the rationale of treating equipoise as a bench-mark of progress for each meditation session.

The common rationale behind these technical steps is to inject control and order by the I in the internal milieu, to facilitate efficient transmutations and accelerate the birth and establishment of the higher self.

Some Differences Between Cognitive And Other Meditations

Those who are conversant with the field of meditation must have noticed quite a few differences between cognitive meditation and other systems. Some of these are dealt with below.

Theory

To start with, most systems have sketchy or no theoretical base. I would not claim that my theory is the last word. Far from it. But at least, I have made an effort. My theory sprang from practice. Naturally, there are bound to be many lacunae. These are filled up by informed speculation. I believe my theory would help the aspirant to understand the various steps of practice and their reasoning. There is nothing arbitrary about meditation. If X is done, Y must follow.

Objectives

All systems of meditation including cognitive meditation have ultimate objectives, variously known as moksha, nirvana, kaivalya, release, liberation, realisation, place near God, etc. Apart from the fact that all these terms have different connotations, such objectives have no relevance for most of us. Normally, our objectives are health, prosperity, good interpersonal relations, professional success, peace.....The former objectives are considered spiritual and the latter worldly. Classical systems cater to the spiritual, while a system like cognitive meditation caters to both the spiritual and the worldly. It is paradoxical that the same system can subserve both the spiritual and the worldly objectives. I will not try to resolve this paradox here, except to say that the worldly can be a prelude to the spiritual. Our worldly day-to-day life, if coupled with meditation, can be a preparation for the higher life

Obviously, there is no scope for monasticism in cognitive meditation. Also, those who cannot face this life are not fit for a higher life.

Secular

Meditation is generally a limb of a religion, cult or philosophical system. It is intimately connected with entities like God, gods, goddesses, saints.

This could turn away intellectuals and scientifically-oriented good humans, who can no longer stand certain traditions. This would be unfortunate. Meditation is as areligious as digestion. In fact, meditation is a specialised metabolism of psychological energies, whose end product is the spirit. Meditation can shine in its true splendor when historical accretions like religion and tradition are scraped off. The basic meditation process of the cognitive variety is non religious, non-cultic, non-philosophical, non-traditional. It is experimental, secular and spiritual.

Cognitive meditation has definite scientific tendencies. To start with, it recognises only three entities — the body, the mind and the I. It is only at a later stage of meditation that the higher self makes its appearance. Even the higher self has nothing to do with God or gods or other religious entities. It is a transmuted psychological self, which in turn is a transmuted physiological self, which in turn is a transmuted material self. Matter to spirit is a variegated continuum whose underlying Reality is **THAT**, which is neither God nor demon, but beyond both. The truth is, an intellectual may be repelled by religion, but is always consciously or unconsciously in search of the spiritual. If a non-denominational meditation is offered, he might accept it gratefully. Cognitive meditation is a modern-day meditation unlike other systems, which are heavily scrambled with religion or tradition.

Asana, Pranayama

Even classical systems like Patanjali Yoga Darshan do not emphasise the role of posture (asana). He wants it to be comfortable and stable. (Woods, Book Second - 46-48). Cognitive meditation agrees.

However, when it comes to pranayama, disciplining of the breath or breathing exercises, there is a parting of ways. The Hindu system is all for control and regulation of breath. In other words, suppression of the normal rhythm of inhalation, exhalation cycle. The Buddhist system does not suppress the breath and its rhythm in any way. The inhalation and exhalation are just observed. This is a part of Buddhist Vipassana System. On this issue, I side with Vipassana, thought partially. The main issue is not suppression, not even of the breath.

In cognitive meditation, the breath is severely left alone. There is neither control nor observation of breath. In cognitive meditation, the I is busy observing the thought-spray. Breathing is completely disregarded. Where the meditation ends with a good equipoise, it is noted that breathing has practically ceased. It is slow, shallow and hardly noticeable. In pranayama, the breath is controlled to control the mind. In cognitive meditation, the stillness of equipoise almost stills the breath.

(In the Second Meditation I provide a technique in which the I is involved in watching the breath instead of the thought-spray).

Progressive Muscular Relaxation

To a certain extent, relaxation still continues to be a buzz word. Its validity is even traced to an asana of Yoga — 'Shavasan'. The 'dead body' posture. Cognitive meditation does not consider relaxation practice as healthy. Its relief is temporary and pushes tension deeper (Chapter I). In the main meditation, the body, like the breath, relaxes by itself The equipoise not only stills the breath but also the body.

However, in the Second Meditation, such automatic relaxation is a distinct result of the breath observation technique. The body relaxes delightfully by itself, without any voluntary effort, just as in the case of sleep (though without falling asleep).

Concentration

It is almost a universal belief that meditation is concentration. This is because some classical systems of meditation are carried out while concentrating on a fixed point, nose-tip or mantra. It is believed that by fixing attention on a single point, in the course of time, all distracting thoughts will subside. This means that other thoughts are suppressed. This is a wrong technique. We now know, through depth psychology, that suppression cannot destroy thoughts. Instead, it perpetuates them in the unconscious, from where they can play mischief. The only way to deal with all thoughts is to face them and transmute them. (See Observation Effect, Chapter VIII). This is the very basis of cognitive meditation.

When all or most thoughts are transmuted and equipoise established, the I is able to concentrate without any distraction or effort. It is meditation that leads to concentration and not the other way.

In the technique of cognitive meditation, there is no concentration on a fixed point. There is only observation of the moving thought-spray, till it is transmuted and stillness pervades.

Analysis

Cognitive meditation goes beyond mere observation. In non-concentrative systems like the Buddhist Vipassana, which are based on observation of the thought-spray, there is no analysis of thought. There is mere passive observation of the rising and subsiding of thoughts. In cognitive meditation, as far as possible and particularly in the case of intense thoughts, analysis is a must. (Chapter VIII). This is in the interest of accelerated transmutation. Why analysis has not been recommended in Vipassana has not been explained. However, even if explicit analysis is not permitted, at least some of it is automatically taking place along with observation. And it is this unintended analysis which works in Vipassana.

External inputs including the Guru

Classical meditation systems give great importance to factors like sacred spots or holy places like temples, where meditation should be performed. Constant companionship of the spiritually advanced is another aid to meditation, strongly recommended. Elevating music is still another aid. While I may not altogether object to such help, I am basically against the use of such inputs. Particularly if an aspirant is going to become dependent on them. I do not believe in 'imports' of tranquility. I firmly believe all spiritual progress should be self-generated. 'Imports' of spirituality from external agencies is substituting one slavery for another. One should enter the spiritual on one's own legs. If somebody or something promises to carry you there, rest assured, you will find yourself in another unsought territory.

This obviously brings us to the role of the guru. It should alert you that any number of gurus are dying to enlighten you. They are prepared to do all the thinking for you. All that is required is surrender, preferably along with all your property. Granting, for the sake of argument, that there is a guru who is really a good human being, I maintain he cannot help you much. And there is always the danger of becoming dependent on him. At the most, he can act as a facilitator, which is altogether a different function.

Talking of external aids, the biggest and the most dangerous is the guru. Struggling to find the way independently by oneself is itself a spiritual activity.

I have written this book to share my experience with you, to set you thinking and experimenting, I have no intention of becoming your guru. I am interested in you. But I am more interested in your own independent struggle. Meditation is an adventure, with all its loneliness, risks, dangers, failures, successes and ultimate success.

One day, you will find that you do have a guru, who happens to reside within you. It is self-awareness.

Asceticism, Hedonism, Transmutation

It is one of the most widespread beliefs that the meditator has to be an ascetic. Many systems of meditation, particularly of the classical variety, are intimately linked with asceticism. I have mentioned in an earlier chapter that asceticism (and also hedonism) is a compulsive drive. Asceticism is a product of ascetic desires. And drives and desires belong to the psychological. Not to the Spiritual. Asceticism, however much respected in certain circles, is a pathology. Meditation powered by such asceticism may produce an altered state of consciousness, but far from one of effortless equipoise. It could be a new and intensified pathology.

It is not so well-known that hedonism is also considered by some groups as an adjunct to meditation. The thinking is, if all the desires could be indulged in and consumed, liberation will follow. Unfortunately, even an emperor cannot satisfy all his likes and dislikes. It's an impractical project. Meanwhile, a life of pleasure will just drag one into the pit. That a life of indulgence would lead to the spiritual is just rationalisation.

I would particularly like to draw your attention to a cult, which passes off as tantra. They believe in ritualised eating, drinking and copulating. In fact, it is a degenerate form of tantra. These days, everyone including some western gurus are offering tantra. There is no end to advertisements in which an aspirant sits in a lotus pose, displaying his six 'chakras', an illustration of tantric anatomy. In the mind of the public, tantra has something to do'with sex. It is oriental, exotic, esoteric, ritualised sex, with a promise of dusky, spiritual women thrown in. For the western sexualist satiated with routine and twisted sex. tantra is a brand new thrill.

Genuine tantra is more difficult than all the yogas put together. Only a greenhorn or the very advanced will attempt it. Tantra is a headlong collision with desire and darkness, with uncertain consequences. Come to think of it, cognitive meditation is a diluted form of tantra, where day-to-day desires have to be observed, faced and transmuted by the I and its self-awareness. In tantra proper, there is a lot of scope for self-deception. I cannot resist repeating the Tibetan saying:

'Some drink in order to perform the ceremony, and some perform the ceremony in order to drink'.

If there is a hell, the pseudo-tantric will certainly find his way there. If not, he will assuredly create one of his own.

If neither asceticism nor hedonism can lead to the right meditation and the consequent liberation, what has one to do?

What one has to do is to recognise the futility of asceticism as the Buddha did. Also, the futility of hedonism which anyone can understand. Both asceticism and hedonism are desires and as such, obstacles to meditation. The only force that can deal with desires is self-awareness. But even self-awareness cannot destroy desires. It can only transmute them into further self-awareness. Self-awareness producing more self-awareness.

So this is a major difference. Not by asceticism, not by hedonism, but by self-awareness can one build the higher self.

Concept of the Spiritual

The classical concept of the spiritual is something to do with God, temples, vows, fasts, pilgrimages, conventional morality, prayers, surrender to God, rising above body and mind by suppressing both, and so on.

For cognitive meditation, the spiritual is something altogether different. It is self-awareness and its various facets like purity, power, higher morality, being and transcendence (Chapter X).

The Identity of the Meditator

Since meditation is a highly practical undertaking, who is the initiator of this activity? Is it the physiological system or the psychological system or the psycho-spiritual system or the spiritual system — like the atma, purusha or spirit?

The first (body) and the last (spirit) are out of the question. The body is incapable and the latter is already perfect, not requiring any meditation. We have to decide between the psychological and the psycho-spiritual systems. The former being 'blind' and inertial is incapable of any non-built-in activity like meditation. The only system left is the psycho-spiritual and it turns out to be ideal. It is the spiritual component, which undertakes the meditation activity. The spiritual component of the psycho-spiritual is the current I. So it is the I (i.e. the Current I here) who initiates the meditation activity.

In most other systems, particularly the classical, there is no official clue as to who is going to practice meditation. In Buddhism, the I is only an apparent entity, there being nothing substantial about it. In Vedanta, both body and mind are illusions. And if the I is going to be considered either unsubstantial or illusory, it certainly cannot undertake a very real and substantial activity like meditation. Similarly, in Samkhya (Patanjal Yoga), the I belongs to the Prakarti system and does not help the purusha to liberate itself. Also, the purusha cannot liberate itself from the coils of Prakarti, as it is incapable of action, by definition. No wonder then, the classical systems quietly shelve the question of the identity of the meditator. Further, some of these systems are derogatory of the I. I am sure some long-winded complicated answer is waiting in the wings. Meanwhile, it is my direct experience, and it will be yours, also that the meditation exercise is undertaken by the I.

The Second Meditation

I am about to introduce you to an extraordinary experience, of which you have not even heard, much less experienced. It does not involve drugs or any direct intentional effort. It just happens, if you carry out a cognitive exercise. This experience is the ecstasy generated in the frontal lobes of the brain.

All practitioners of meditation look forward to some unique altered state of consciousness. The conventional meditator expects to reach a deep state of stillness and tranquility. Those practicing progressive muscular relaxation try to reach a state free from all muscular tension. Those dabbling in drugs are mad after their 'highs'. Zen practitioners cultivate their paradoxical, liberated consciousness, leading to the ecstasy of the 'no-mind'.

I have already dealt with the experience of equipoise through cognitive meditation. It is a facet of the deeper and wider dynamics of the higher self (Chapter X).

I will try to familiarise you with the concept of the Second Meditation, with reference to the main meditation.

Main and the Second Meditation

In both meditations, the operating agent is common, i.e. the I (the current I). Also, in both meditations, the process involved is cognition. In the main meditation, the I is the observer and the thought-spray is the observed. In the Second Meditation, the same I is the observer but the observed is the breath - its inhalation and exhalation cycle.

In the case of the main meditation, the thought-spray is transmuted. In the case of the Second Meditation, it is the state of breath and of the frontal lobes of the brain that is transmuted.

The transmutation of the thought-spray leads to the dynamics of self awareness -- purity, power, higher morality, being and transcendence. The actual spiritual marker is equipoise. The transmutation of the state of the frontal lobes leads to a cerebral and physiological rejuvenation. The actual physiological marker is cerebral and physiological ecstasy.

The main meditation is all-comprehensive. It can lead to very advanced stages, which may not be required for the man of the world. The Second Meditation is tailor-made for the modern harried executive:

The Second Meditation may also serve as a starter and a foundation for a higher activity like the main meditation. It can also be accomplished in a shorter period than the main meditation.

Mistaken Comparisons

The Second Meditation can be easily mistaken for Vipassana meditation or progressive muscular relaxation or yoga nidra.

The Second Meditation, like the main one, based on cognition and the consequent observation effect, leading to a dialectical leap into the opposite and the higher (transmutation). Progressive muscular relaxation and yoga nidra are not based on cognition. They are suppressive techniques, trying to push tension deeper and attaining superficial tranquility. Vipassana no doubt is based on cognition, but the fruits of the second meditation, particularly relating to the frontal lobes, are different from those of Vipassana. Hence, both are not the same.

As far as progressive muscular relaxation and yoga nidra are concerned, we have to understand the difference between relaxation and equipoise.

Relaxation is produced by consciously, directly and voluntarily trying to loosen our already tensed up muscles. Here the muscle may be relaxed, but not by cleansing the tension. In any case, any energy including that of tension cannot be destroyed, only transformed. In this exercise, the tension is simply displaced from the muscles, to perhaps the blood stream, by transfer of concerned chemicals. In the first instance, tension must have traveled through related chemicals from the blood stream to the muscles. In subsequent relaxation, this movement is reversed.

Equipoise is a different phenomenon altogether. In the case of a turbulent thought-spray, under cognition, the same is transmuted (not displaced) into the opposite and the higher, as per the dynamics of the observation effect (Chapter VIII). Thus, turbulence itself becomes tranquility (equipoise). The energy of turbulence is restructured into that of tranquility (equipoise). In order to distinguish this phenomenon from that of muscular loosening, the former is called equipoise and the latter relaxation.

Also in the case of the Second Meditation, the frontal lobes are not 'relaxed'. We cannot consciously, directly and voluntarily reach them. Hence, there is no question of relaxing them. Still, the frontal lobes (and the rest of the body) do attain extraordinary easing. This is derived from the cognition of the breath and the consequent observation effect, which ends up in the frontal lobes.

The question that immediately arises is, how does observation of breath transmute the state of the frontal lobes. This happens because our breath is a bridge between the body and the mind. Changes either in body or mind bring about change in the breath. And change in the breath brings about change in the body and/or mind.

Breath alchemy can take place, as long as it is just observed and not controlled, as in the pranayama of hatha yoga. The moment it is controlled and its spontaneous rhythm regulated, it is not observation but disciplining. And all disciplining is suppressive.

In the case of Vipassana there is no control of breath but only detached observation. It is very similar to the Second Meditation. However, the fruits of Vipassana are not present in the second meditation, particularly the ecstasy of the frontal lobes. Hence, Vipassana and the Second Meditation are different entities.

Fruits of the Main and the Second Meditation

I have already described the results of the main meditation in Chapter X. They are the facets of self-awareness - purity, power, higher morality, being and transcendence.

However, if one is on the lookout for a ready reckoner or a marker, it is equipoise. The depth of equipoise is always a good indicator of our spiritual state. In general terms the fruits are psychological and spiritual health.

The fruit of the Second Meditation, however desirable, are of a different order. The most important is equipoise and an ecstasy of the frontal lobes of the brain; a condition not heard of in the fields of meditation. The equipoise of the frontal lobes spreads over the eyes, the face, the trunk, the limbs, i.e. the entire body. It bathes the body with freshness and delight. This is a kind of physiological equipoise and ecstasy. The physiological well-being generates freshness, energy, immunity and consequent longevity. Also, the very process of cognition of the breath contributes, to a certain extent, to the further development of self-awareness and its allotropes. Thus, even though the benefits are predominantly physiological, a certain spiritual component is also involved. The Second Meditation is ideal for neutralising the toxins generated by modern stress. In fact, they .are transmuted into benign substances.

Second Meditation Procedure

Having described the nature and fruits of the second meditation, we come to its procedure.

1. To decide whether you are in a position to practice both the main and second meditations. If you have got time for only one, to decide which one. If you decide in favour of only the second meditation, what time? Morning or evening?

2. If it is morning, ensure that the mind is quite fresh after a night of restful sleep. If you choose evening, you have to take into account the wear and tear and the consequent fatigue of the day. In case of evening fatigue, after the day's work, it is essential to rest for about twenty minutes in bed, in a darkened room. If you attempt this meditation in .a state of fatigue, you will only end up with a headache. No solid food, one to one-and-half hour before starting the meditation. . Also a shower just before beginning the. Meditation session is essential.

3. The posture for this meditation is different from that for other meditations. It is lying on one's back in bed. The pillow should be as low as possible. There should be another pillow just below the

knees. This makes the lying down posture very comfortable, even if it lasts for an hour. The legs should be spread out, at about 30 degrees. Arms resting on the bed, with the palms touching the bed.

4. To start with the eyes will remain open, but as one continues to meditate they will close by themselves. As far as possible, the body should remain still, with occasional unavoidable movements.

5. Now comes the main procedure.

    You should start watching the inhalation and expiration of the breath, at the level of the nostrils. When you inhale, you count one and when you exhale, you count two. When you reach fifty, it constitutes one round. At the time of inhalation, you observe the entry and upward passage of the breath. And at the time of exhalation, watch the downward and outward movement of the breath.

6. There should be absolutely no attempt of any kind to control the breath in any way, either while inhaling or exhaling. At any given time, the breath will have its own rhythm. One should try to distance oneself from this rhythm and observe it in a detached way (after certain practice, one will find that the rhythm of the breath will change by itself, with mere observation by the I, in an unidentified way). No tinkering with the breath. It should be left entirely to itself. Once observation is on, results will just happen.

7. At the beginning of this meditation exercise, the I will be identified, with the inhalation, exhalation rhythm of the breath. But as observation/cognition proceeds, a growing separation will develop between the observer (the I) and the observed (the breath). The better you observe, the better the separation between the I and the breath. And better the separation, better the transmutation.

8. You have to ensure that you do not slide into a state of sleep. To begin with, a fresh brain will help. Counting the number of inhalations and exhalations will help further. Also, counting the completed rounds.

9. To start with, this exercise should be done for one round only, twenty five inhalations and twenty-five exhalations. Once mastery is obtained over one round, other rounds may be, gradually added. Like this, one should be able to carry on for ten to twelve rounds.

10. As you proceed with the rounds, around the eighth to the twelfth round, an unusual experience wilt start taking place. The area

behind the forehead, most probably the frontal .lobes of the brain, starts relaxing (the correct term would be equipoising). When advanced equipoising takes place, a profound experience of easing, releasing, relaxing, equipoising, happiness, bliss, ecstasy takes place in the frontal lobes. Once experienced, you will always try to re-experience it. This is the heart of the second meditation.

With practice, the rounds will come down from twelve to eight to six. In more earthy terms, this experience will lead to washing off the days wear and tear, making you feel extraordinarily fresh. If you perform this meditation in the evening, you will experience a second morning on the same day. If you are a night worker, you will have added two more fresh hours to the day. .

11. Once a deep stage of the equipoising of the frontal lobes is reached, the counting of inhalations and exhalations should cease. While dwelling on the equipoise state of the frontal lobes, further experiences will start taking place. The equipoise from the frontal lobes will travel .to the eyes and then to the face When the face is equipoised, for the first time you will realize how tensed your face was. From the face, the equipoise will travel to the trunk, both the dorsal and ventral areas, and from the trunk to the legs and the arms.

Thus equipoise will spread from head to toe.. The entire body will be drenched in a feeling of wellbeing.

12. Feel the experience. Enjoy the feeling. Stay with it for as long as your lifestyle permits you. Ideally ten minutes will be sufficient. You may now open your eyes and sit up within a minute or two and resume your routine.

13. The major effects of the second meditations are physiological. The most important one being the profound equipoising. and calming of the frontal lobes of the brains. And from this follow the equipoising of the eyes, face and the rest of the body. Soaking of the entire body in a feeling of well-being, incidentally, improves vitality, immunity and consequently longevity. The face and the body become more fresh and youthful.

However, the effects are not restricted to the physiological level only. The calming of the frontal lobes leads to the calming of the psychological level, also making its transmutation into the spiritual, easier and quicker.

14. If the professional executive, under high pressure, with unending tasks and decisions riddled with deadlines, has to choose between the two meditations main or the second, I would recommend the latter. At least as a starter. It would take ten times to master and meets the immediate requirement and above all, lays a solid foundation for the main meditation. It is tailor-made for the executive at risk.

15. I have narrated quite a few unusually beneficial effects of the second meditation. What is more unusual is that no direct effort is made to achieve them. They cannot be produced by voluntary action. They just happen. There is no suggestion no anti-suggestion or so-called positive thinking involved. The meditator just becomes positive, which leads to positive thinking and not vice-versa.

    But effort is involved. It is indirect and of a different kind. It is the sustained observation / cognition by the I of the rhythm of breathing (non-I). In other words, it is once again the observation effect; self-awareness (the I) restructuring non-self-awareness (the breathing rhythm and the pre meditation state of the frontal lobes). Once the state of the frontal lobes is beneficially restructured, all other beneficial states automatically follow.

16. The paradox. Intense activity should lead to further active developments. Here the intense activity of cognition leads to calming of the frontal lobes. Activity into equipoise. (The same happens also in the main meditation under the gaze of self-awareness, the turbulent psychological becomes equipoised and transmuted into the spiritual)

    In both the meditations, it is the play of self-awareness and its alchemy.

APPENDIX I

THE RISE AND FALL OF THE THOUGHT-SPRAY

The phrase is 'Stream of Consciousness'. I have shown earlier, it is not the stream of consciousness, but the stream of thoughts observed by consciousness. (In my terminology, self-awareness). Going one step further, I find that it is not a stream of thoughts but a spray of thoughts. Contemplate a fountain. How the waters rise and fall. Therefore, a spray of thoughts, which rises and falls.

This spray is constantly rising and falling, even in sleep. It is this spray which leads to the comparison of the mind to a monkey.

A couple of related issues will be considered. To start with, why do the thoughts rise? Where do they start and where do they go? It is obvious, it is an involuntary activity.

My explanation for the rising of thoughts is as follows:

I have already pointed out that all thoughts are derivatives of the various drives harbouring in the preconscious and the unconscious (Chapter IX). In fact, I have called them mini-drives. These drives and their derivatives are self powered. They derive their energy from the big bang, uncoiling via the material, the physiological (instincts) and the psychological, in the form of drives. The further uncoiling of the drives leads to the formation of mini-drives or thoughts. Thus, thoughts are self-powered entities.

The upward movement .of uncoiling from the material to the physiological to the psychological continues. The drives rise into thoughts and the thoughts continue their upward direction. Thoughts rise because they are uncoiling in the upward direction.

When the rising thoughts reach the outskirts of the I and its self-awareness, they get perceived by the I. The I becomes conscious (self-aware) of the thoughts. Here comes the snag. The I becoming conscious of the thoughts is misreported as the thoughts becoming conscious The truth is all thoughts belong to the psychological system and as such are non-self-aware and can never become conscious. It is the light of self-awareness beamed on the thoughts, which creates the mal-observation of .the thoughts becoming conscious. What has happened is the thoughts have come within the range of the cognition of the I and hence get registered.

When the thoughts rise to the surface, they are in a queue. The topmost thought is pushed by the one below it, which in turn is pushed by another one below it.

Now the thoughts rising from the preconscious and particularly from the unconscious lose a part of its energy in the act of rising. The thought which is uppermost has lost more energy than the one just below it. The consequence is, the uppermost thought is pushed aside by the one just below it, which now becomes uppermost. This in turn is also pushed aside by another one just below it. Thus the queue moves upwards, constituting the upward flow of the spray.

Having understood the upward movement of the thought-spray, it is easy to understand its downward movement. What is pushed aside falls back into the reservoir from which the spray arose -- the preconscious.

This is how the upward and downward chain of thoughts incessantly continues, frequently causing turbulence, loss of peace and exhaustion. No wonder the world always dreams of stilling the thoughts, loosely called the 'stilling of the mind'.

All thoughts that have risen need not necessarily become a part of the downward flow. A thought which has arisen to the top can also have an extraordinary prospect. If the I focuses its cognition on it, as also analyses it, it gets transmuted as per the dynamics of the observation effect (Chapter VIII). It takes a dialectical leap, ceases to be a specific thought and becomes undifferentiated self-awareness of the I. The non-I becomes the I. The non-self-aware becomes the self-aware. One more tiny step in the direction of the cosmic evolution.

Taking cognisance of a thought in a focused way, analysing it, and transmuting it is called meditation.

APPENDIX II

CONSERVATION OF ENERGY

I have been talking all the time of transmutation. Basically, it has been the transmutation of the energy from one form to another, an opposite and higher form. The starting point has been physical energy, which by a series of dialectical leaps reaches the final stage of spiritual energy.

When there is transmutation of physical energies into physiological energies, there is a decrease in physical energies and an increase in physiological energies. This is what observation means. It is the same for other levels too.

Both science and classical meditation believe in conversation of energy. But in a limited way, as compared to cognitive meditation.

Science accepts conservation of energy from the physical to the physiological to the psychological, but not to the spiritual level because science, as of today, does not believe in the spiritual level.

Classical meditation will also accept conservation of energy from the physical to the psychological levels. But not from the psychological to the spiritual level. This is so for a reason different from that of science. Classical meditations, unlike science, do believe in the spiritual. But for these meditations, there is a hiatus between the non-spiritual and spiritual levels.

There is no continuity and communication between the two. Consequently, there is no energy exchange between the two levels. For example, the atma of Vedanta has no concept of connectivity with the body or the mind. Both will constitute independent, exclusive and non-communicating systems. Hence, there is no conservation of energies between the body and mind on the one hand and atma on the other. Though the concept of the spiritual will vary from one classical meditation to another, the exclusivity of the spiritual will hold in all cases and, therefore there is no concept of energy exchange between the non-spiritual and the spiritual.

For me, the position is altogether different. I believe in the spiritual level, but the concept is distinct from that of classical meditations. For me, the spiritual is the end level of the cosmic evolution, which starts with the physical level. The spiritual was potentially present in the physical and eventually emerged from it. This means that the spiritual of cognitive meditation is also, however contrary it may be to the physical, a part of the manifested universe. Entities like atma are conceived to be beyond the manifested universe. It is never explained how they ever come into a relationship with the physical, physiological and psychological, which belong to the manifested universe.

There are two kinds of spiritual levels. One conceived by classical meditation and the other by cognitive meditation. The former has no connectivity with body or mind and hence no energy exchange between the two sides takes place. In the latter there is a continuation and communication between body, mind and spiritual, and therefore energy exchange exists right from the physical to the spiritual.

An entity like atma is a fixed quantity. It neither increases nor decreases. Much less is born or dies. It is beyond all description. It is supposed to be entirely without quantity and quality. Though in the next breath, there is no compunction in describing it as existence, consciousness and bliss. The spiritual of cognitive medication can increase or decrease. There is conservation of energy from the physical to the spiritual. If the spiritual increases, the physical decreases and vice-versa. There is also no problem of connectivity. However much the levels from the physical to the spiritual may differ, there is a common underlying reality – THAT.

The atma which does not increase or decrease can still merge into the Brahman thus cease to be an individualised entity. The higher self, which belongs to the manifested universe, also merges into THAT, but not without taking a final dialectical leap.

In the classical meditation systems, there are two energy systems, while in cognitive mediation there is only one. The non-manifested and the manifested is a common energy pool, only the expression of this Energy vary and differ. Energy might move from one expressions to another. Because of this, there can be waning and waxing of the expressions, but the underlying total of Energy remains constant. The manifested universe is just an expression of THAT, which in turn has so many sub-expressions. However insignificant we may be, we are throbbing parts of a seamless whole. Conservation of energy leads to a holistic version, embracing the

Non-manifested and the Manifested. Tantra has symbolised this concept in the image of the Devi, which is Shakti (Energy) incarnate.

When aggression is refined into sport, it is called sublimation. This is a typical and common case of conservation of energy.

But here is another case, which goes much beyond refinement. A conversion into the opposite and the higher, which I call a dialectical leap. Take the case of anger. It can be, with the aid of self-awareness, converted into deep calm. Into the opposite and the higher. I have called this transmutation.

Most of us think that the more the energy, more the activity even to the extent of turbulence. This is not necessarily so. When anger is transmuted into the calm, all activity ceases and a kind of silence prevails. This does not mean that the calm is a non-energy state. The calm is as 'energetic' as anger. Only, structurally, it is a different kind of energy.

A transmutation is always fundamental. From the non-I to the I. From non-self-awareness to self-awareness. In more concrete term, from bondage to liberation.

APPENDIX III

THE MEANING OF MEANING – A STORY TO END WITH

This particular African Chief ruled one of the lesser known countries of Africa. He was not keeping well. Somehow, a physician from a country, whose name is better not divulged, reached the Chief. He taught the Chief a mantra for his health, to be repeated three times a day. It was 'Every day, in every way, 1 am becoming worse and worse'. The Chief, who did not understand the meaning, not knowing the language, religiously recited the mantra three times daily. Soon he improved and became healthy and ruddy. One day, another doctor who knew English reached the Court of the Chief. He. soon came to know about the remarkable turn-around in the Chief's health. But when he came to learn about the mantra, he was shocked beyond belief and conveyed his misgivings to the Chief. The consequence was the Chief's health again began to deteriorate. Then the new doctor taught him the 'improved' mantra - 'Every day, in every way, I am getting better and better'. Soon the Chief once again recovered his health and handsomely rewarded the doctor.

Comment: The above imaginary tale is true throughout the world. The nature of faith, belief, suggestion, superstition, cousins all, raises a number of questions. In what kind of soils do they grow? What are their short-term and long-term advantages and disadvantages? In what spheres of life are they operative? And so on.

Right now, I am concerned here with a limited issue ---- what is the relationship between the non-material and the material.

Come to think of it, meaning is an entity, which has no length, no width, no height and no weight. It can be called 'non-material'. On the other hand, the physiological effects - improvement and deterioration are material entities.

The question immediately arises, how can a 'non-material' entity interact with and modify 'material' entities? They belong to different and exclusive categories and as such cannot interact. They live in their worlds and just cannot interact. Since logic is a part of life and life is not a part of logic, it will have to give way to a fact, which is a constituent of life. The fact is, meaning which is supposed be 'non-material' can modify physiological tissues, which are supposed to be 'material'.

The very fact that meaning and matter can interact shows that there is a hidden connection between the two. Analogically, we had noted that, though the physical self and the spiritual self are contrary to each other, they can interact (Chapter III). This was shown to be possible because the source of both is the same- THAT. Both the selves are different expressions of the same underlying Reality. At a deeper level, both are the same. Hence the interactivity. It is the same with meaning and physiological modifications. Both are expressions of the same underlying Reality---THAT. Being basically the same, they can and do interact. Neither 'non-matter' nor 'matter' are irrevocably such and nothing else. Their roots descend into a deeper stratum, which is common for both. It is a case of a hidden thread, keeping together a 'variety of jewels and stones ---- a necklace, sparkling, shimmering and shadowing, all the time.

NOTE ON THE FELDTRON

The feldtron (from 'feld', archaic for field) is a circular assembly of various circular components. Different configurations of this circular assembly are possible. Water and colours - white and black, play an important part.

The feldtron consists of two dials — circular assemblies, identical in all respects, except for the locations, which are different. One of the dials acts as the master dial and the other as the slave dial. The feldtron is a product of pure empirical activity based on trial and error. It took birth from an accidental observation.

The experiments with the feldtron lead to six significant conclusions.

1. Because of identical geometry, a geometric resonance (I cannot think of a better term) develops between the two dials across space. This means identical fields in both the dials (but susceptible to difference because of local environment of each dial).

    When a change is brought about in the field of the master dial, with the help of an additional circular component, the same is immediately reflected in the slave dial, even without the additional circular component. (with a suitable assistant, this can be done, without any circular components, by a simple mental act which would mean telepathy). The fields, either in the master dial or the slave dial, cannot be read with physical senses of experimenter. They are read with the help of a pendulum, which is an ESP procedure. Reading the change in the slave dial with the help of a pendulum, the experimenter can describe the change in the master dial without any physical means. This is the heart of the experiment.

2. In short, the experimenter can find out the changes in the master dial, without any physical means, by simply reading the changes in the slave dial by an ESP procedure. This establishes the existence of ESP.

3. The experiment reveals an exciting interface between the geometry of the dials and the success rate of the ESP readings. Certain geometries give a higher success rate and others a low or nil success rate. This opens the possibility of modulating the success rate by modifying the geometry alone, without any improvement in the ESP ability. This also discloses a continuum between the physical entities — the components and the behaviour of the ESP forces.

4. Only ten readings with five options are taken at a time. More than ten readings at a time can 'curdle' the fields, leading to mistakes. (More than ten readings at a time are possible with improved geometry).

   This experiment does not involve thousands of readings to be statistically evaluated later, which establishes the existence of ESP by a fractional success rate, which does not convince few critically inclined.

   In the feldtron experiment success can be as high as seven to ten, out of ten readings.

5. Apart from the geometric resonance, the success rate is modified by the impinging of the personal field of the assistant to the experimenter on the master dial. The assistant is required to change the master dial field to be subsequently read in the slave dial, by ESP, by the experimenter. Some assistants can produce wonderful success rates and some disastrous. An empirical observation is lean assistants give better results than obese ones. Much more work is necessary, regarding the impact of the assistant's personal field on the success rate.

6. The field of the master and slave dials are also sensitive to magnetic and electromagnetic fields; but not so much as the personal field of the assistant. Similarly, fields of so called inert masses and shapes can also interfere powerfully. All the interfering fields, human or otherwise, can be neutrliased by suitable geometry.

   Current Activity – Currently, I am trying to work out geometries which can neutralize the impact of the assistant's personal fields, or magnetic and other fields, to improve the success rate.

BIBLIOGRAPHY

"The wise man reads both books and life itself'

Lin Yutang

"In science, read by preference, the newest works, in literature, the oldest. The classic literature is always modern".

"Of making many books there is no end, and much study is a weariness of the flesh".

Ecclesiastes 12:12

"One must be rich in thought and character to owe nothing to books, though preparation is necessary to profitable reading, and the less reading is better than more, bookstruck men are of all readers least wise, however learned".

A.B.Alcott

If you are intent on roughing out your way to the final stages of meditation, entirely on your own, without taking any help from humans or books, you are on the most correct path. Only, one life span may not be enough. You may have to compromise, and your major independent effort will have to be validated by the thinking and experiences of others, to expedite the meditative process. Otherwise, you will have to continue your efforts in the next birth.

There are two kinds of 'books on meditation. Those intimately and directly connected with the goals and procedures for learning meditation; and those indirectly connected with the vast and far-reaching background of meditation. Mysticism and modem science, aerobics and psychosomatics, psychology and psychiatry, popular literature and highly technical approaches, physiology and spirituality, stress management and insight procedures, physics and metaphysics, management — personal and professional, consciousness and matter, so on and on. All these subjects are indirectly but pertinently connected with meditation. Knowledge of such literature enhances our meditation skills.

This bibliography which is divided in two parts, caters to both the requirements.

I regret that the quality of books included in the bibliography is not even, especially those directly concerned with meditation. The very nature of the subject is such that a wide spectrum of quality is involved. If titles of uneven quality are included, this is so because I do not want to sit on judgment on them.

The various texts do not necessarily represent my views. Most of the time, they do not. These titles are included so that the reader may have access to the variety of concepts and thinking generated over different periods.

Titles indirectly concerned with the vast and far-reaching background of meditation are the works that really matter. Some of them are classics. The word 'meditation' may not occur in them, but they do refer to the various processes and phenomena which will lead to the overall comprehension of the meditative activity. These titles reflect modern times and can infuse much needed updating on various aspects of meditation.

261

Titles intimately or directly connected with the goals and procedures for learning meditation.

Carrington, P., *"Releasing"*, William Morrow, New York, 1984.

Carrington, Patricia, *"Freedom in Meditation"*. Anchor Press/Doubleday, New York, 1977.

Charlesworth, Edward A. and Nathan, Ronald G., *"Stress Management, A Comprehensive Guide to Wellness"*, Ballantine Books, New York, 1987.

Conze E., *"Buddhist Meditation"*, Harper Torchbooks, New York, 1969.

Cowan, Tom, *"Shamanism as a Spiritual Practice for Daily Life"*, The Crossing Press, Freedom, California, 1996.

De Mello, Anthony S.J., *"Awareness"*, Doubleday, Image Books, 1992.

Ed., Kiyota, Minoru, *"Mahayana Buddhist Meditation"*, Motilal Banarasidas, Delhi, 1978-1991.

Erdelyi, Matthew Hugh, *"Psychoanalysis, Freud's Cognitive Psychology"*, W. H. Freeman and Company, New York, 1985.

FarrowE. Pickworth, *"A Practical Method of Self Analysis"*, George Allen & Unwin Ltd., London, 1948.

Frankl, Victor E., *"Man's Search for Meaning"*, Pocket Books, Washington Square Press, New York, 1985.

Freud Sigmund, *"Introductory Lectures on Psychoanalysis"*, 1915-1917, Penguin Books, 1991.

Gendlin, Eugene T., *"Focussing"*, A Bantam New Age Book, New York, 1980, 1983.

Goldstein, J., *"The Experience of Insight"*, New Science Library, Shambhala, 1983.

Goldstein, Joseph, *"Insight Meditation"*, Sharnbhala, Boston, 1993.

Goleman Daniel, *"Emotional Intelligence"*, Bantam Books, New York, 1996.

Goleman, Daniel, *"The Meditative Mind, The Varieties of Meditative Experience"*, Jeremy P. Tarcher, Putnam, 1988.

Groddeck, George, *"The Book of the It"*, Vintage Books, New York, 1949.

Gunaratana, Henepola, *"The Path of Serenity and Insight, An Explanation of the Buddhist Jhanas"*, Motilal Banarasidas, Delhi, 1985.

Gyatso, Geshe Kelsang, *"The Meditation Handbook"*, Motilal Banarsidas Delhi, 1999.

Hamilton-Merritt, *"A Meditator's Diary, A Western Woman's Unique Experiences in Thailand Monasteries"*, Penguin Books, Harmondsworth, Middlesex, England, 1979.

Hanh, Thich Nhat, *"A Guide to Walking Meditation"*, Fellowship Publications, New York, 1985.

Hanh, Thich Nhat, *"Our Appointment with Life, The Buddha's Teaching on Living in the Present"*, Full Circle, New Delhi, 1997.

Hanh, Thich Nhat, *"The Miracle of Mindfulness, A Manual on Meditation"*, Beacon Press, Boston, 1987.

Hanh, Thich, Nhat, *"Being Peace"*, Parallax Press, Berkeley, 1987.

Horney, K., *"Self Analysis"*, Norton Library, New York, 1968.

Humphreys, Christmas, *"Concentration and Meditation"*, The Buddhist Lodge, 1935.

Huxley, Laura, *"You are not the target. A practical manual of how to cope with a world of bewildering change and uncertainty including thirty recipes to help you"*, Heinemann, London, 1964.

Kornfield, Jack, *"A Path with Heart, A Guide through the Perils and Promises of Spiritual Life"*, Bantam Books, New York, 1993.

Le Shan, Lawrence, *"How to Meditate, A Guide to Self-Discovery"*, Bantam Books, 1975.

Luthe, W., *"Stress and Self-regulation, Introduction to the Methods of Autogenic Therapy"*, International Institute of Stress, Pointe-Claire, Quebec, 1977.

Maharshi, Sri Ramana, *"Talks with Sri Ramana Maharshi in Ramanasramam"*, Tiruvannamalai South India, 1955 (3 volumes).

Maslow, A., *"The Farther Reaches of Human Nature"*, Viking New York, 1971.

Matthews, Caitlin and John Matthews, *"The Western Way, A Practical Guide to the Western Mystery Tradition"*, Arkana, Penguin Books, Penguin Group, London, 1986, 1994.

Mc Kenna, M., *"Revitalize Yourself: The Techniques of Staying Youthful"*, Hawlhorn Books, Inc., New York, 1972.

Mc. Kinnon, Pauline, *"In Stillness Conquer Fear, Overcoming Anxiety through Meditation"*, Collins Dove, Melbourne, 1989.

McQuade, W., & Aikman, *"Stress: What it is, What it can do to your health, How to Fight Back"*, E. P. Dutton & Co., Inc., New York, 1974.

Mishra, Rammurti, S., *"Yoga Sutras"*, Anchor Books, New York, 1973.

Monks of the Ramkrishna Order, "*Meditation*", Sri Ramkrishna Math, Madras.

Nicholson, R.A., Rumi, "*Poet and Mystic*", George Allan and Unwin Ltd., London, 1950.

Osborne, Arthur (Ed.), "*The Teachings of Bhagwan Sri Raman Maharshi. In his own words*", Sri Ramanasramam, Tiruvannamalai, South India, 1988.

Osborne, Arthur, "*Raman Maharshi and the Path of Self-knowledge*", Rider & Co., London, 1963.

Progoff, Ira, "*At a Journal Workshop*", Jeremy P. Tarcher, New York, 1992.

Radhakrishnan, S., "*The Bhagavadgita*", George Allen& Unwin Ltd., London, 1953.

Radhakrishnan, S, "*The Principal Upanishads*", Indus, An imprint of Harper Collins, Publishers India Pvt. Ltd., New Delhi, 1996.

Rainwater, Janette,"*You are in Charge, A Guide to Becoming Your Own Therapist*", Turnstone Press Ltd., U.K., 1981.

Ram Dass, "*Be Here Now*", Lama Foundation, New Mexico, 1971.

Ram Dass,"*Journey of Awakening A Meditators Guide Book*", Bantam, New York, 1990.

Saraswati, Swamy Satyananda,"*Yoga Nidra, (Yogic Sleep)*", Bihar School of Yoga, Munger, Bihar, India, 1984 (fifth edition).

Shankaracharya,"*Vivekacudamani Translated by Swami Madhavananda*", Advaita Ashrama, 5, Delhi Entally Road, Kolkata —700 014, 1982 (Eleventh Reprint).

Silva J. and Miele, P., "*The Silva Mind Control Method*", Simon and Schster, New York, 1977.

Steiner, Rudolf, *"Knowledge of the Higher Worlds and its attainment"*, Rudolf Steiner Publishing Co., London, 1937.

Swahananda Swami, *"Meditation and Other Spiritual Disciplines"*, Advaita Ashrama, Calcutta, India, 1983.

Taimini, I.K., *"The Science of Yoga, The Yoga Sutras of Patanjali and Commentary"*. The Theosophical Publishing House, Madras, 1974.

Tart, C.,T., *"Waking Up"*, New Science Library, Shambhala, Boston, 1987.

Thera Soma, *"The Removal of Distracting Thoughts"*, Buddhist Publication Society, Kandy, Sri Lanka, 1972.

Thera, Nyanaponica,*"The Power of Mindfulness"*, The Buddhist Publication Society, Kandy, Sri Lanka, 1976.

Under hill Evelyn, *"Practical Mysticism"*, J.M. Dent, London, 1914.

Von Durekheim, K., *"Daily Life as Spiritual Exercise, The Way of Transformation"*, Perenial Library, New York, 1972.

Woods, James Haughton,*"The Yoga-System of Patanjali"*, The Harvard University Press, Cambridge Massachusetts, 1927.

Woolfolk, R.I. and P.M. Lehrer (Ed.), *"Principles and Practice of Stress Management"*, Gailford, New York, 1984.

Titles Indirectly Connected with the Vast and Far Reaching Background of Meditation.

Abraham, F., *"Psychosomatic Medicine"*, W. W. Norton & Co., New York, 1950.

Ahern Geoffry, *"Spiritual/Religious Experience in Modern Society"*, Alastair Hardy Foundation, Oxford, 1990.

Alexander, Charles N., Ellen J. Langer Eds., *"Higher Stages of Human Development"*, Oxford University Press, Oxford 1990.

Alexander, F., *"The Scope of Psycho-analysis"*, Basic Books, New York, 1941.

Anderson, Walter Truett, *"The Upstart Spring: Esalen and the American Awakening"*, Addison — Wesly Reading, Mass., 1983.

Anthony, D., Ecker, B., and Wilbet, E., Eds., *"Spiritual Choices, The Problem of recognising authentic Paths, to inner transformation"*, Paragon, New York, 1987.

Antoine and Jacob Needleman Eds., *"Modern Esoteric Spirituality"*, Crossroad, New York, 1995.

Arasteh, Reza A., *"Rumi The Persian, The Sufi"*, Routledge & Kegan Paul, London, 1974.

Arberry, A. J. *"Discourses of Rumi"*, John Murray, London, 1961.

Arberry A. J. *"Tales from the .Masnavi"*, Unesco Collection of Representative Works, Persian Series, George Allen and Unwin Ltd., London, 1961.

Arberry, A. J. *"More Tales from the Masnavi"*, Unesco Collection of Representative Works, Persian Series, George Allen and Unwin Ltd., London, 1963.

Arberry, A. J. *"Sufism, An account of the Mystics of Islam"*, Allen and Unwin, London, 1972.

Arberry, A. J. *"Sufism"*, Mandala Books, Unwin Paperbacks London, 1979.

Ashvagosha, *"The Awakening of Faith"*, Translated by T. Richard, Charles Skilton, London, 1961.

Assagioli R., *"Psycho-synthesis"*, Viking, New York, 1971.

Assagioli, Roberto, *"The Act of Will"*, Penguin Books, London, 1974.

Assagioli, Roberto, *"Psychosynthesis, A Collection of Basic Writings"*, Penguin Books, 1976.

Assagioli, Roberto, *"Transpersonal Development, The Dimension beyond Psychosynthesis"*, The Acquarian Press, 1991.

Aurobindo, Sri, *"The Problem of Rebirth"*, Sri Aurobindo, Ashram, Pondicherry, India, 1952.

Avalon, Arthur, *"The Great Liberation, (Mahanirvan Tantra)"*, Ganesh & Co., (Madras) Ltd., Madras, Third Edition, 1953.

Avalon, Arthur, *"The Serpent Power"*, Ganesh & Co., Madras, 1958.

Bader, Jonathan, *"Meditation in Sankara's Vedanta"*, Aditya Prakashan, New Delhi, 1990.

Bailey, Alice, A., *"Letters On Occult Meditation"*, Lucis Publishing Company, New York, 1922, 1993 (fifteenth printing).

Barber, T., et al, Eds — *"Biofeedback and Self-Control"*, Aldine-Alkerton, Chicago, 1971.

Baars, Bernard, J., *"In the Theater of Consciousness"*, Oxford University Press, Oxford, 1997.

Barret, William, *"Irrational Man. A Study in Existential Philosophy"*, Doubleday New York, 1958.

Beck, A.T. *"Cognitive Therapy and the Emotional Disorders"*, Meridian, 1976.

Beck, A.T. and-Emery Gary, *"Anxiety Disorders arid Phobias A Cognitive Perspective"*, Basic Books, New York, 1985.

Beesing, Maria, Robert J. Nogosek, Patrick H.O. Leary,*"The Enneagram. A Journey of Self Discovery"*, Dimension Books Inc., New Jersey, 1984.

Bennet, J.G., *"The Dramatic Universe"*, Vols. 1-IV, Hodder & Stoughton, London, 1966.

Bennett, J.G., Gurdjieff: *"Making a New World"*, Turnstone Book, London, 1973.

Benoit, Hubert, *"The Supreme Doctrine"*, Routledge & Kegan Paul, London, 1950.

Benson, Herbert, *"The Mind-Body Effect"*, Simon &Schuster, New York, 1979.

Benson, H., *"Your Maximum Mind"*, Random House, New York, 1987.

Bernal, J.D., *"The Origin of Life"*, Weidenfeld & Nicholson, London, 1969.

Berne, E., *"Games People Play"*, Grove Press, New York, 1967.

Bharati, Agehananda,*"The Tantric Tradition"*, Garden City, Anchor Books, Doubleday, New York, 1970.

Bharati Agehanand, *"The Light at the Centre, Context and Pretext, of Modern Mysticism"*, Ross Erikson, Santa Barbara, 1976.

Blanchard, K. and N.V. Peale, *"The Power of Ethical Management"*, Morrow, New York, 1988.

Blanck, Gertrude and Rubin, *"Ego Psychology, Theory and Practice"*, Columbia University Press, New York, 1974.

Blanck, Gertrude and Rubin, *"Ego Psychology, Vol. II, Psychoanalytic Developmental Psychology"*, Columbia University Press, New York, 1979.

Blanck, Rubin and Gertrude, *"Ego Psychology, Developmental Object Relations Theory"*, Columbia University Press, 1986.

Blofeld, John, *"Gateway to Wisdom. Taoist and Buddhist Contemplative and Healing Yogas adapted for Western Students of the Way"*, Unwin Paperbacks, London, 1990.

Bloomfield, Harold et al, TM — *"Discovering inner energy and overcoming stress"*.

Blyth, R.H., *"Zen in English Literature and Oriental Classics"*, The Hokuseido Press, 1942.

Borysenko, Joan, *"Minding the Body, Minding the Mind"*, Bantam Books, New York, 1988.

Borysenko, Joan, *"Fire in the Soul, A New Psychology of Spirtual Optimism"*, Warner Books Inc., New York, 1993.

Bowker, John, *"The Problems of Suffering in Religions of the World"*, Cambridge University Press, London, 1970.

Bowl by, J., *"Attachment and Love"*, Basic Books, New York, 1969.

Bronkhorst, Johanees, *"The Two Traditions of Meditation in Ancient India"*, Motilal Banarsi Dass, Delhi, 1993.

Brown, Barbara, B., *"New Mind, New Body, Biofeedback: New Directions for the Mind"*, Harper and Row, New York, 1974.

Brown, Barbara B., *"Stress and the Art of Biofeedback"*, Bantam Book, New York, 1979.

Brown, Barbara, "*Super Mind, The Ultimate Energy, How to awaken your super mentality for a more productive future*", Bantam, New Age Books, New York, 1983.

Brown, Norman, O., "*Life Against Death*", Routledge and Kegan Paul, London, 1959.

Bucke, Richard Maurice, "*Cosmic Consciousness, A Study in the Evolution of the Human Mind*", E. P. Dutton and Company Inc., New York, 1969.

Buddhaghosa, Visuddhimagga, "*The Path of Purification*". Translated by Bhikkhu Nanamoli, R, Semage, Colombo, Sri Lanka, 1956.

Burckhardt, Titus, "*Alchemy: Science of the Cosmos, Science of the Soul*", Trans. William Stoddart, Stuart and Watkins, London, 1967.

Campbell, Joseph (Ed.), "*The Mysterious, Papers from the Eranos Year Books*", Bollingen Foundation, Princeton University Press, Princeton, 1990.

Cannon, Walter B., "*The Wisdom of the Body*", Kegan Paul, London, 1932, 1947.

Cannon, W.B., "*Bodily Changes in Pain, Hunger, Fear and Rage*", Charles T. Branford Co. Boston, 1953.

Capra, Fritjof, "*The Tao of Physics*", Bantam, New York, 1984.

Castaneda, Carlos, "*The Teachings of Don Juan, A Yaqui Way of Knowledge*", Simon and Schuster, New York, 1973.

Cattell R.B. and J.H. Scheier, "*The Meaning and Measurement Neuroticism and Anxiety*", Ronald Press, New York, 1961.

Chadwick, A.W., "*A Sadhu's Reminiscences of Raman Maharshi*", Sri Ramanasram, Tiruvannamalai, India, 1966.

Chakraborty S.K., Ed., "*Human Response Development: Exploring Transformational Values*", Wiley Eastern, New Delhi, 1990.

Chang, C.C. Garma, *"The Practice of Zen"*, Perenial Library, New York, 1970.

Chuang Tzu,*"Basic Writings, translated by Watson Burton"*, Columbia University Press, Year 1996.

Churchland, Paul M., *"Matter and Consciousness"*, A Bradford Book, The MIT Press. Cambridge, Massachusetts Fifih printing, 1993.

Claxton, G. L., *"Wholly human, Western and Eastern Visions of the self and its perfection"*, Routledge and Kegan Paul, London, 1981.

Cooper, K. H., *"The Aerobics Program for Total Well Being"*, Bantam Books, New York, 1983.

Cooper, Robert, K.E. Ayman Sawal, *"Emotional Intelligence in Business"*, Orion Business Books, 1997.

Coue´, E., *"Self-Mastery through Conscious Auto suggestion"*, New York, 1922.

Cousins, Norman, *"Anatomy of an Illness"*, Bantam, New York, 1981.

Cousins, N., *"The Healing Heart"*, W.W. Norton, New York, 1983.

Cox, Harvey, *"Turning East, The Promise and Peril of the New Orientalism"*, Allen Lane, London, 1977.

Cox, Tom, *"Stress"*, Macmillan Press Ltd., 1978.

Crick, Francis, *"The Astonishing Hypothesis, The Scientific Search for the Soul"*, Touchstone Books, New York, 1994, 1995.

Danto, Arthur C., *"Mysticism and Morality, Oriental Thought and Moral Philosophy"*, Basic Books, New York, 1972.

David-Neal, A., *"Magic and Mystery in Tibet"*, Penguin Books, New York, 1971.

Davids, Rhys, T.W., *"Dialogues of the Buddha"*, Motilal Banarasidas, Delhi, 2000.

Davidson, R.J., and J. M. Davidson, Eds. *"The Psychology of Consciousness"*, Plenum, New York, 1980.

Davis, Martha, E. R. Eshelman, M. Mckay, *"The Relaxation & Stress Reduction Workbook"*, Jaico Publishing House, Bombay, 1990.

De Chardin, T., *"The Phenomenon of Man"*. Harper Torchbooks, New York, 1965.

Dean, S. R. Ed., *"Psychiatry and Mysticism"*, Nelson-Hall, Chicago,1975.

Deikman, Arthur J., *"The Observing Self: Mysticism and Psychotherapy"*, Beacon Press, Boston, 1982.

Dennett, D. C., *"Brain Storms"*, MIT Press Cambridge, 1978.

Dennett, Daniel C., *"Consciousness Explained"*, Penguin Books, London, 1993.

Descartes, Rene´, *"Meditations"*, Bobbs, Merrill, New York, 1960.

Dhammasudhi,*"The Venerable Chao Khun, Phera, Sobhana, Insight Meditation"*, The Committee for the Advancement of Buddhism, London, 1968.

Dilman, Ilham, Freud, *"Insight and Change"*, Basil Blackwell, Oxford, 1988.

Dominguez, Joe and Vicki Robin, *"Your Money or your Life"*, Viking Press, New York, 1992.

Doore, Gary. *"What Survives? Contemporary Explorations of Life after Death"*, Jeremy P. Tarcher, Inc. Los Angeles, 1990.

Dossey, Larry, Space, *"Time and Medicine"*, Shambhala, Boston, 1982.

Dossey, Larry, M.D., *"Recovering the Soul"*, Bantam, New York, 1989.

Drever, James, "*A Dictionary of Psychology*", Penguin Books Harmondsworth, England, First Edition, 1952.

Duval, S., and Wicklund R.A., "*A Theory of Objective Self-awareness*", Academic Press, New York, 1972.

Easwaran, Eknath, "*The Dhammapada Arkana*", Penguin Books, London, 1987.

Eccles, J.C., Ed., "*Brain and Conscious Experience*", Springer, New York, 1966.

Eccles, J.C., "*Brain and Freewill, in Consciousness and the Brain, A Scientific and Philosophical Inquiry*", Eds., G.C. Globus, G. Maxwell and I. Savodnik, Plenum Press, New York, 1976.

Eccles, John, Sir, "*The Human Mystery*", Routledge Kegan Paul, London, 1979.

Eccles, John C., "*Evolution of the Brain. Creation of the Self*", Routledge, London, 1989.

Eccles, John, Sir, "*The Human Psyche*", The Gifford Lectures, 1978-79, Routledge, London, 1992.

Eds., Blackmore, Colin and Greenfield, Susan, "*Mindwaves*" Basil Blackwell, Cambridge, Massachusetts, 1989.

Edwards, H., "*Thirty Years a Spiritual Healer*", Jenkins, London, 1968.

Elgin, Duane, "*Voluntary Simplicity, Toward a Way of Life that is outwardly simple, inwardly rich*", William Morrow, New York, 1981, 1993.

Eliade, M., "*Yoga: Immortality and Freedom*", Princeton University Press, Princeton, 1970. .

Eliade, Mircea, "*Shamanism, Archaic Techniques of Ecstasy*", Bollingen Series, Princeton University Press, Princeton, 1974.

Eliade, Mircea,"*Patanjali and Yoga*", Schocken Books, New York, 1975.

Ellis, A. and Harper, R.A."*New Guide to Rational Living*", Prentice-Hall, New York, 1975.

Emery, Gary and Campbell, James."*Rapid Relief from Emotional Distress*", Rawson Associates, New York, 1986.

Evans-Wentz, W.Y., "*Tibetan Yoga and Secret Doctrines*", Oxford University Press, London, 1958.

Evans-Wentz W. Y., "*The Tibetan Book of the Great Liberation, or the Method of Realising NIRVANA Through Knowing the Mind*", Oxford University Press, London, 1968.

Evans-Wentz W.Y. Trans., "*The Tibetan Book of the Dead*", Oxford University Press, Oxford, 1970.

Evola, Julius, "*The Hermetic Tradition, Symbols and Teachings of the Royal Art*", Inner Traditions International, Vermont, 1995.

Ferrucci, P., "*What we may be*", Tarcher, Los Angeles, 1982.

Fingarette Herbert, "*The Self in Transformation*", Harper, New York, 1977.

Fisher, Joe, "*The Case for Reincarnation*", Bantam Books, New York, 1985.

Ford, Norman D, "*Minding Your Body*", Autumn Press, Massachusetts, 1981.

Foreyt, J. P. and D. P., Rathjen, (Eds.),"*Cognitive Behaviour Therapy*": Research and Application, Plenum, New York, 1978.

Frager, Robert, James Fadiman, "*Personality, & Personal Growth*", Longman, New York, 1998.

Freud, Sigmund and Joseph Breuer, "*Studies in Hysteria*", 1895, Penguin Books, 1988.

Freud, Sigmund, *"Beyond the Pleasure Principle"*, 1920, in On Metapsychology Penguin Books, 1991.

Freud, Sigmund, *"The Ego and the Id"*, 1923, in On Metapsychology Penguin Books 1991.

Freud, Sigmund, *"New Introductory Lectures on Psychoanalysis"*, 1933, Penguin Books, 1991.

Friedman, Meyer, M. D. and Ray Rosenman M.D., *"Type A Behavior and Your Heart"*, Fawcett, New York, 1985.

Fromm E., Ed., *"Zen Buddhism and Psychoanalysis"*, Grove Press, New York, 1960.

Fromm, Erich, *"Psychoanalysis and Religion"*, Bantam Books, 1950.

Funkenstein, D.H., King, S.H., Drolette M.E., *"Mastery Of Stress"*, Harward University Press, Cambridge, 1957.

Gaibraith, Dr. Paul, *"Meditation Rejuvenate. The Definitive Handbook on Releasing Stress Naturally"*, Media Masters, Singapore, 1997.

Goldberger, C., and Breznitz, S., (Eds.) *"Handbook of Stress: Theoretical and Clinical Aspects"*, Macmillan, 1982.

Govinda, Lama Anagarika, *"Foundations of Tibetan Mysticism"*, E.P. Dutton, New York, 1960.

Govinda, Lama Anagarika, *"Creative Meditation and Multidimensional Consciousness"*, the Theosophical Publishing House, Wheaton, III, 1978.

Green E., and Green, A., *"Beyond Biofeedback"*, Delacorte Press, New York, 1977.

Grof, S., Ed., *"Ancient Wisdom and Modern Science"*, State University of New York Press, Albany 1984.

Grof S., *"The Adventure of Self-discovery"*, State University of New York Press, Albany, 1988.

Grof, Stanislav and Christina GrofEds. *"Spiritual Emergency, When Personal Transformation becomes a Crisis"*, Jeremy Tarcher, Los Angeles, 1990.

Grof, Christina and Grof, Stanislav, *"The Stormy Search for the Self"*, Thorsons, London, 1991.

Gross, N.E., *"Living with Stress"*, McGraw— Hill Book Co., New York, 1958.

Grossman, Carl M, M.D., and Sylva Grossman, *"The Wild Analyst"*, Barrie and Rockliff, London, 1965.

Guenlher, H.V., *"The Life and Teaching of Naropa"*, Oxford University Press, Oxford, 1963.

Guenther, H.V., *"Yuganaddha The Tantric View of Life"*, Chowkhamba Sanskrit Series, Banaras, 1952.

Gunaratna V.F., *"Rebirth Explained"*, The Wheel Publications No.167/169, Buddhist Publication Society, Kandy, Sri Lanka, 1971.

Gyatso Geshe Kelsang, *"Clear Light of Bliss"*, Wisdom Publications, London, 1982.

Gyatso, Geshe Kelsang, *"Understanding the Mind, An Explanation of the nature and functions of the mind"*, Therpa Publications, London, 1993.

Hanson, V., Ed., *"Approaches to Meditation"*. The Theosophical Publishing House, Wheaton, Ill., 1973.

Happold, F.C., *"Mysticism, A Study and an Anthology"*, Penguin Books, 1963.

Harding, Esther,*"Psychic Energy, Its Source and Its Transformation"*, Bollingen Series X Pantheon Books, 1948, 1963.

Hardy, Alastair, *"The Spiritual Nature of Man"*, Oxford University Press, Oxford, 1979.

Hardy, Sir Alister,*"The Living Stream, Evolution and Man"*

Hart, William, *"The Art of Living, Vipassana Meditation, as taught by S.N. Goenka"*, Vipassana Research Institute, Igatpuri, Maharashtra, India, 1987.

Hartmann, Edward Von, *"Philosophy of the Unconscious"*, Routledge & Kegan Paul Ltd., London, 1869, 1950.

Hartmann, Heinz,*"Essays on Ego Psychology, Selected Problems of Psychoanalytical Theory"*, International Universities Press, New York, 1964.

Hawley, Jack, *"Reawakening the Spirit in Work, The Power of Dharmic Management"*, McGraw-Hill, New Delhi, 1994.

Head, Joseph and S.L. Cranston, (Eds.), *"Reincarnation, an East-West Anthology"*, The Theosophical Publishing House, Wheaton, Ill., U.S.A., 1985.

Heisenberg, W., *"Physics and Philosophy"*, Harper and Brothers, New York, 1958.

Henderson, C.W., *"Awakening, Ways to Psycho-Spiritual Growth"*, Prentice Hall, Inc., New Jersey, 1975.

Hendricks, Gay and Russel Wills, *"The Centering Book, Awareness Activities for Children, Parents and Teachers"*, Prentice Hall, 1976, 1986

Herrigel, Eugen, *"The Method of Zen"*,Vintage Books, New York, 1974.

Herrigel, E., *"Zen in the Art of Archery"*, Routledge and Kegan Paul, London, 1975.

Hiriyanna, M., *"The Essentials of Indian Philosophy"*, Motilal Banarasidas, Delhi, 1948, 1995.

Hoch, E.M., *"Sources and Resources, A Western Psychiatrist's Search for Meaning in the Ancient Indian Scriptures"*.

Hodgkinson, Liz,*"The Personal Growth Hand Book"*, Platkus, London, 1993.

Hofstoder, D., and Dennet D.C., *"The Mind's I - Fantasies and Reflections, on Self and Soul"*, Basic Books, New York, 1987.

Horgan, John, *"The End of Science"*, Little Brown and Company, London, 1997.

Horney, Karen, *"Our Inner Conflicts"*, Norton, New York, 1945.

Horney, K., *"The Neurotic Personality of our time"*, Norton Library, New York, 1968.

Hughes, John,*"Self Realisation in Kashmir Shaivism"*, Sri Satguru Publications,' Delhi, 1997. .

Hume, Robert Ernest,*"The Thirteen Principal Upanishads"*, Oxford University Press, Delhi, 1995.

Humphrey, Nicholas,*"A History of the Mind"*, Simon & Schuster, London, 1992.

Humphreys, Christmas, *"Zen Buddhism"*, Macmillan, New York, 1949.

Humphreys, Christmas, *"Karma and Rebirth"*, Curzon Press, London, 1983.

Humphreys, Christmas,*"A Western Approach to Zen"*, Unwin Paperbacks, London, 1985.

Husserl, E., *"Ideas: General Introduction to Pure Phenomenology"*, Macmillan, New York, 1981.

Huxley, Aldous, *"The Perenial Philosophy"*, Harper & Row, 1944.

Huxley, Aldous, *"The Doors of Perception, and Heaven and Hell"*, Penguin Books, London, 1959.

Huxley, Julian, *"Religion without Revelation"*, New American Library, New York, 1957.

Inge, W.R., *"Christian Mysticism"*, Meridian Books, New York, 1956.

Iqbal, Mohammad, *"Secrets of the Self"*, Published by Gulati Vazirani for Arnold Heinemann, New Delhi, 1978.

Ishiguro, H., *"The Scientific Truth of Zen"*, Zenrizaku Society, Tokyo, 1964.

Iyengar, B.K.S., *"Light on Yoga"*, Schocken Books, New York, 1965.

Iyengar, B.K.S., *"Light on Pranayam"*, Crossroad, New York, 1981.

Jabobson, Edmund, *"You must Relax, A Practical Method of Reducing the Strains of Modern Living"*, Mcgraw Hill Book Company, Inc., London, 1934, 1948 (Third Edition).

Jacobs, Hans, *"Western Psychotherapy and Hindu Sadhana"*, George Allen & Unwin Ltd., London, 1961.

James, W., *"The Varieties of Religious Experience"*, New American Library, New York, 1958.

Jaynes, Julian, *"The Origin of Consciousness in the Breakdown of the Bicameral Mind"*, Penguin Books, 1976, 1979.

Johansson, R.E.A., *"The Psychology of Nirvana"*, Anchor, New York, 1970.

Johnson, Raynor C., *"The Imprisoned Splendour, An Approach to Reality based upon the Significance of Data drawn from the fields of Natural Science, Psychical Research and Mystical Experience"*, Hodder and Stoughton, London, 1953.

Johnson, Willard, *"Riding the Ox Home"*, Beacon Press, Boston, 1986.

"A History of Meditation from Shamanism to Science".

Jung, Carl,"*Modern Man in Search of a Soul*", Harcourt Brace, New York, 1955.

Jung, C., "*Memories, Dreams, Reflections*",Vintage Books, New York, 1961.

Jung, C.G., "*On Psychic Energy - The Structure and Dynamics of the Psyche*", Tr., R.F.C. Hull, Routledge and Kegan Paul, London, 1960.

Jung, C.G., "*Psychology and Alchemy, in Collected Works*", Vol. 12, Princeton University Press, Princeton, 1968.

Kakar, Sudhir, "*The Analyst and the Mystic, Psychoanalytic Reflections on Religion and Mysticism*", Viking Penguin Books, 1991.

Kakuzo, Okukara,"*The Book of Tea*", Charles E. Tuttle, Company, Tokyo, 1963.

Kapleau, Roshi Philip, "*Zen merging of East and West*", Anchor Books, New York, 1989.

Kapleau, Philip, Ed., "*The Three Pillars of Zen*", Anchor, Doubleday, New York, 1980.

Kapleau, Philip,"*The Wheel of Life and Death*," Rider, London, 1990.

Khin, U.B., "*The Essentials of Buddhist Dhamma in Meditative Practicare*".

Kinsbourne, Marcel, "*Integrated field theory of Consciousness*", in Marcel,

A.J., and Bisiach, E., Eds., "*Consciousness in Contemporary Science*", Oxford, 1994.

Kobayashi, Shi Shigeru, "*Creative Management*", American Management Association, Inc., New York, 1971.

Koestler, Arthur, "*The Act of Creation*", Macmillan, New York, 1964.

Koestler, A., "*The Ghost in the Machine*", MacMillan, New York, 1967.

Koestler, Arthur and J.R. Smythis,"*Beyond Reductionism*", The Alpbad Symposium, Hutchinson & Co., London, 1969, 1972.

Kornfield, Jack and Paul Breiter, "*A Still Forest Pool, Quest*", Wheaton III, 1985.

Krishnamurti, J., "*Commentaries on Living*", Ed. D. Rajagopal, Victor Gollancz, London, 1962.

Kuhn, Thomas, S., "*The Structure of Scientific Revolutions*", 22nd Edition, The University of Chicago Press Chicago, 1962, 1970.

Laing, R.D., "*The Divided Self*", Penguin, London, 1959.

Laing, R. D., "*Politics of Experience*" Penguin.

Langer, Ellen J., "*Mindfulness*", Addison-Wesley, Reading Mass., 1989.

Langley Noel, Ed., "*The Hidden History of Reincarnation*", A.R.E. Press, Virginia Beach, Va., 1965.

Laski, Marghanita,"*Ecstasy, A Study of Some Secular and Religious Experiences*". Cresset Press, London, 1965.

Lazarus, R. S., "*Psychological Stress and the Coping Process*", McGraw Hill Book Co., Inc., New York, 1966.

Le Shan, Lawrence, "*The Medium. The Mystic and the Physicist. Toward a General Theory of the Para normal*", Viking Press, New York, 1974.

Leary, T., Metzner, R., and Alpert, R., "*The Psychedelic Experience*", University Books, New Hyde Park, N.Y., 1964.

Leary, Timothy, "*High Priest*", The World Publishing Company, New York, 1968.

Levi, L., "*Stress: Sources, Management, and Prevention*", Liveright Publishing Corporation, New York, 1967.

Lifson, Lawrence E., *"Understanding Therapeutic Action, Psychodynamic Concepts of Cure"*, The Analytic Press, London, 1996.

Lonergan, B., *"Insight, A Study of Human Understanding"*, Philosophical Library, 1970.

Low, Albert, *"Zen and Creative Management"*, Anchor Books Garden City, N.Y., 1976.

Lowen, Alexander, *"Bioenergetics, The Revolutionary Therapy that uses the language of the body to heal the problems of the mind"*, Penguin, Harmondsworth, England, 1978.

Lowen, Alexander, *"The Spirituality of the Body"*, Macmillan, New York, 1990.

Luk, Charles, *"The Secrets of Chinese Meditation"*, Rider & Co., London, 1964.

Luthe, W., *"Autogenic Therapy"*, Vols. 1-5, Grune and Stratton, New York, 1969.

Lyons, William, *"The Disappearance of Introspection"*, A Bradford Book, The MIT Press, Cambridge, Massachusetts, 1986.

M., *"The Gospel of Sri Ramakrishna"*, Vivekananda Centre New York, 1952.

MacGregor Geddes, *"Reincarnation in Christianity, A New Vision of the Role of Rebirth in Christian Thought"*, The Theosophical Publishing House, Wheaton, Ill. U.S.A. 1981.

MacGregor, Geddes, *"The Christening of Karma"*, The Theosophical Publishing House, Wheaton, Ill., 1984.

Madhavanand, Swami, *"Translator of Vivekacudamani of Sri Sankaracarya"*, Advaita Ashrama, Calcutta, 1978.

Maharshi Mahesh Yogi, *"The Science of Being and Art of Living"* International SRM Publications, London, 1963, 1966.

Marcel, A.J., and Bisiach, E., Eds.,*"Consciousness in Contemporary Science"*, Oxford University Press, Oxford, 1994.

Martz, Louis, L., *"The Poetry of Meditation"*, Yale, New Haven, 1954.

Maslow, A.H., *"Motivation and Personality"*,Harper and Brothers, New York, 1 954.

Maslow, Abraham, *"Religions, Values, and Peak Experiences"*, The Viking Press, New York, 1970.

Masters, Robert, and Jean Houston, *"The Varieties of Psychedelic Experience"*, Halt, Rinehart, and Winston, New York, 1966.

Matsushita, K., *"Not for Bread alone, A Business Ethos, a Management Ethic"*, PHP Institute, Tokyo, 1984.

May, Rollo, *"Meaning of Anxiety"*, Ronald Books, New York, 1950.

May, Rollo, *"Love and Will"*., Dell, New York, 1969.

McDougall, W., *"The Energies of Men, A Study of the Fundamentals of Dynamic Psychology"*, Methun & Co., Italy London, 1932.

Meckel, Daniel, J., and Robert I. Moore, *"Self and Liberation, The Jung — Buddhism Dialogue"*, Paulist Press, New York, 1992.

Medard, Boss, *"A Psychiatrist Discovers India"*, Oswald Wolff, London, 1965.

Meichenbaum, D.H., *"Cognitive Behaviour Modification: An Integrative Approach"*, Plenum, New York, 1977.

Meichenbaum, D.H, and Jaremko, M.E., (Eds.), *"Stress Prevention and Management, A Cognitive Behavioral Approach"*, Plenum, New York, 1982.

Merrell-Wolff, F., *"Pathways through Space, A Personal Record of Transformation in Consciousness"*, Richard R. Smith, New York.

Mishra, Kansalakar, *"Kashmir Saivism, The Central Philosophy of Tantrism"*, The Satguru Publications, Delhi, 1999.

Moliner, E. Ramon,*"The Conscious State of Matter"*, Vintage Press, New York, 1994.

Moyers, Bill, *"Healing and the Mind"*, Doubleday, New York, 1995.

Mukerjee, Radhakamal, *"Astavakragita, The Song of the Self Supreme"*, Motilal Banarasidas, Delhi, Reprint, 1997, 2000.

Murphy, M., and S. Donowan, *"The Physical and Psychological Effects of Meditation, A Review of Contemporary Meditation Research with a Comprehensive Bibliography"*, 1931, 1988, Esalen Institute, San Rafael, 1988.

Muss, Caroline, *"Anatomy of the Spirit"*, Bantam Books, New York, 1997.

Mustofsky, D-1, (Ed.), *"Behaviour Control and the Modification of Physiological Activity"*, Prentice Hall, Englewood Cliffs, N.J. 1976.

Myres, F.W.H., *"Human Personality and its Survival of Bodily Death"*, Longman, Green, and Co., London, 1906.

Naranjo, C., and Ornstein R.E., *"On the Psychology of Meditation"*, Viking Press, New York, 1973.

Naranjo, Claudio,*"Ennea — type Structures, Self-analysis for the Seeker"*, Gateways/IDHHB Inc. Publishers, Nevada city, L.A.

Nemeck, Francis Kelly and Marie Theresa Coombs. *"The Spiritual Journey, Critical Threshholds and Stages of Adult Spiritual Genesis"*, Michael Glazier, Wilmington, Delaware, 1968.

Neumann,*"Depth Psychology and a New Ethic"*, Shambhala, Boston, 1990.

Neumann, E., "*The Origin and History of Consciousness*", Princeton University Press, Princeton, 1973

Nissanka, H.S.S., "*Buddhist Psychotherapy, An Eastern Therapeutical Approach to Mental Problems*", Vikas Publishing House, New Delhi, 1993.

Nunn, Chris,"*Awareness, What is It, What It does*", Routledge, London, 1996.

Nyanaponika, M., "*The Heart of Buddhist Meditation*", Rider, London, 1962.

O'Flaherty, Wendy Doninger (Ed), "*Karma and Rebirth in Classical Indian Traditions*", Motilal Banarasidas Delhi, 1983.

Ornish Dean, "*Dr. Dean, Ornish's Program for Reversing Heart Disease*", Ballantine Books, New York, 1990.

Ornstein, E., Robert, "*The Psychology of Consciousness*", Penguin Books, Harmondsworth, England, 1975.

Ostrander, Sheila, and Schroeder, Lynn, "*Psychic Discoveries behind the Iron Curtain*", Prentice Hall, New Jersey, 1970.

Otsu, D. R., "*The Ox and his Herdsman*", Hokuseido Press, Tokyo, 1964.

Otto, Rudolph,"*The Idea of the Holy*", Oxford Galaxy Books, New York, 1958.

Otto, R., "*Mysticism East and West, Translated by B. L. Bracey and R.C. Payne*", MacMillan Co., New York, 1960.

Ouspensky, P.D., "*In Search of the Miraculous*", Routledge and Kegan Paul, 1949.

Ouspensky P.D., "*The Psychology of Man's Possible Evolution*", Hodder and Stoughton, London, 1951.

Ouspensky P. D., "*The Fourth Way*", Vintage, New York, 1971.

Paul, G. L., *"Insight Vs. Desensitization in Psychotherapy"*, Stanford University, Stanford, 1966.

Peale, N.V., *"The Power of Positive Thinking"*, Fawcett Crest, Greenwich, Connecticut, 1956.

Peck, M. Scott, *"The Road less Traveled"*, Simon & Schuster, 1979.

Pelletier, K., and Garfield C., *"Consciousness . East and West"*, Harper and Row, New York, 1976.

Pelletier, K.R., *"Mind as Healer, Mind as Slayer"*, Dell, New York, 1977.

Penfield, Wilder, *"The Mystery of the Mind"*, Princeton, University Press, Princeton, New Jersey, 1972, 1975.

Penrose, Roger, *"The Emperor's New Mind"*, Vintage, London, 1990.

Penrose, Roger, *"Shadows of the Mind"*, Oxford University Press, New York, 1994.

Perls, F.S., *"Ego, Hunger, Aggression"*, Vintage Books, New York, 1969.

Peterson, Severin, *"A Catalog of the Way People grow"*, Ballentine.

Pierrakos, Eva, *"The Pathwork of Self transformation"*, Bantam Books, New York, 1990.

Pirsig, Robert M., *"Zen and the Art of Motor Cycle Maintenance"*, A Corgi Book, London, 1978.

Platanov K., *"Psychology As You Like It"*. Progress Publishers, Moscow, 1965.

Popper Karl, *"Unending Quest"*, Fontana, 1976.

Popper, Karl and Eccles, John C., *"The Self and Its Brain"*, Springer International, Heidelburger, 1977.

Progoff, Ira, *"The Death and Rebirth of Psychology"*, The Julian Press, New York,1956.

Progoff, Ira, *"Depth Psychology and Modern Man"*, Dialogue House Library, New York, 1970.

Quick, J. C., and Quick J. D.,*"Organisational Stress, and Preventive Management"*, McGraw Hill, 1984.

Rai, Ramkumar, (Translator), *"Kularnava Tantra"*,Prachya Prakashan, Varanasi.

Rangdrol, Tsele, Natsok, *"Lamp of Mahamudra, Tr. By Erik Pema Kunsang"*, Shambhala, Boston & Shaftesbury, 1989.

Reber, Arthur S., *"Dictionary of Psychology"*,Penguin Books, Second Edition, 1995, Harmondsworth, England.

Reich Wilhelm, *"Selected Writings: An Introduction to Orgonomy"*, Noonday Press, New York, 1961.

Rele, Vasant C, *"The Mysterious Kundalini"*, D.B., Taraporevala Sons & Co., Bombay, 1931.

Reps, Paul, Zen Flesh, Zen Bones, *"A Collection of Zen & Pre-Zen Writings"*, Charles E. Tuttle Co., Tokyo, 1965.

Rhine, J. B., *"The Reach of the Mind"*, Apollo, 1947.

Rhinehart, L-l, *"The Book of Est."*, Holt, Rhine Hart, and Winston, New York, 1976

Richardson, H.W., and Cutler D.R., Eds., *"Transcendence"*, Beacon Press, Boston, 1969.

Roger's Carl R.,*"A Therapist's View of Psychotherapy, On Becoming a Person"*, Constable, London, 1969, 1989.

Rose Steven, Ed., *"From Brains to Consciousness? Essays on the New Sciences of the Mind"*, Allen Lane, The Penguin Press, London, 1998.

Rosen, G.M., *"The Relaxation Book"*, Prentice Hall, Englewood Cliffs, N.J., 1977.

Rosenfeld, F., *"The Book of Highs"*, Times Books, New York, 1973.

Ross, Nancy Wilson, *"The World of Zen, An East West Anthology"*, Vintage Books, New York, 1960.

Rossi, Ernest Lawrence, *"The Psycho-biology of Mind-Body Healing"*, Norton, New York, 1986.

Rossi, I., Ed.,*"The Unconscious in Culture"*, E. P. Dutton and Co., New York, 1974.

Royal Canadian Air Force, *"Exercise Plans for Physical Fitness"*, Pocket Books, New York, 1962.

Rumi, Jalaluddin, *"Selected Lyric Poetry of Jalaluddin Rumi, Translated by Edmund Helminski"*, Threshold Books, Putney, Vf: 1984.

S. Arthur, Joyce Berger (Eds.), *"Reincarnation: Fact or Fable"*, The Aquarian Press, London, 1991.

Sachdeva, I. P.,*"Yoga & Depth Psychology"*, Motilal Banarasidas, Delhi, 1978.

Saint John of the Cross, *"Ascent of Mount Carmel"*, Doubleday and Co., Garden City, 1958.

Saint John of the Cross, *"Dark Night of the Soul, Translated by E. Allison Peers"*, Buns and Oats, 1976.

Salk, Jonas, *"Man Unfolding"*, Allied Publishers Pvt. Ltd., Bombay, 1972.

Sankaracarya, Sri, *"Self-Knowledge, Tr. By Swami Nikhilananda"*, Sri Ramkrishna Math, Madras, India.

Sankaracarya, Sri, "*Vivekacudamani Tr. By Swami, Madhavananda*", Advaita Ashram, Calcutta, India, 1982.

Satprem, Sri Aurobindo, "*The Adventure of Consciousness, Translated by Tehmi*", Sri Aurobindo Society, Pondicherry, India, 1970.

Sayadaw, Mahasi, "*The Progress of Insight, A Treatise on Buddhist Satipatthana Meditation*". Buddhist Publications Society, Kandy Sri Lanka, 1978.

Schutz, W. C., Joy, "*Expanding Human Awareness*", Souvenir Press, London, 1971.

Schwarz Jack, "*Voluntary Controls, Exercises for Creative Meditation*", Arkana, 1992.

Schwartz, Tony, "*What Really Matters, Searching for Wisdom in America*", Bantam Books, New York, 1995.

Scott David & Doubleday, Tony, "*The Elements of Zen*", Element Books, Shaftstesbury Dorset, U.K., 1992.

Searle, John R., "*The Rediscovery of the Mind*", A Bradford Book, The MIT Press, Cambridge, Massachusetts, U.S.A., 1995.

Searle, John, Minds, "*Brains and Science*", B.B.C., London, 1984.

Selye, H., "*Stress without Distress*", Hodder London, 1975.

Selye, Hans, "*The Stress Of Life*", McGraw Hill Book Co., New York, 1956, 1978.

Shah, Idris, "*Tales of Derwishes*", Jonathan Cape, London, 1967.

Shah, Idris, "*The Way of the Sufi*", Jonathan Cape, London, 1968.

Shah, Idris, "*The Sufis*", Doubleday, 1971.

Shapiro, D. H., "Meditation: Self regulation Strategy and Altered States of Consciousness", Aldine, New York, 1980.

Shapiro, D. H. and Walsh R. N., *"Beyond Health and Normality: Explorations in exceptional psychological well-being"*, Van Nostrand, New York, 1982.

Shapiro, D. and Walsh R., Eds., *"Meditation: Classical and Contemporary Views"*, Aldine, New York, 1984.

Shattock, E.H., *"An Experiment in Mindfulness"*, Rider & Company, London, 1958.

Sheldrake Rupert & Fox Matthew, *"Natural Grace, Dialogues on Science & Spirituality"*, Bloomsbury, London, 1997. .

Sherrington, C., *"Man on His Nature"*, Cambridge University Press, Cambridge, 1963

Skinner, B. F., *"Beyond Freedom and Dignity"*, Jonathan Cape, London, 1972.

Skinner, B.F. *"Science and Human Behaviour"*, Macmillan, New York, 1953.

Smith, J. C.,*"Meditation: A New Way"*, Research Press, Champaign, Illmois.

Smith, J. C. *"Relaxation Dynamics: A Cognitive Behavioral Approach to Relaxation"*, Research Press, Champaign Illinois, 1985, 1989.

Snellgrove, David, *"Four Lamas of Dolpo"*, Harward University Press, Cambridge, Mass., 1967.

Soma, Bhikkhu, *"The Way of Mindfulness"*, Buddhist Publication Society Kandy, Sri Lanka.

Spurgeon, Caroline F.E., *"Mysticism in English Literature"*, Kennikat Press, London, 1970.

St. Teresa of Avila, *"Interior Castle Translated and Edited by E. Allison"*, Peers, Image Books, New York, 1961.

Staal, Frits, *"Exploring Mysticism"*, University of California Press, Berkeley, 1975.

Stace, W., *"Mysticism and Philosophy"*, Tarcher, Los Angeles, 1987.

Stevenson, 1.,*"Twenty Cases Suggestive of Reincarnation 2ndEd".*, University of Virginia Press, Charlottesville, 1974.

Stevenson, Dr. Ian, *"Casesof the Reincarnation Type (Vols. 1-4)"*,University Press of Virginia, Charlottes Ville,1975-1983.

Stewart, W.S., *"The Divided Self, The Healing of a Common and distressing nervous disorder, the personal account of a highly intelligent patient"*, George Allen & Unwin Ltd., London, 1964.

Storr, Anthony, *"Human Aggression"*, Athenium, New York, 1968.

Sullivan, Lawrence E., (Ed.) *"Hidden Truths: Magic, Alchemy, and the Occult"*, Collier Macmillan Publishers, London, 1989.

Sutherland, Stuart, *"The International Dictionary of Psychology"*, The Crossroad Publishing Company, Second Edition, New York, 1996.

Suzuki, D.T., *"Living by Zen"*, Sanseido Press, Tokyo, 1949.

Suzuki D.T., *"The Zen Doctrine of No-Mind"*, Rider, London, 1949.

Suzuki, D.T., *"Mysticism: Christian and Buddhist"*, Harper, 1957.

Suzuki, D.T.,*"Manual of Zen Buddhism"*, Grove Press, New York, 1960.

Suzuki, D.T., Erich Fromm, Richard de Martino, *"Zen Buddhism and Psycho-analysis"*, George Allen & Unwin, London, 1960.

Tart, C.T., Ed., *"Altered States of Consciousness"*, John Wiley and Sons, Inc., New York, 1969.

Tart, C.T., *"States of Consciousness"*, F. P. Dutton, New York, 1975. .

Tart, C.,"*Transpersonal Psychologies*". Harper Collins, New York, 1992.

Thoreau, C.B., "*Walden*", Princeton University Press, Princeton, 1971.

Thurman, Robert A.F., "*The Holy Teaching of Vimalakirti*", Pennsylvania State University Press, 1976.

Tipler, Frank, "*The Physics of Immortality*", Pan Books, London, 1994.

Tirth, Swami Shivom, "*A Guide to Shaktipat*", Devatma Shakti Society, Dahisar Village, Thane, Maharashtra State, India, 1985.

Toffler, "*A, Future Shock*", Random House, New York, 1970.

Toynbee, Arnold, et al.,"*Life after Death*", Weidenfeld & Nicholson, London, 1976

Trevor, M.H., "*The Ox and his Herdsman*", Hokuseido Press, Tokyo, 1956.

Trungpa, Chogyam, "*Cutting through Spiritual Materialism*", Shambhala, Boston, 1973.

Tucci Giuseppe, "*The Theory and Practice of the Mandala*", Rider, London, 1961.

Tzu, Chuang, "*Trans*"., Herbert A. Giles, George Allen & Unwin, London, 1961.

Tzu, Lao, "*Tao Te Ching, Translated by D. C. Lao*", Pelican Books, Harmondsworth Middlesex, U.K., 1963.

Udupa, K. N., "*Stress and its Management by Yoga*", Motilal Banarasidas, Delhi, 1985.

Underhill, E., "*Mysticism*", New American Library, New York, 1974.

Underwood, G. and Stevens, R., (Eds) "*Aspects of Consciousness, Vol. 1, Psychological Issues*", Academic Press, 1979.

Underwood, G. and Stevens, R. (Eds.) *"Aspects of Consciousness, Vol. 2, Structural Issues"*, Academic Press, 1981.

Underwood, G. (Ed.)*"Aspects of Consciousness, Vol. 3, Awareness and Self-awareness"*, London, Academic Press, 1982.

Varenne, Jean,*"Yoga and the Hindu Tradition"*, University of Chicago Press, Chicago, 1976.

Vaysse, Jean, *"Toward Awakening, An approach to the teaching left by Gurdjeff"*, Harper & Row", New York, 1979.

Vivekananda, Swami *"Vedanta, Voice of Freedom"*, Advaita Ashrama, Calcutta, India, 1997.

Waddell, E., *"The Desert Fathers"*, University of Michigan Press, Ann Arbor, Michigan, 1957.

Waley, Arthur, *"The Way and Its Power, A Study of the Tao Te Ching and its Place in Chinese Thought"*, George Allen & Unwin Ltd., London, 1956.

Walker, K., *"A Study of Gurdjeff's Teaching"*, Jonathan Cape, London, 1969.

Walpe, J., *"Psychotherapy by Reciprocal Inhibition"*, Stanford University Press, Stanford, 1958.

Walsh, Roger, *"Staying Alive: The Psychology of Human Survival"*, New Science Library, Shanbhala, Boston, 1984.

Walsh Roger, Vaughan Frances; Eds., *"Paths Beyond Ego, The Transpersonal Vision"*, Jeremy P. Tarcher Inc., Los Angeles, 1993.

Watson, Lyall, *"The Romeo Error, A Matter of Life and Death"*, Anchor Press, New York, 1975.

Watts, Allan W., "The way of zen" A Mentor Book, New York, 1959.

Watts, Allan, W., *"This is It and other Essays on Zen"*, Pantheon Books 1960.

Watts, A., *"Psychotherapy East and West"*, Pantheon New York, 1961.

Watts, A.W., *"The Book on the Taboo against knowing who you are"*, Abacus, London, 1973.

Watts, Alan, *"TAO, The Watercourse Way"*, Pantheon Books, New York, 1975.

West, Michael A., Ed., *"The Psychology of Meditation"*, Oxford University Press, Oxford, 1991.

White, John, Ed., "The Highest State of Consciousness", Anchor Books, Garden City, New York, 1972.

White, J., Ed., *"What is Meditation"*, Anchor Books, New York, 1974.

Whyte, L.L., *"The Next Development in Man"*, The Cresset Press, London, 1944.

Zweig, Stefan, *"Mental Healers, Franz Anton Mesmer, Mary Baker Eddy, Sigmund Freud"*, Cassel and Company Limited, London, 1933.

Whyte, L.L., *"The Unconscious before Freud"*, Basic Books, New York, 1960.

Whyte, William H., "The Organisation Man", Penguin Books, 1963.

Wilber, Ken, Jack Engler and Daniel Brown, *"Transformation of Consciousness"*, Science Library, Boston, 1986.

Wilber, Ken, *"The Atman Project, A Transpersonal View of Human Development"*, Theosophical Publishing House, Wheaton Ill., 1989.

Wilber, Ken, *"The Spectrum of Consciousness"*, Quest Book, Wheaton, 11, U.S.A., 1993.

Wilhelm, R., *"The Secret of the Golden Flower"*, Routledge and Kegan Paul, 1969.

Williams, E. William, *"Unbounded Light, The Inward Journey"*, Nicolas-Hays-Inc York Beach ME, 1992.

Wing, R.L. *"The Tao of Power. A new translation of the Tao Te Ching"*, The Aquarian Press, 1986.

Yazaki, Katsuhiko, *"The Path of Liang Zhi"*, Future Generations Alliance Foundation, Kyoto, Japan, 1994.

Zaehner, R.C., *"Mysticism: Sacred and Profane"*, Oxford Paperbacks, London, 1961.

Zaehner R.C., *"Our Savage God — The Perverse Use of Eastern Thought"*, Sheal and Ward, Mission, Kansas, 1975.

Zimmer, H., "Philosophies of India", Princeton University Press, Princeton, 1969.

Zohar, Danah, *"The Quantum Self"*, Bloomsbury, London and William Morrow, New York, 1990.

Zohar, Danah and Marshall, Ian, S.Q., *"Spiritual Intelligence, The Ultimate Intelligence"*, Bloomsbury, London, 2000.

Zukov, Gary, *"The Dancing Wu Li Masters. An Overview of New Physics"*, Bantam Books, New York, 1980.

Printed in the United States
By Bookmasters